BEYOND THE FRONT DOOR

BEYOND THE FRONT DOOR

Embracing Nature for a Happier and Healthier Family

Josée Bergeron

Dedication

To my children, who help me see the wonders of nature,
and to all parents bravely stepping beyond
the front door with their children.

The recipes and activities contained in this publication are intended for general informational purposes only and do not address individual circumstances. The author and publisher are not responsible for any adverse or allergic reactions to ingredients used throughout this book. Plants and fungi that are deemed to be poisonous, including derivatives thereof, should not be ingested in any form. Please exercise caution and provide parental supervision.

Morehouse Publishing
19 East 34th Street
New York, NY 10016
www.churchpublishing.org

Morehouse Publishing is an imprint of Church Publishing Incorporated.

Cover design by David Baldeosingh Rotstein
Interior design by Alison Cnockaert
Typeset by Westchester Publishing Services

ISBN 978-1-64065-855-4 (paperback)
ISBN 978-1-64065-856-1 (eBook)

Library of Congress Control Number: 2025944828

AUTHOR'S NOTE

Parts two through five of this book are packed with seasonal activities, projects, recipes, and ideas. They're fun ways to connect with nature—not professional advice. Every family, child, kitchen, and nearby nature spot is different. Please read the entire activity or recipe first, note any safety instructions, set up your space, and adjust for your comfort, gear, weather, and your children's ages. Parents and caregivers: Please supervise children and assign age-appropriate tasks. In the kitchen, wash hands and tools, avoid cross contamination, and cook foods to safe internal temperatures. When you head outside, check your local forecast and advisories, know the terrain, bring the essentials, and be kind to wildlife and plants. If something doesn't feel right for your family, tweak it, scale it back, or skip it.

TABLE OF CONTENTS

PART FOUR: AUTUMN

PART FIVE: WINTER

PART SIX: GOING FORTH

Part One

RECONNECTING FAMILY & NATURE

CHAPTER 1

The Night I Slipped Away

I WAS DISCONNECTED. Not the weekend warrior style of *let's turn off our phones and traipse through the wilderness for a couple days* sort of disconnected. It was the opposite of that. I was plugged in, strapped in, locked in to the day-to-day parenting grind, the way North American parents do it best. In my early days as a mother, I had naively promised myself that I wouldn't become *that* parent. I've discovered in the world of parenting that the moment you swear you'll never do something, you seem bound to do it.

I promised myself that I would never let my toddler sit in front of a screen. That didn't happen. I promised myself I would never give my toddler sweets. That didn't happen either. I promised myself I would never have a large age gap between my kids. My eldest is thirteen years older than my toddler. There I was, feeding my toddler cake for breakfast as she watched her favorite show, telling my teenage son to watch her like a hawk so that I could jump in the shower, barking various orders at my other two children all the while running through a mental list of everything I had to do that day. Truthfully, I had become *that* parent, sleep-deprived, caffeine driven, somewhat crazed . . . and pregnant with my fifth baby.

Every morning was the same, setting the stage for the day to come, more of the same. As I chauffeured my children from activity to activity, cursing under my breath at the slow traffic and the steady march of minutes, I started to feel like I was trapped at an amusement park. I hate amusement parks. The thought of being locked into rides that spin, twist, and catapult while being suffocated by the heat and strange smells makes my stomach roil. The nonstop blur of drop-offs, pickups, errands, and extracurricular activities felt eerily similar. Moments that should have been treasured rushed by, yet I felt trapped inside, unable to escape from the frenzy.

Even at night there was no rest. My sleep was punctuated with moments of panic. I would startle awake convinced I heard a cry, but it was only my rapid heartbeat echoing in my ears. In these moments I tried to gulp down deep breaths to quell the rising anxiety, but I was drowning. Every morning before I got up out of bed, I was free-falling.

I hadn't always been this way. As a new mother, I watched the throng of parents rushing, stressing, and disconnecting, and promised myself I wouldn't become one of them. Instead, I took a page from my own childhood. I grew up in a suburban neighborhood tucked away in the northern interior of British Columbia, Canada, where I spent most of my free time outdoors climbing trees, playing with the neighborhood kids, and exploring the forested ravine across the street from my home.

It was a treasured childhood, and it gave me the courage to resist North American parenting pressures, saying no to extra lessons, sports, and extracurriculars for my three young children. Instead, I filled our days with hours of outdoor play, weekly visits to the library, and regular meetups with friends. I stood strong against the current of modern parenting culture, but slowly its rushing waters eroded my will and my beliefs, until I could no longer recognize myself or my family.

As my first three children grew older, they wanted to do the same things as their friends. Slowly our days filled up with activities, commitments, and appointments. By the autumn of 2022, there wasn't a single day on my calendar that was free from several scheduled activities. Not one. Everything my children were enrolled in had value. They were all *good* things. I didn't realize, however, that with each added extracurricular activity, I was letting go of walks in the forest, picnics on the lawn, and snuggles in the hammock—connection.

TWO PEAS IN A POD: PARENTING AND STRESS

As I spent more and more time indoors, stressing about lists and laundry, driving my kids everywhere and trying to keep them from climbing walls, I noticed a steady uptick in my stress levels and more problems with my health. I was constantly getting sick with colds and flus. I was exhausted but couldn't sleep and my body ached incessantly. I was suffering from stress and anxiety.

At first, I attributed these problems to being a busy parent. I accepted the truth that raising four kids and being pregnant with a fifth should make me feel terrible. After all, isn't that what our society preaches? Parenting and stress are two peas in a pod, and feeling this way is *a badge of honor.*

It's true that moments of stress are part of living, life's curveballs so to speak, like when your toddler has an accident on a walk so you fashion a pair of pants out of your sweater, or finding out you're pregnant with your fourth baby a week after getting a puppy, or moving to a new city away from family and friends. For sure, those things are stressful, but I'm talking about the gripping, relentless stress haunting parents, day in and day out. The kind of pressure that creates coffee addicts, mommy wine culture, and influencers claiming the solution is "self-care."

Since the late 1980s parenting has become more intense. Parents are much more involved in optimizing their children's day-to-day lives along with constantly protecting them. While these behaviors might seem like parenting progress, they have insidious consequences: parental stress.

Parental stress is an epidemic. It has become such a significant problem that in August 2024 the U.S. Surgeon General published a Surgeon General's Advisory on the mental health and well-being of parents titled *Parents Under Pressure*. This advisory declared that parental stress has increased over the last decade, with 41 percent of parents reporting that they are stressed most days and 48 percent of parents reporting that their stress is completely overwhelming.[1]

With stress on the rise, parental burnout is becoming a problem as well. In 2019, the World Health Organization included "burnout" in the 11th edition of the International Classification of Diseases (ICD-11) as a syndrome marked by exhaustion, increased feelings of negativity, and reduced professional efficacy.[2] The WHO insisted that burnout is only a "work" related phenomenon, but professor of psychiatry Gordon Parker and researcher Gabriela Tavella from the University of New South Wales (UNSW) point out that burnout also happens in those that aren't "formally employed" like parents and caregivers.[3] In a study of forty-two countries around the world, the ten countries experiencing the *highest* prevalence of parental burnout were the United States, Belgium, Poland, Canada, Burundi, France, Lebanon, Russia, Finland, and Switzerland (sex-weighted estimates).[4]

Parents Under Pressure shares a tidy summary of the seven groups of parental stressors impacting parental mental health and well-being: financial strain, time demands, children's health, children's safety, loneliness, social media, and cultural pressure. These are all serious issues, which I will explore in upcoming chapters, but something important is missing in the pages of this report.

I RAN AWAY FROM HOME

In the fall of 2022, I was heavily pregnant with my fifth baby. My stress, anxiety, and overwhelm were at an all-time high. I was burned out, and it all came crashing down on me one September evening as summer catapulted into autumn. Maybe it was the pregnancy hormones that tipped the scale, but I know for a fact that I had been standing on a precipice for some time. This was the culmination of three years, and it happened right before supper.

"I'm home," my husband Jeremie called wearily through the front door of our small log home. It was four o'clock in the afternoon, and he had come home early to help with supper and chauffeuring kids to evening activities.

I didn't reply, but it didn't take him long to spot me in the kitchen. I saw his gentle smile in my peripheral vision as he approached to embrace me. I shifted my pregnant body away before I could get caught up in his strong arms.

"Supper's almost ready," I said stiffly, stirring the potato-leek soup and trying to ignore the pained look in his blue eyes. Even though my body was swelling with new life, I felt brittle like a delicate layer of ice over a puddle. I tried to say something to him, an apology on the tip of my tongue, but the clamor of the toddler screaming, older children bickering, and dog whining were a crescendo in my ears. That's when it happened.

Without warning, I was gripped with a terrifying urge to flee into the hills and live among the whispering pines. I felt a deep longing to run away, and my body responded instinctively. I turned the soup to a simmer, walked to the front door, slipped on my coat and boots, and waddled away.

There was no fanfare. My family didn't even notice me leave. Since running, even walking, was an awkward and slow affair, I drove instead, but before backing out of the driveway I turned off the locator app on my phone—a decision I would soon regret.

I drove with no specific goal in mind and ended up at one of my favorite spots, a rocky knoll that dips down into deep gray freshwaters of Okanagan Lake. There in the parking lot tears came, a cacophony of gut-wrenching sobs. The salty tears left my eyes feeling puffy and gritty. For a long time, I sat paralyzed in my vehicle, watching the sun slip behind the hills and the last car leave the parking lot.

In the descending darkness, I stepped shakily onto a gravel path. Waddling slowly but purposefully over the hill, I carefully picked my way through the patches of prickly pear, down to the pebbly shore. I stood there for a moment, transfixed by the orange, purple, and blue colors mingling in the sky. Then a single thought burst into my consciousness, "I want to *feel* again." I'm not sure where this thought came from, but it forced me down to the ground desperately removing my well-worn boots and socks.

Without a second thought, I stepped into the silvery lake—an act of rebellion. I knew the water would be frigid, but I needed to *feel* the piercing grip of water on my skin. The lake embraced me. It held me as tears flowed again. This simple moment between myself and nature broke through my numbness and jolted me awake. In many ways it was my baptism, my moment of rebirth. I had become lost, but now I was *home*.

Although the frigid water made my feet ache, I didn't move. I rooted myself in place by digging my toes into the rocky lake bed, plugging myself into *Land*, recharging. The air thickened with periwinkle. A hush of icy air pulled at my long, dark hair and set my teeth chattering, urging me not to linger.

I didn't want to return to my life of chaos. I knew that something had to change, but I didn't know what or how. The more pressing problem, however, was the loss of feeling to my feet, the need to return to shore, the limited light, and the fact that nobody knew where I was. Worry and guilt crashed down on me.

I turned toward the edge of the lake. I had only waded out a little way, but my legs felt leaden, which added awkwardness to my already awkward pregnant body. Slipping into the lake would not be good. If I injured myself nobody could help me. I did what seemed like the safest bet. I rolled up my sleeves, squatted down low and lumbered back to shore like a bear. It seemed fitting somehow—being humbled by nature.

In the three years leading up to this moment, I gave little thought to my relationship with the natural world. I had developed a close bond with nature as a child, thanks to my Métis father and my mother, who both encouraged plenty of outdoor play. I assumed it would always stay that way, but clearly I was wrong.

My bond had frayed like an abused rope, a lifeline precariously close to snapping. To make matters worse, I was not living authentically. I had been writing about the importance of getting outside for over a dozen years on my blog and elsewhere. If ever there was an impostor, it was me.

How did this happen?

The question probed the corners of my mind as I navigated the encroaching darkness back up the hill to the parking lot and made the tortuous return to a life that was slowly breaking me apart.

THE *REAL* BACKWOODS MAMA

Ten years earlier, in 2012, my husband and I uprooted our family from our hometown of Prince George, British Columbia, and moved over 435 miles (700 km) south to the sleepy lakeside town of Okanagan Falls. Possessed by the promise of new opportunities and sunshine, we abruptly left behind our family and friends. To this day, I wonder at the foolish bravery of our decision. Our children were four, two, and six months at that time and we were leaving all our supports and community all while I suffered a silent war with undiagnosed postpartum anxiety.

As our vehicle descended into the Okanagan Valley, my breath caught. Although I'd seen this view before, it never failed to capture my heart. There, before me, a long, sparkling lake surrounded by a mix of forests, grasslands, orchards, vineyards, and desert shrublands lay on the valley floor. As I rolled down my window, the August sun warmed my face and the torrid breeze carried notes of pine and sagebrush into my nose. It was a symphony for my senses, a song of welcoming. However, the moment we crossed the small bridge over the outlet of the lake into town, a wave of anxiety rose through my body. It crested high, building pressure behind my eyes.

This is the stupidest decision I've ever made.

That's when the tears came.

"Hon?" said Jeremie, probing gently, as he sat by the waterfall next to him.

"Can we go back home?" I sobbed, knowing full well that this wasn't an option. Contracts were signed—a job and a house.

"Let's give it a year, OK?" he said. I nodded, wiping tears from my eyes.

I soon discovered that being new in a small town isn't easy. The friendly locals held me at arm's length. As a tourist hot spot, new people come and go. Perhaps they assumed I wouldn't stay long, or their lives were already filled with meaningful relationships and they didn't need more. I struggled with loneliness in a way I'd never experienced—a mother of three young children, no family or friends around, a sojourner in a strange *Land.* I felt adrift like sea kelp, tossed around without anchor, support, or safety.

Perhaps the lack of friendship or a need to get my rambunctious children out of the house drove me outdoors. Regardless, during my first year in Okanagan Falls, while I struggled with loneliness and lingering postpartum anxiety, I sought refuge outside.

Initially, I explored the nature close to our home. We fell in love with a beautiful king maple hugging our home and planted a few tulip bulbs that would sprout next spring. Then we started to wander around the quaint neighborhood. We walked the same route day after day and still discovered something new every time. Eventually we started adventuring further from home and discovering the wilder nature that surrounded us.

The ecosystem around our new home felt alien to me. I grew up in a subboreal spruce ecosystem, a city within a mixed forest of white spruce, lodgepole pine, subalpine fir, trembling aspens, and paper birch. The winters there were long and cold, but the autumns were a splendid kaleidoscope of color.

I found myself in a shrub-steppe grassland ecosystem: hot, dry, yellow, and gray. I didn't recognize the native flora, and the snakes and spiders terrified me. Together my children and I wandered cautiously through open forests of towering ponderosa pine and swathes of waving grass. We wondered why sagebrush bloomed yellow and how quail parents kept track of all their young. As we filled our pockets with rocks, nature filled our hearts.

Of course, we had plenty of misadventures along the way.

"Ow ow ow! Owwww! Maman! Mamaaaan!" screamed three-year-old Theo. He had taken a shortcut down a deer path to catch up to his older siblings and had fallen onto his bottom.

"What happened?" called five-year-old Claire, backtracking to help her little brother. Both of us reached Theo at the same time.

"Bummmm!" Theo howled.

I picked him up and there stuck to his backside was an enormous prickly pear, sharp spines pierced through his clothing into his butt cheek.

"Oh ouch!" I blurted out, catching his hand before he could grab the cactus. "Stay still and I'll pull it off."

I pinched the bottom of the cactus between my fingers and gave it a swift yank. The fruit went flying through the brush, taking most of its spines with it. The few that were left behind I yanked out to the sound of Theo's yelps and screams.

"His bum is bleeding!" Claire pointed out as I checked the damage. Several pinprick marks were all that remained of his cactus encounter.

Prickly pears, I would later learn, spread by attaching themselves to animals or unsuspecting children. Tossed into a new area, when the conditions are right, they take root and grow. Just as we'd been doing.

I shared many of our adventures, misadventures, and lessons learned on my personal website Backwoods Mama. Since I could find little information about local trails online, my children and I explored the nearby wild together and I posted our discoveries online to help other families in the area.

One year after moving to Okanagan Falls, I felt more at home in my new town. I had discovered a group of wild mamas that took their children into the woods and celebrated the seasons. They welcomed me into their group, and I learned much from them. One mama taught me how to recognize the song of a red-winged blackbird. Another how to weave flower crowns with willow branches. For eight years, my family grew deep roots both to people and *Land*. I felt connected, grounded—the real *Backwoods Mama*.

THE BEGINNING OF A LIE

"Kids, come and sit beside us for a bit," said my husband.

We were in an airport in Guangzhou, China, returning from a

family trip to Bali, Indonesia. Still buzzing from our adventures there, my husband and I figured we could ride that wave into our next adventure.

"We have some exciting news to share with all of you," he went on.

My three children gathered round, chattering excitedly. It was the fall of 2019, and they were seven, nine, and eleven years old. Felix our eldest, spoke up first.

"Are we going on another trip?" he said.

"Not exactly . . ." I replied.

"Are we getting a dog?" Claire asked, wanting to add to her menagerie of animals.

"Nope, no dog," said my husband. We looked at each other and I bit my lip. He forged on, "We're moving."

Their reactions were like autumn leaves on the forest floor, some bright others dark.

"Cool!" replied Felix, his easygoing, down-to-earth personality meant even big changes rarely ruffled his feathers.

"Ummm OK," said seven-year-old Theo nervously, reaching out for my hand.

"What?" exclaimed my daughter, swiftly bursting into tears.

We explained that a move to a new city beckoned us. My husband was offered an exciting career opportunity. We would live on the same acreage as their grandparents. Maybe we could even get a dog—a consolation prize for my daughter. My daughter was devastated, and my own feelings were a tangled web.

Within two months of that conversation, we moved from Okanagan Falls to the city of Kelowna, downsizing to a small 1,200-square-foot two-bedroom log home on my parents' two-acre lot.

Before saying our final goodbye to our bigger home in Okanagan Falls, my son and I dug up a small maple sapling in our yard. It had seeded itself from the mother tree that my children had spent hours climbing in and playing under. Like that sapling, we pulled up our roots and relocated, but this move turned out nothing like we imagined.

CHAPTER 2

Last Parent in the Woods

SHORTLY AFTER MOVING to Kelowna, a trifecta of surprises came my way: a pandemic, a puppy, and a pregnancy. All three happened in the same week, throwing my world off axis, spinning, careening me into survival mode. Sludging through a thick haze of fatigue and confusion, I longed for normalcy. Instead of setting down roots in my new community like I had done in Okanagan Falls, getting to know the people and *Land* that surrounded me, I withdrew into the cocoon of my home, secretly glad the world had come to a sudden and painful halt.

In 1993, a moth and butterfly expert, Robert Pyle, proposed a theory in his book *The Thunder Tree: Lessons from an Urban Wildland*. He suggested that we are all losing direct connection with nature—an experience that makes us aliens in our own home, a separation that breeds apathy, anxiety, and contempt for nature. He called this phenomenon "the extinction of experience."[1]

The "extinction of experience" proposed by Pyle was largely ignored for more than twenty years, but not completely forgotten. Richard Louv brought attention to this issue in 2005 with *Last Child in the Woods: Saving Our Children from Nature-Deficit Disorder*. In this book Louv introduced the idea of a nature-deficit disorder, not a true medical condition, but the idea that there is a growing gap between children and nature that's negatively impacting their well-being and development.

It wasn't until 2016 that this "growing gap" or "extinction of experience" became a more commonly discussed topic around researchers' campfires. I'm assuming, of course, that the people researching, writing, or learning about this stuff enjoy a good campfire chin-wag just as much as I do. Since 2016, however, the chitchat has become louder and more insistent. Overall, it's becoming clear that children's connection to nature is slipping away. But what about parents?

One evening, during the start of the pandemic, I scanned my bookshelf for a diversion. Richard Louv's *Last Child in the Woods* stared back at me. I slipped the book off the shelf and held it in my hands. At that time, many of our local parks, trails, and nature areas were closed from the public, so the growing gap Louv wrote about felt more like an impassable chasm. In that moment, book in hand, a flood of frustration, anger, and sadness overwhelmed me. I wanted to jump on an airplane, fly to Louv's house, and ask him:

"What about us *parents*? What about our nature-deficit disorder?"

Somewhere along the way we forgot about the last *parent* in the woods. Six years after *Last Child in the Woods*, Louv published *The Nature Principle: Human Restoration and the End of Nature-Deficit Disorder* and wrote: "After the book's [*Last Child in the Woods*] publication, I heard many adults speak with heartfelt emotion, even anger, about this separation [from nature], but also about their own sense of loss."[2] This "growing gap" or "extinction of experience" isn't something that's unique to our children. It's happening to parents. It happened to me.

I DON'T BELONG HERE

My separation from the natural world didn't occur all at once. Like a fissure in a boulder, it started as a hairline crack, imperceptible at first, that grew wider and deeper as my choices and experiences trickled into it. Occasionally certain events would add extra pressure to the crack—geologists call this frost wedging—and the gap would quickly widen, pushing me away, making me feel like I didn't belong in nature. One of these events happened on a blue-skied, sunshiny spring day.

Feeling recovered from the birth of my fourth wildling, I made good on my promise to take my three children pond dipping. Just so we're clear, pond dipping has nothing to do with swimming, and everything to do with curiosity. It involves dipping, or trawling, small pond nets in shallow pond areas to catch, observe, and release pond-dwelling creatures like frogs, tadpoles, newts, mosquito larvae, leeches, dragonfly nymphs, and diving beetles.

The pond my kids had in mind lay in the middle of the city, surrounded by remnants of a black cottonwood and water birch forest. Many years ago, the pond was part of a larger ecosystem that was destroyed by urban development, agriculture, and the channeling of streams and rivers.[3]

We had visited this small pond and walked the flat pathway that encircled it a few times. My children enjoyed watching the waterfowl, raptors, and majestic blue heron that made this spot their home, but their curiosity didn't stop there. They wanted to know more about the pond and knew that just below the pond's reflective surface a magical world of minibeasts was waiting to be discovered.

With clean nets and buckets in hand we made our way to the nearby pond. The moment we arrived my children burst out of the van and ran wildly toward the pond. When I say "wildly," I mean it. There were shouts of glee and nets waving all around.

"Turtles, turtles!" my nine-year-old son Theodore shouted. He had spotted a line of western painted turtles sunning themselves on a floating log in the pond. I smiled, holding his outburst of joy close to my heart. We have a family habit of celebrating sun-basking turtles whenever we see them.

I quickly unpacked the van, buckled baby Alice into a stroller, and made my way to the edge of the pond where my older children lingered; however, as I neared the water a middle-aged woman intercepted me.

"You're not allowed to net the turtles. It's illegal," she informed me pointedly.

"We aren't here to catch turtles," I replied, taken off guard. "We're here to go pond dipping, to look at invertebrates swimming in the water. Anything we scoop up will be gently returned into the pond."

"You can't touch the turtles," she repeated, eyes filling with anger.

"We aren't here to net turtles," I insisted. "We are here to look at pond invertebrates, but if we accidentally catch a turtle, I promise it will be gently returned into the water."

I could tell that my attempt to alleviate her concern fell on deaf ears, so I gave her a kind smile and walked toward my children.

"What was that woman saying to you?" my daughter asked, seeing a troubled look on my face.

"She's worried we're here to net the turtles and take them away," I calmly replied.

"Why would we do that?" Theodore asked anxiously. "This is their home."

"It's also illegal," Felix pointed out and then looked back at the woman.

I wished that woman could have overheard our conversation and realized we were all on team turtle.

"Why is that woman taking pictures of us?" my daughter asked.

I pivoted around. I couldn't believe my eyes. The woman stood in place, camera in hand, taking photos of us and then swiftly walked to the parking lot. I would later discover that she was on the hunt for our license plate.

"Maybe today isn't going to be the day for pond dipping," I decided. "Let's put away our gear and go bird-watching instead. I saw a juvenile hawk circling the pond just a moment ago." My kids groaned with disappointment, but soon they were chatting up local birders.

Over the next few days two things happened. First, a story about "turtle-nappers" hit the local news, and then a message from the conservation officer landed in my voicemail.[4] I was shocked. Apparently, the day before our arrival at the pond a woman and son were trying to catch turtles. I'm not sure what their intentions were, perhaps they too were pond dipping or maybe they had other plans.

"I'm here twice a day every day taking photographs," one nature enthusiast said during an interview, "so I'm keeping a very good watch out [for people] now."

I had inadvertently walked into the perfect storm. We hadn't even dipped our nets into the pond and people were leaving nasty comments on social media about how kids "shouldn't touch nature with their grubby little fingers" and how they "didn't belong there." The hate was real.

I recalled a story from Linda Åkeson McGurk's book *There's No Such Thing as Bad Weather: A Scandinavian Mom's Secrets for Raising Healthy, Resilient, and Confident Kids* when McGurk was fined by a police officer for letting her children play in a creek. She had violated a state code that "makes it illegal to wade or swim in any public waterway unless it's a 'designated swimming beach or pool.'"[5]

Would this be my very own "creek incident"?

I returned the conservation officer's call straightaway and prepared to stand my defense. "Hello officer, I believe you left me a message," I said a bit too quickly.

"Oh hello, thank you for calling me back. I must follow-up on a complaint I received. Were you by chance removing turtles from a city pond?"

I dove in and explained the whole situation, from beginning to end.

"If you weren't taking turtles away then we're done here. Also, what you are doing is great. Keep bringing your kids outdoors."

"Oh . . . thank you," I replied. This is not how I expected this conversation to go.

Despite the officer's encouragement, I never returned to that pond with my children. In fact, it would be years before I would take them pond dipping again.

APPROACHING EXTINCTION

As the pandemic restrictions started to ease, I fully expected that I would return to a pre-pandemic "normal." That didn't happen. Instead of nets dipping into ponds, I flitted between driving three older children to various activities, wrangling a firecracker toddler, and keeping tabs on an energetic Australian shepherd. Instead of weaving nature crowns for my children to wear as they climbed trees, I wove through traffic to get everyone to their activities on time. It didn't occur to me that I was fast approaching extinction from nature.

Researchers have identified two significant themes that cause "the extinction of experience." The first is that we have fewer opportunities to interact with nature (loss of opportunity) and the second is that there is less interest in nature (loss of orientation). Which came first, fewer opportunities or less interest? I think it's safe to say that these two realities are as intertwined as the vines of a Virginia creeper.

Loss of Opportunity: The Big Three

Many parents would agree that their children have fewer opportunities and/or less interest in interacting with nature compared to when they were children themselves. There are many reasons for this new reality, but in my research on the "extinction of experience" three major themes came up. I call these "the big three" and they are: cities (urban living), (over)scheduled lives, and screens. Let's unpack each one and see how they impact families.

URBAN LIVING (CITIES)

During the eight years that my family and I lived in the rural town of Okanagan Falls, I balked at the idea of moving to the city. The few times a year that I visited left me exhausted. The traffic was ridiculous and the parking atrocious. I promised myself that I would never move there, which, as you already know, is exactly what we ended up doing.

Families moving to cities is a growing trend. More than half of the world's population lives in urban areas and that number will only increase to an estimated 68 percent by 2050.[6] We all need somewhere to live, and cities have some distinct advantages. They have more jobs and education opportunities along with better access to health care. Two of those three reasons were why we moved to a bigger city.

However, cities have a significant impact on nature. Urban landscapes disrupt natural environments and ecosystems, dropping the number and diversity of plants, insects, and animals.[7] As a result, nature in urban areas can be limited and fragmented, especially in highly dense metropolitan areas, making it challenging for families to find opportunities to access and interact with nature. When families don't have easy access to nature, it's much more difficult to connect with it.

(OVER)SCHEDULED LIVES

Before moving to the city, a busy *week* had more than six activities or commitments. By 2022, after the pandemic restrictions eased, each *day* had four to six activities scheduled in.

When parents were asked about the reasons that prevented them from getting outside with their children, *lack of time* was one of the most mentioned reasons.[8] Between working, shuttling kids to school then extracurricular activities, making meals, and doing chores, families are overscheduled. While extracurriculars, also called enrichment activities, can be good for children, too much isn't a good thing. Unfortunately, many children have no time left in their day for unstructured outdoor play or to be in nature, and neither do parents.

SCREENS

While I'm not "anti-screens," I can't deny the impact that screens have had on my children and my own "extinction of experience" from 2019 to 2023. Many opportunities to interact with nature were lost in exchange for time in front of screens.

In his book *Reconnection: Fixing Our Broken Relationship with*

Nature, Miles Richardson, professor of human factors and nature connectedness, noted that "as technology advances, nature becomes more distant."[9] Screens have had a significant impact in pulling our families away from nature.

Technology, especially screens—smartphones, tablets, gaming devices, computers, streaming services—as we use them presently, steal a lot of time from us. The average American, ages eight and older, spends an average of 7.5 hours a day staring at a screen.[10] Screens also shift our focus away from connecting with others and with nature and narrows us into a very specific way of experiencing life, one that is often lonely and isolated.

Loss of Orientation: Biophobia

The Insectarium in Montreal, Quebec, is home to over 3,000 insects, most of which are dead and on display. The Great Vivarium, however, is a year-round living kingdom where butterflies are reared and insects thrive. On a trip to Montreal, my children and I walked through this area with wonder and curiosity. A few steps behind us two young adults followed close by.

As my children noticed all the variety of butterflies, yelps sprung up from behind us. Suddenly, the young folk were thrashing about and cowering in fear every time a gentle butterfly swooped over their heads.

"What's wrong with those people?" Theo, then eleven years old, whispered beside me.

"I think they're afraid of the butterflies," I said.

"Why? Don't they know that these butterflies won't harm them?" he asked.

"Maybe this is their first time being close to butterflies," I replied.

My kids thought the situation was comical, because obviously the butterflies weren't going to hurt them, but I felt more than a little concerned. Fears of certain animals and insects are normal, true, but I had never seen a fear of butterflies until that moment.

As our connection with nature weakens, our fear of nature

deepens. Fear of nature is called biophobia. Some scientists believe a specific fear of nature can be genetic, a protective mechanism deeply embedded into humanness; however, a general feeling of distrust toward nature seems to be more a product of our disconnection.[11] It makes sense to be cautious of a poisonous snake sunning itself in the middle of a trail, but what about a butterfly flitting from flower to flower? And does it even matter?

CHAPTER 3

Families and Nature Flourishing Together

"MAYBE WE COULD meet up for a walk by the creek?" I suggested tentatively.

Even though I had lived in Kelowna, British Columbia, for two years already, I had very few connections in the community. I blamed the pandemic restrictions, but the truth was that as restrictions eased, my days filled with extracurricular activities, and I had no *time* to make new friends. Yet I longed for the close friendships that were a part of our daily lives in Okanagan Falls. I knew I had to at least *try* to meet new people.

"There's a nice trail that ends at a park down by the pool . . ." I went on. The mother I spoke to had four boys who were the same ages as my three older children. They seemed like fun and energetic kids that would enjoy a good romp through a forest.

"I don't *do* nature," she replied nonchalantly. "It's not my thing."

I stared at her blankly, attempting to process what I just heard. Before I could go on to explain that it was an easy wide trail about half a mile long (1 km), she turned away from me and whisked her boys into their van. Although I saw her several more times after this encounter, she ignored me completely.

That encounter, as awkward as it was, had me pondering an even stranger reality, one that has embedded itself into our views of nature—that some people are "into" nature and others are not. That some people are "outdoorsy" and others are not. That some people are "tree huggers" and others not.

For many people, nature has been reduced to a weekend hobby, a value system, a political stance, or a cult following, something we can choose to be interested in or not. But does a disconnection from nature even matter? Maybe a disconnection from nature negatively impacted me, but do all parents and children really *need* nature to thrive? This question was also asked by Scott D. Sampson, renowned paleontologist, in his book *How to Raise a Wild Child.* "Here in the twenty-first century, can we be healthy without meaningful experiences of nature?"[1]

It's a question worth answering, but before I do, let's backtrack. What exactly is *nature*?

NATURE, WHAT IS IT?

When you read the word *nature*, what's the first image that comes to your mind? For me, it's a forest. Not just any forest, it's the forest of my childhood. Across the street from my suburban home, a mixed forest of evergreen and deciduous trees sheltered a deep ravine where a small creek trickled toward the mighty Fraser River. I remember its woodsy smell, the prickly feeling of needles under my bare feet, the chattering squirrels, and the sticky sap perpetually stuck to my hands.

There are many different views of what nature is or is not. For instance, some people believe that nature is only found outside of cities in wild or untouched places. Others view nature more holistically. In my Métis Indigenous tradition, nature, or *Land*, is seen as an animated, spiritual, and interconnected being of water, earth, air, and sky that encompasses all plants, animals, insects, fungi, rocks, humans, and more.[2]

For the pages ahead, it might be easier to understand nature as *the world of living things and the outdoors.*[3] It's the dirt beneath our feet, stars shining in the night sky, dandelions growing in sidewalk cracks, birds on utility poles, and a puddle on a sidewalk. Nature surrounds and sustains us. It's the rush of air that fills our lungs with every in-breath, the cool water that quenches our thirst, and the food that fills us at mealtimes. Nature is *everywhere.*[4]

BIOPHILIA: AS A FISH TO WATER

My ancestors were *voyageurs*, men who transported goods and furs along the rivers and lakes of the Northwest for fur trading companies, and the beautiful Indigenous (Cree) daughters of the *Land.* When voyageurs and Indigenous women came together in the Red River region of what is now known as Manitoba and beyond in the late 1700s, a distinct People was born—the Métis Nation. The Métis people developed a close relationship with *Land* thanks to the Indigenous women that became mothers of the Métis people.

In many ways, I feel like my own connection with nature was passed down to me by my Métis father. As a child, my father took me and my siblings on plenty of adventures, often close to home, and encouraged us to spend plenty of time outside. My mother also showed us a love for nature in the way she grew flowers and vegetables in our yard—something I also came to love. When I think back on those days, and my Métis heritage, I often wonder if my love of nature was something I was born with, or if it was something learned along the way. Is a connection to the natural world genetic or learned?

In 2022, a study of twins showed that the way we connect to and experience nature is inherited, but our environment plays a crucial role in igniting that connection.[5] This finding supports a trending idea among researchers: Our genes play a role in our love of nature, but access to nature, time in nature, and learning about nature play an even bigger role.

Just like a dormant seed, each of us is born with a natural pull toward nature—a love of all living things (biophilia)—but we need to nurture that seed for it to sprout and grow strong. The wonderful thing about biophilia is that it can be nurtured at any point in time no matter where you live. If you didn't develop a connection to nature as a child, that's OK—you can begin as an adult even in the city. However, when we help that seed sprout in childhood, something magical happens.

CHILDREN *NEED* NATURE

My five children are energetic, boisterous, and playful. In other words, they're kids! From an early age they would bounce on beds, catapult off couches, and climb onto counters. I knew one thing for sure: Keeping my kids between four walls wasn't the best thing for them or myself.

Parents have known for ages that the outdoors can be restorative for children, but now science confirms it: Spending time in and interacting with nature makes children happier, healthier, and smarter. While entire books could explore this important connection, I'll give you a brief overview—enough information to confidently say "yes" to more outdoor time for your child.

Let's start with the physical benefits. We know that children from coast-to-coast, north-to-south, don't move their bodies enough. They aren't running down hills, climbing trees, or jumping over logs. A study of 5,844 nine- to eleven-year-olds from twelve countries around the world, Canada and the United States included, discovered that children's average sedentary time is 8.6 hours each day, and all that sitting around isn't doing our kids any favors.[6]

Obesity rates have skyrocketed in children. Between 1971 and 1974, 16.4 percent of American children ages two to nineteen experienced excessive weight, but by 2017 and 2018, that number jumped to 41.5 percent based on the National Health and Nutrition Examination Survey (NHANES).[7] In Canada, 31.8 percent of children and youth ages five to seventeen were overweight or had obesity in 2015.[8] It's true that excess weight in childhood has numerous causes, but the two main factors contributing to childhood obesity are diet and physical activity.

To help children have healthier body weights, the Centers for Disease Control and Prevention (CDC) and the Canadian 24-Hour

Movement Guidelines both recommend that children between the ages of five to seventeen engage in sixty minutes or more of moderate-to-vigorous physical activity each day.[9] While it might be tempting to increase the amount of time our kids are physically active by scheduling in more extracurricular activities, one of the best ways to increase physical activity in children is *unstructured outdoor play.*[10] A 2015 meta-analysis found that children who spend more time outside are more physically active and less sedentary.[11] In a day care study of two-to-three-year-olds, children were about four times more likely to be in moderate-to-vigorous activity outdoors than indoors and much less sedentary outdoors.

Not only does getting outside increase physical activity but it also improves children's motor development and physical literacy skills. The outdoors provides children with an inexhaustible list of opportunities to develop fine and gross motor skills. Collecting rocks, gathering sticks, balancing on a log, running on grass, digging in the dirt, jumping over streams, and climbing trees all seem to help younger children develop motor skills in ways that can't be replicated indoors.[12]

The benefits of time outdoors extend beyond physical health; nature also profoundly nurtures a child's emotional and mental well-being. Among my own five children, one suffers from anxiety, which happens to be the second most common mental health disorder among American children ages six to eleven after behavior disorders.[13] Unfortunately, anxiety and depression have been increasing in children. According to the American Academy of Pediatrics, "nearly 20 percent of children aged 3–17 years have a mental, emotional, and behavioral disorder."[14] Canadian children and youth aren't any better off. The Canadian Paediatric Society reports that "twenty per cent of Canadian children and youth will experience mental illness."[15]

Time in nature, even passive exposure to nature, seems to have a positive effect on the mental and emotional well-being of children. I'm not saying that nature is a "cure-all," but time outside can help reduce stress, improve coping skills, and build resilience in children.[16] It also has a significant impact on improving attention and hyperactivity, reducing the symptoms of attention deficit disorder (ADD) and attention deficit hyperactivity disorder (ADHD).[17]

The open-endedness of nature also *invites* children to develop creative thinking and problem-solving skills. For example, a stick can transform into a fishing pole, a flute, a writing utensil, a sword, a wand, or a guitar through the imagination of a child.

Research on nature and creative thinking in children is relatively new, but a 2018 study of young children going to nature preschools versus non-nature preschools found that the children going to nature preschools had a significant growth in creative thinking over the year.[18] Another study of two natural outdoor classrooms found that children's creativity and imagination blossomed when they had plenty of access to the outdoors with open-ended nature materials and supportive adults.[19] And another study of two childcare centers found that children engaged in more independent play, using more creativity and problem-solving skills, when their outdoor play spaces were improved to include more nature.[20]

CO-PARENTING *WITH* NATURE

I will never forget the first time my child "prescribed" me nature time. I was flustered, impatient, and downright grumpy. The house was a mess, and I barked at my children to pick up their toys while angrily vacuuming crumbs off the floor for the umpteenth time.

"Why can't the house just stay clean?" I ranted.

My eldest son, about ten years old at the time, scowled at me and said, "I think you need a time-out in nature."

In that moment, my eldest reminded of something important: Nature isn't just a gift for our children, it's a lifeline for parents. When parents embrace nature, it can transform us and the way we connect with our children.

I turned off the vacuum, looked at Felix, and smiled with a mixture of surprise, pride, and embarrassment. Of course, he was right. The moment I stepped outside, my need for a perfectly clean home was replaced with a healthy dose of dirt under my fingernails.

There has been a great deal of focus on the importance of nature for children and adults, but the impact of nature on parents and parenting is also very important. Like children, when parents spend time outside, they feel happier, healthier, and more grounded, and nature can even have a greater impact than income, education, and religiosity.[21] Personally, when I take time in and with nature I feel settled and refreshed—a more engaged parent—and I lean in to nature as a co-parent.

I can't remember the first time I came across the idea of co-parenting with nature, also called nature-connected parenting, but the concept is deeply rooted in various cultural traditions, especially of Indigenous peoples. In many Indigenous traditions there is a sacred reciprocal relationship with nature, which is often seen as "Mother"—an important partner in raising children. Drawing from this perspective, as well as the idea from the "Six Touchstones for Wild Pedagogies in Practice," I like to think of co-parenting *with* nature as seeing the natural world as an active partner and co-teacher in raising and nurturing my children and making time to listen to, engage with, and learn from the natural world in a way that fosters mutual flourishing.[22]

Co-parenting with nature is about *shared experiences* that foster connection, curiosity, and growth as a family. It's about improving parent-child-nature relationships.

When I co-parent with nature, I've noticed something eye-opening and humbling—I am a better parent. Nature helps me feel more present, calm, and grounded. I'm less distracted by household chores, endless to-do lists, or my smartphone and can focus on being present with my children.

Emerging research supports these observations. Studies show that time outdoors can improve parent-child communication and responsiveness.[23] For example, Dina Izenstark from San José State University found that when mothers and tween daughters spend time outside together, their communication improves and they get along better.[24] Similarly, Jillisa Overholt of Warren Wilson College discovered that fathers and their children who participated in an Outward Bound family course experienced positive shifts in their relationships.[25] While research on the parent-child-nature relationship seems to be in its early phase, these studies are showing that nature can improve the way parents connect with and relate to their children.

LEAVING NATURE *BETTER* THAN WE FOUND IT

Little legs ran ahead of me, padding down the gentle forest trail. Without warning they veered off-trail and settled onto a thick mat of dried evergreen needles below a mighty ponderosa pine. Together three-year-old Alice, my fourth child, and her cousin grasped handfuls of prickly forest floor and tossed them into the air like stardust. All was magic, for a moment.

"What are you doing there?" a voice barked from down the trail. The sound snatched the moment like a thief.

There, coming up the trail, a man postured, fists on his hips. His tall frame towered aggressively, but something was off. He was dressed head to toe in a blue costume.

Is he a dolphin? No, it looks more like a . . .

"Just so you know," his voice boomed, "you're not supposed to go *off*-trail. You could get a hefty fine for what you're doing."

This angry dude is wearing a narwhal costume!

My mind does this thing in the face of confrontation. I don't cower. I don't lash out. Time slows and I notice odd details. I dissociate.

Oh . . . he's got a group of children with him, how fun!

"Is that right?" I ventured noncommittally, still wondering about the costume and children, trying to piece the scene together. He glared at me for a moment, and I stared at the white plush tusk perched on his head. Eventually, he scoffed and stomped off with a pack of children in tow. The cadence of time picked back up.

I think I was just scolded by an early childhood educator dressed in a narwhal costume for letting two toddlers play with pine needles under a tree by the trail.

My sister-in-law hovered close to my elbow and whispered nervously, "Will he report us?"

"No," I said. "I never saw any signs . . ." but I started second-guessing myself.

The nature area we visited, tucked into a city neighborhood, is well loved by families. Signs of nature play are spread throughout, from impromptu forts to hand-painted rocks with the word *happy* written on them. Apart from a few areas of restoration that are *clearly* signed and fenced off, children are allowed to sit under trees and play with sticks. In fact, forest yoga classes are held among the peaceful stands of trees and families are encouraged to take part in the annual "pick up the sticks" event to remove deadfall from the forest as a fire prevention strategy. My previous knowledge about this area of nature collided with this man's angry warnings.

Before you assume that my children trample over sensitive nature areas without regard, know that this is not the case. I am both respectful and aware of situations where nature needs a gentle touch or space to flourish. However, since becoming a parent, I've lost track of how many times my children have been scolded by strangers, educators, and other parents for their hands-on interactions with nature. With everything from collecting rocks along the shore to playing with sticks, the message has been more insistent over the years—"Nature is *not* for touching."

The "Leave No Trace" Movement

In the 1960s outdoor recreation exploded in the United States. It became so popular, in fact, that some said Americans were "loving their parks to death."[26] Regulations were put into place to help protect wildlands. These were met with some resistance, so the focus shifted from regulation to education around backcountry "manners."

Between the 1970s and 1980s, programs and guides like the Sierra Club's *Walking Softly in the Wilderness* (1977) helped camping and hiking enthusiasts learn how to tread gently through wild spaces with some success, but by the early 1990s some felt that there needed to be consistent messaging at a national level. That's when the U.S. Forest Service (USFS) partnered with the National Outdoor Leadership School (NOLS) to create Leave No Trace, a wilderness education program that provided in-depth courses along with clear principles for guiding those exploring wild spaces.[27]

Over time, Leave No Trace has evolved, and new principles were added. Eventually it became a nonprofit organization—a movement—that spread beyond American borders to Canada, South America, and beyond.

Presently, there are seven Leave No Trace principles:[28]

1. Plan Ahead and Prepare
2. Travel and Camp on Durable Surfaces
3. Dispose of Waste Properly
4. Leave What You Find
5. Minimize Campfire Impacts
6. Respect Wildlife
7. Be Considerate of Others

Leaving *More* Ethical Traces

From the moment he could walk, Felix, my eldest son, had a fascination with frogs. His favorite stuffy was a fuzzy lime green frog, and his preferred bedtime stories were *Frog and Toad* by Arnold Lobel. I fully expected his frog obsession to fade away with time, but it didn't. By the age of ten, my son announced that he wanted to build a frog pond in our backyard. Not knowing where to start, we visited the local pond shop.

"I want to build a frog pond," my son announced confidently to the kindly older man.

"Well, I think that's wonderful," the owner replied. "I have a small piece of pond liner that I can sell you at a discounted price."

My son paid from his own savings and started digging a hole in the corner of our backyard as soon as he arrived home. After three days of hard solitary work, he had a hole big enough for his liner which he laid in place and secured with large rocks. He secured it with large rocks from our friends' property and covered the bottom with smooth pond rocks. Then, he filled the pond with water and waited.

"Do you think they'll come?" he asked me, concerned all his work was for nothing.

"I think they will," I said, hopefully.

Within days of having finished his pond, the first frog appeared, and soon the ruckus mating calls of many frogs echoed through our neighborhood—very loudly I might add! Other critters moved in too: mayfly larvae, water gliders, and water beetles. Birds swooped by for a sip and butterflies rested on the nearby flowers. To my happy surprise, my son had created a thriving microecosystem; he had left an ethical trace.

The Leave No Trace (LNT) principles are helpful for guiding people toward ethical wilderness behavior and greater care for nature. After all, I've seen my fair share of disregard for wild spaces. However, here's where I'm going to resist (a skill well-honed by my Métis ancestors): While LNT does good, it's also problematic.

Over the past decade, I've noticed a shift in the way adults view children's interaction with nature. As I mentioned in my opening story, I've seen an increasing trend toward telling children that *nature is not for touching.* At first, I dismissed these comments, but when I noticed social media influencers preventing their little ones from playing with a rock on the shore or a stick in the forest in the name of Leave No Trace, that's when I started asking questions and received some interesting replies.

During a conversation with Sean Blenkinsop, professor in the Faculty of Education at Simon Fraser University, and founder of two outdoor public schools in Vancouver, British Columbia, I offhandedly asked about Leave No Trace. It wasn't the focus of our discussion, but his reply stuck with me.

"The Leave No Trace movement is entrenched in a western romantic understanding of nature," he said. "Instead [of Leave No

Trace] we should strive for a mutually beneficial flourishing between humans and the more-than-human world of nature."

Often when we think of nature flourishing, it's in the absence of families. This way of thinking, however, is based on the idea that we are separate from nature.[29] Chris Loynes, emeritus professor in human nature relations at the University of Cumbria, points out that the Leave No Trace movement distances people from nature while also ignoring the traces we leave while traveling to wild places and living everyday life.[30] Instead, he argues that we should consider a more "hands-on" approach with nature that seeks to leave reasonable, proportional, and ethical traces that help humans and nature flourish.[31]

This idea is echoed by Ryan Lumber, father of the Five Pathway framework for nature connection, when he urges families to engage with nature in a "respectful, moral way—one that acknowledges that we are part of it" and that "spending time in nature, touching, smelling, and experiencing it is how we get to know the world, and it ultimately helps us protect it."[32]

This "hands-on" approach with nature is especially important for our children. Contact with and in nature, being "hands-on," plays a key role in helping children bond with the natural world, something called *nature connection*, which I'll delve into in the next chapter, and when this bond forms it goes on to motivate children and parents to care for nature.[33]

CHAPTER 4

The Five Pathways to Reconnecting with Nature

NATURE CONNECTION, OR nature-connectedness, refers to our *relationship* with the natural world. It's how we feel, think, and experience nature.[1] When we feel connected to nature, we see ourselves as part of something much bigger—that we *belong* to a wider natural community.[2]

Nature connection is a relatively new area of study that started showing up in the early 2000s and has become an established area of research that involves psychology, public health, neuroscience, ecology, as well as social science—nature connection isn't pop psychology! Researchers use scientific methods to better understand how humans relate to the natural world and how this relationship impacts the health and well-being of adults, children, and our planet.

One thing that makes nature connection interesting is that it isn't the same experience for everyone. Nature connection is a *subjective* experience. It's influenced by our personality, our way of thinking, our emotions, our experiences, our beliefs, and our community. The way I might feel connected to nature will be different than my children's connection, and my father's connection. That's very normal—we all experience relationships differently. However, even though the experience of connection can be different for every one of us, connection with nature gives parents and children a greater sense of happiness, purpose in life, and desire to care for nature (pro-environmental attitudes).[3] These benefits are unique to feeling connected to nature, which is different than contact with nature.

It's important to mention that nature connection isn't the same as *contact with* or being exposed to nature. Yes, being in contact with nature is good for our family's health and well-being, but it's possible to be in nature but not feel connected to nature. I've experienced this myself.

For several years, I struggled to understand how I could be *in* nature but still feel so disconnected. It's not that I didn't go outside at all during that period, but when I did, I treated nature as a backdrop for various activities. It wasn't until I began reconnecting with nature as *home*—while learning about the science of nature connection and rediscovering my Indigenous Métis understanding of *Land*—that I moved beyond seeing nature as a backdrop. From that point, I began the journey of forging a deeper connection with the natural world by following my children down the pathways to greater nature connection.

THE FIVE PATHWAYS TO NATURE CONNECTION

I rushed out the front door into the coolness of the evening, following the rocky pathway to the gardens. The air was heavy with moisture, and the lawn was drooping under wetness. I stepped off the pathway and skidded through the wet lawn, enjoying the moisture on my bare feet while running through a mental list of the garden chores I needed to complete. Just before launching myself into work, a shimmering brown object caught my eye in the grass.

Is that a penny?

I crouched down getting a closer look. No, not a penny. It was a mini house mover, a slowpoke wanderer, a slug with a backpack—a snail! It slow-danced through the dripping grass and weaved through the blooming clover. Eyes searching, tentacles probing. I watched the snail closely, enthralled.

Moments later Claire and Theo spotted me crouching in the grass and gathered around.

"What are you looking at?" Claire asked.

"Come and see," I whispered.

"What a beautiful shell," she said.

"Will you move it to safety?" asked Theo.

"Let's just see what happens," I said, trying not to break this magical moment.

We inched through the wet grass, following the snail as it led us deeper into nature.

In 2017, Ryan Lumber, Miles Richardson, and David Sheffield documented five pathways that draw us closer to nature.[4] These pathways were initially developed by Ryan Lumber for his PhD in 2016 by testing the nine values of biophilia, from *The Biophilia Hypothesis*, to see which ones led to a greater connection with nature—*contact*, *meaning*, *emotion*, *compassion*, and *beauty* became the Five Pathway framework.[5] Since then, these pathways have been reaffirmed by research and shared by major organizations around the world to help others reconnect with nature.[6]

Pathway One: Experiencing Sensory Contact with Nature

My children and I crouched down in the wet grass, getting eye-to-eye with the snail. Suddenly our world shifted. Grass blades seemed enormous, and the world smelled of wet earth. We could almost hear grass bending as the tiny traveler scaled stems, leaving licks of slime in its wake.

Humans are sensuous beings. Touching, tasting, smelling, seeing, and hearing are how we gather information about our surroundings and make connections to our world. This explains why sensory contact is crucial for connecting with the natural world. Contact with nature is the fundamental starting point for parents and children—"Engage your senses first!"[7]

Ways to explore sensory contact with nature:

- Walking on the ground barefoot.
- Feeling the wind on your skin.
- Nibbling on herbs or wild edible berries.
- Rubbing a hand over a soft patch of moss.
- Balancing on a log.
- Listening to birdsongs.
- Smelling wildflowers.
- Watching the sun set.

Pathway Two: Engaging with Nature's Beauty

The copper swirl of the snail's shell, perfect like a penny, moving through droplet-bejeweled blades of grass, captivated my children and me. How could something so small and simple be so beautiful?

The beauty of nature, both in its grandiose mountains, sunsets, and waterfalls, and in its minuscule creepy crawlies, have captivated the hearts of poets and artists for thousands of years. Children have an eye for noticing and engaging in nature's beauty, and are open to seeing beauty that's often overlooked, like a snail. When we engage with the beauty in nature—its colors, shapes, and forms—and allow the beauty of nature to inspire our art, music, and poetry, it deepens our connection to the natural world.[8]

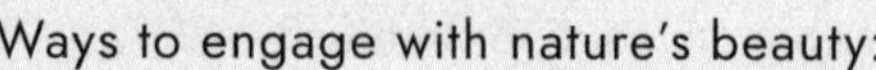

Ways to engage with nature's beauty:

- Slowing down and noticing nature up close.
- Looking for opportunities to celebrate and experience the beauty of nature, like watching a sunset, counting the stars, noticing a rainbow, or visiting a botanical garden.
- Taking photos of nature.
- Nature journaling.
- Creating arts and crafts with and in nature.
- Appreciating nature in fine art, music, and poems.

Pathway Three: Fostering an Emotional Bond with Nature

The snail's long march across our front yard drew various emotions from its onlookers. Worry that it would fall prey to a bird or the heavy footfall of a human, wonder that it was so persistent and brave, and joy that we could witness such a shy creature.

Nature can stir up a host of emotions in us. Even a brief experience in nature, as short as fifteen minutes, can make us feel happiness, joy, peace, and awe.[9] Nature can also make us feel sad, angry, afraid, or frustrated. All these experiences deepen our connection with nature. As a parent, I have always appreciated the safe, nonjudgmental space that nature provides to explore emotions, both for myself and my children, and when we take time to process emotions, both those that nature stirs within us and those we bring along, we rediscover how to express ourselves *through* nature.

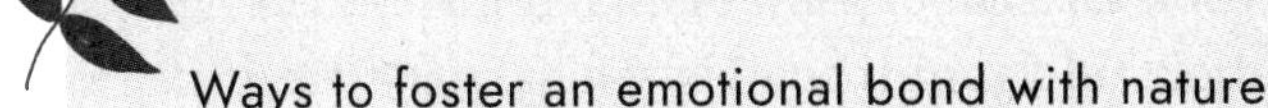

Ways to foster an emotional bond with nature:

- Noticing good things in nature and how they make you and your children feel.[10]
- Talking about how you or your children feel before, during, and after time outside.
- Discovering how contact with different animals, plants, or landscapes make you and your children feel.
- Recognizing emotions that arise in nature (seeing a dead animal, litter on the ground, etc.).
- Processing emotions like sadness and grief in nature.

Pathway Four: Showing Compassion and Care for Nature

My son's concern for the snail, a creature despised by gardeners for their veracious vegan appetite, warmed my heart. As dusk settled, he gently urged the snail into the rocky border, where it would be safe for the night.

Often people think caring for nature means "reducing, reusing, and recycling." Yes, reducing our impact on the planet by buying less, fixing and repurposing items, conserving water, biking or taking public transit, and planting trees all help care for our planet. However, compassion for nature goes beyond the 3Rs. It means developing a sense of loving care for our natural world, a desire to heal and support nature close to home, and extending that same compassion to ourselves and to our children.

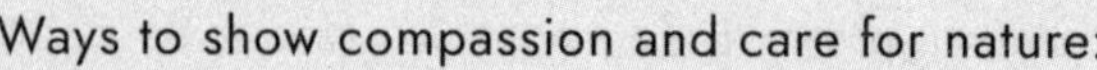

Ways to show compassion and care for nature:

- Providing food or shelter for wildlife such as setting up a bird feeder and building a bat home or mason bee home.
- Caring for the "unloved" things in nature like insects, snails, and earthworms.
- Planting and caring for trees, flowers, and plants in your yard, balcony, or inside your home.
- Volunteering at a community garden or with an organization that helps rewild nature close to home.
- Embracing compassion toward nature, your child, and yourself.

Pathway Five: Finding Meaning in Nature

With the snail safely tucked away, Theo wandered back indoors, walking slowly to the steady beat of a nursery rhyme he'd remembered from long ago:

Slowly, slowly, very slowly
Creeps the garden snail.
Slowly, slowly, very slowly
Up the garden rail.

Finding meaning in nature embraces that sense that we are part of something much bigger than ourselves. This pathway can seem abstract at first, but we can discover meaning through the stories we tell and share with others about the natural world as well as through celebrations, festivals, traditions, art, poetry, words, and songs.

Ways to find meaning in nature:

- Incorporating seasonal nature celebrations and rhythms into family life such as the spring equinox, summer solstice, autumn equinox, winter solstice, and seasonal midpoints.
- Celebrating natural events like full moons, meteor showers, and solar eclipses.
- Learning about how our ancestors understood and experienced nature.
- Connecting with local Indigenous (First Nations, Métis, Inuit, Indigenous American) peoples to listen to their traditional stories of *Land*.
- Reading stories, legends, and myth about animals and plants.
- Singing or listening to songs about nature.
- Telling stories about your own experiences in nature to friends, family, and one another.

Parents Hold the Key to Children's Connection with Nature

As parents and caregivers, we play a pivotal role in children's connection with the natural world. Research consistently shows that parents, and their own connection with nature, influence children's bond with nature. For instance, Holli-Anne Passmore, associate professor and department chair of Psychology at Concordia University of Edmonton, found in her study of 209 Canadian children that the strongest predictor of children's connection with nature was household adults' (parents and caregivers) connection with nature.[11] Similarly, in a longitudinal study of 398 Chinese children, parents' nature orientation positively impacted not only children's nature-connectedness but also their social relationships.[12] And in the United Kingdom, research on 216 children attending nature pre-schools found that parental nature connection was an important factor of children's nature connection, especially for children that don't go to nature preschool.[13]

I've often felt frustrated that parents are overlooked when it comes to connecting children and nature. It's part of what urged me to write this book! The truth is parents and caregivers have an incredible role in fostering the child-nature connection. We hold the key—quite literally—to going beyond the door into the wild, wonderful world of nature, to *Land*, and to our home.

In the next four sections of this book, I hope you will join me on a journey through spring, summer, fall, and winter. In each season, we will explore the rhythm of nature, gain a better understanding of the natural world, and discover simple ways to nurture the wild and precious bond between parents, children, and nature.

Part Two

SPRING

CHAPTER 5

Welcoming Springtime

WHEN THE FINAL patches of snow disappeared under the warming spring sun, my children burst outside and leapt across the front lawn, shedding their coats, boots, and socks in heaps along the way. I ventured outside more tentatively.

It had been six months since I ran away from home to the lake's edge, and three months since the birth of my fifth child. Instead of leaping and running, I sat on the front steps, wrapped in a thick wool blanket and held my sleeping baby to my chest. With my face turned to the sun, I breathed.

It seemed right that the slow suturing between nature and myself started in early spring. After all, for thousands of years humans living in the northern and southern midlatitudes of our planet have embraced spring as a season of new beginnings, awakening, and rebirth. They had survived winter, no easy feat for those living in colder climates. I too had survived winter, not in the same way as my Métis ancestors living on the plains of Manitoba, Canada, but more figuratively. I had survived a challenging period of my life, a winter away from nature, and welcomed spring with an open heart.

Whether you are at the beginning of your journey to reconnect with the natural world or well on your way, I invite you and your family to open your doors, windows, and hearts and welcome the season of spring.

WHEN DOES SPRING BEGIN?

Spring officially begins on the *spring equinox*, also called the vernal equinox, which marks a specific moment when the sun crosses over the Earth's celestial equator. In the Northern Hemisphere, the spring equinox happens on March 19, 20, or 21 when the sun moves from south to north over the equatorial line. In the Southern Hemisphere, the spring equinox happens on September 22 or 23 when the sun moves from north to south over the equatorial line. On this first day of spring, the amount of daylight and darkness are *almost* equal, and from this day onward light will flood nature, springing it to life.

SPRINGTIME CELEBRATIONS AND TRADITIONS FOR FAMILIES

Across continents, cultures, and ages, humans have welcomed the beginning of spring with celebrations, traditions, songs, and stories. Many still do today. Seasonal celebrations act like anchor points through the year, helping us stay in tune with seasonal rhythms by giving us a sense of *meaning* about the natural world and our place in it.

Often spring celebrations are interwoven with religious rituals. *Passover*, the Hebrew celebration of the Hebrew peoples' freedom from slavery in ancient Egypt; *Easter*, the Christian celebration of Jesus' resurrection; *Holi*, the Hindu celebration of color; and *Ostara*, the pagan celebration of spring, all take place around the spring equinox. In fact, Easter and Passover are celebrated on or after the full moon closest to the spring equinox; that's why the dates for these holidays change year-to-year. Of course, you don't need to be religious to celebrate spring. Spring celebrations and traditions are for all; seasonal celebrations are for everyone.

Your Family's Spring Celebrations

My childhood celebrations of spring were strongly influenced by my French-Canadian Catholic and Indigenous Métis cultural backgrounds. Many of these traditions I've passed along to my children, but I've collected a few others along the way. Rituals like enjoying a stroll outside on the spring equinox to search for signs of spring or dancing around the maypole have become part of our family's repertoire of spring celebrations.

What's important to remember, however, is that seasonal celebrations and traditions are meant to be rooted in *your* family values, cultural heritage, and *Land* you live on, whether that's an urban neighborhood or a rural hillside. What I mean by that is there is no one way of celebrating the seasons, but many wonderful ways. The point of this chapter is to help you to discover ways of celebrating spring that are meaningful to you and your children.

If you're unsure how to go about celebrating spring, here are a few prompts to get you started:

- What spring celebrations and traditions were part of my childhood? Do I want to pass down these traditions to my child?
- What is my cultural background? Are there specific spring traditions associated with my culture that I would like to adopt?
- What are my religious or spiritual beliefs? How are these incorporated into seasonal celebrations?
- How has spring been celebrated by the Indigenous peoples living on the *Land* I call home? Are there any opportunities to take part in these celebrations?
- How does the *Land* I call home respond to spring? What kind of flowers are in bloom? What are the animals doing? How can I take part in these spring changes?

I encourage you to embrace simplicity when adding new spring celebrations and traditions to your family's seasonal calendar. Try one new thing and see if it resonates before adding more.

Spring Equinox (March 19, 20, or 21)

The spring (vernal) equinox is the first day of spring, and in our home we welcome it by heading outdoors together, often to a sunny slope, to watch for early signs of spring, like the first blush of a sagebrush buttercup.

Easter (varies, between March 22 and April 25)

Easter celebrates the resurrection of Jesus Christ, but many Easter traditions and symbols find their roots in other ancient celebrations—egg dyeing, hot cross buns, and even the Easter bunny—all family favorites!

Passover (varies, typically March or April)

Passover commemorates the Hebrews' freedom from slavery in ancient Egypt and aligns with the start of the barley harvest. In the days leading up to this celebration, homes undergo spring-cleaning and ceremonial purification.

Earth Day (April 22)

Established in 1970, Earth Day reminds us to care for our planet. Each year our family picks a green project, like picking up litter along a favorite trail, planting a tree, hanging a bird feeder, or simply pausing to notice nature's small wonders.

Arbor Day (varies by region, late April/May)

Arbor Day celebrates trees and honors the vital role of trees in our ecosystems. Many families plant a young sapling or join community tree-planting events, a wonderful hands-on way to nurture the land and teach children the importance of trees.

May Day (May 1)

May Day is rooted in the ancient Greek festival of Chloris and the Roman celebration of Floralia—both honoring flowers and renewal. On this special day our family wears colorful clothes, makes flower crowns, and dances around the maypole. Other families might tuck flower baskets on neighbors' doorsteps, plant spring bulbs, picnic in a meadow, or build a small bonfire.

Beltane (May 1)

One of the four ancient Gaelic festivals, Beltane marks the beginning of summer with fire rituals. Traditionally people danced around bonfires and leapt through flames for purification and blessing. Many families celebrate by lighting a small fire and sharing stories.

SIGNS OF SPRING NATURE WALK

Depending on where you live, the first day of spring, the spring equinox, may not feel like springtime at all. The ground may be hard and unyielding, covered with ice and snow, or soft and wet from unceasing rain. Winter may be clinging to the shadows of your home, making an unwelcome appearance when least expected. Alternatively, spring might be well on its way and may even feel like an early summer's day.

One of my children's favorite ways to celebrate the spring equinox is to go outside and search for early signs of spring. It's a simple tradition that can be done anywhere: walking to or from school, strolling around the neighborhood or down a nearby park or nature trail. If possible, find a spot to sit with your child and notice how the nature looks, sounds, smells, feels, and tastes.

Early signs of spring:

- Deciduous tree buds swelling
- Pussy willows popping out in wetlands

- Skunk cabbages emerging from the ground
- Sap running and being collected from maple trees
- Snowdrops and crocuses blooming in parks and gardens
- Wildflowers beginning to bloom
- Honeybees leaving their hives to perform "cleansing flights" (they hold in their excrement all winter long!) and search for food
- Peeping and croaking sounds of frogs and toads looking for mates
- Calls of the red-winged blackbird—"*konk-ke-ree*"
- Woodpecker birds knock-knock-knocking on trees and telephone poles
- American robins singing "*cheerily, cheer up, cheer up, cheerily, cheer up*"
- Black-capped chickadees going "*hey, sweetie*" and "*chickadee-dee-dee*"
- Flocks of geese and ducks flying north
- Squirrels and chipmunks emerging from dens
- Turtles coming out of hibernation
- Woolly bear caterpillars awakening

SETTING UP A SPRING NATURE TABLE

A nature table, also called a seasonal table, is a place in your home where you and your children can display treasured items gathered from nearby nature or sourced ethically from local stores. Although the term "table" is typically used, any surface inside your home that can hold space for nature works well. For many years I used the top of our credenza and later the top of our buffet. These days I use an entryway table near our kitchen.

Nature tables were very popular in primary schools in the early and mid-twentieth century. Typically, they were small tables on one side of the class where natural objects were displayed for children to interact with.[1] These days, you can still find nature tables in many Waldorf, Montessori, and forest schools, but this tradition has unfortunately fallen out of fashion in most North American schools.

Children are most engaged with nature tables that have items that are animated (it's alive!), are novel in appearance (it's unique!), are somewhat familiar (it's something I've seen!), have interesting color, shape, texture, and size (it's pretty! It's soft!), and foster emotional engagement (it reminds me of . . . , it makes me feel . . .).[2]

Here are some spring nature items to keep an eye out for on your walks through the nearby wild or visit to the local garden nursery.

- **Painted lady butterflies:** Raise painted lady caterpillars into butterflies to experience the wonders of metamorphosis. This is one of my children's most loved spring experiences, one that we've done for many years. Painted lady butterfly rearing kits are typically ordered online in late winter or early spring from reputable suppliers.
- **A miniature worm farm:** Poke holes in the base and lid of a plastic yogurt container, place a couple pieces of damp shredded newspaper, a handful of dirt, a few bits of food waste (carrot peels, chopped apple core), and four or five night wriggler worms (composting worms) inside and discover the incredible lives of worms.
- **Spring flowering branches:** Branches from flowering trees can be *forced* to flower in early spring by placing them in a jar or vase of warm water. Apple, cherry, peach, plum, pear, pussy willow, and forsythia branches work best and are often discarded during late winter or early spring pruning.
- **Flowering bulbs:** A pot of crocuses, daffodils, tulips, or hyacinths brings bright colors and lovely scents into the home.

- **Eggs and egg holders:** Dyed chicken eggs, painted wooden eggs, wool felted eggs, and fragments of eggs from hatched birds (found on the ground) all make lovely spring decorations. Add a few new eggs to your collection each year to replace the few that were broken by little hands. I like to display our eggs with egg holders purchased from local thrift stores.
- **Nests:** Handmade nests made of twigs, mud, and string.
- **Snail shells, unique rocks, and catkins:** Empty snail shells, rocks with interesting features, catkins, and pussy willows add shape, color, and texture to spring nature tables.
- **Spring picture books:** A few beautifully illustrated spring picture books welcome children to step into spring stories.
- **Play silks:** Waldorf schools drape colorful play silks on their nature tables or use them as backgrounds.

Nature tables are living spaces, always evolving as the season unfolds. When items are no longer being appreciated by your child, return them to nature or store them away until next spring.

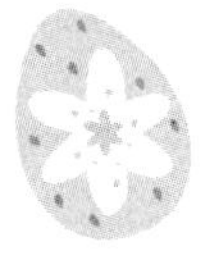

ONION-SKIN NATURE PRINTED EGGS

There's something satisfying about creating a colorful cast of eggs from household items such as onion skins, purple cabbage, beets, turmeric, and tea. While there's a whole list of natural items that can be used to dye eggs, onion skin is a traditionally used material that creates a beautiful deep orange-red hue on white chicken eggs. When you pair this method of dyeing eggs with using bits of nature to create nature prints on the eggshells, the result is magical.

Known as *lystovka* in Ukrainian, eggs dyed with onion skins and printed with bits of nature are simple to make. The most challenging part is saving up a pile of dried yellow or purple onion skins a few weeks before doing this project. Alternatively, buy a bulk bag of onions and rub off a bunch of onion skins. I fill up a gallon-sized plastic bag with onion skins, which is about the equivalent of a dozen onions.

When it comes to choosing bits of nature for printing the eggs, I suggest picking smaller items that will lay flat on the egg: cilantro, flat parsley, strawberry leaves, cedar twigs, sage leaves, and violets work well. You can also experiment with items like lace and string.

EQUIPMENT:

- Medium pot
- Sieve
- Scissors
- String
- Bowl

MATERIALS:

- 1 dozen white eggs
- 1 gallon bag dry yellow or purple onion skins from about a dozen onions
- 4–6 cups water (*approximate*), plus extra cold water to cool the eggs
- ¼ cup white vinegar
- 1 pair of thin nylons
- 12 bits nature (parsley, cilantro, strawberry leaves, flowers, etc.)
- olive oil (optional)

INSTRUCTIONS:

1. **Boil the onion skins:** Place the onion skins in a medium-sized pot and cover with approximately four to six cups water. This isn't an exact science. Just make sure the water covers the onion skins. Bring the water to a boil and simmer on low for 30 minutes.

2. **Prep the eggs:** Place a small leaf or flower flat against the surface of each egg. Cut a square of nylon large enough to wrap the egg

completely. Lay the egg (with the leaf or flower in place) inside the nylon, then gather the open edges up and tie a piece of string tightly around each end to hold the nylon snugly against the shell.

3. **Strain the dye:** Pour the onion skin dye through a sieve to remove the skins and place the dye back into the medium pot.

4. **Add the vinegar:** Add ¼ cup vinegar to the dye and stir to combine.

5. **Dye and cook the eggs:** Place the eggs gently into the pot of dye. Bring the dye to a boil. Turn the heat off and let the eggs cook in the hot liquid. Remove the eggs from the hot dye at six minutes for a soft-boiled egg, eight minutes for a medium-boiled egg, and ten minutes for a hard-boiled egg. Place the eggs in a bowl of cold water to cool the eggs.

6. **Remove the nylons:** Cut or untie the nylon from the eggs.

7. **Rub eggs with olive oil (optional):** Rub the eggs with olive oil to give them a nice shine.

Since these naturally dyed eggs are hard-boiled, they should be refrigerated and eaten within seven days.[3] If you're worried that the onion skins will make your eggs taste onion-y, they won't. Your eggs will still taste perfectly eggy.

One final suggestion, when it's time to consume the eggs, get the whole family involved in an egg-tapping competition. Each person takes turns tapping (hitting) their egg onto another person's hard-boiled egg, top or bottom, or both! If the egg cracks that person is eliminated.

TASTING SPRING AT HOME

When grocery stores sell strawberries in December and apples in April, it can be easy to forget that fruits and vegetables have seasonal rhythms too. These rhythms depend on where you live, of course, but by tuning into the seasons and making a conscious decision to eat locally sourced foods, we can reconnect our family to the natural world and her cycles.

Typically, spring is the season for the sweetness of strawberries, lip-puckering rhubarb, and vibrant asparagus, peas, and spinach. In the nearby wild, dandelions, nettles, wild violets, ramps (wild garlic), and morels can be found. While this isn't a recipe book, I will share seasonally connected recipes that have become staples in our home.

STRAWBERRY-RHUBARB PIE

The tang of rhubarb combined with the sweetness of strawberries results in an explosion of spring flavors. I make three or four of these pies each spring and they disappear as soon as they are cool enough to eat.

Prep Time: 45 mins (dough) + 45 mins (pie)
Cook Time: 50–60 minutes
Servings: 12 slices

All-Butter Pie Dough (Double Crust)

INGREDIENTS:

- 1 cup frozen unsalted butter (use salted butter and omit salt if preferred)
- 2 ½ cups all-purpose flour
- ⅓ cup cold water + 1–4 Tbsp extra (if the dough is dry)
- 3 Tbsp sour cream or plain yogurt
- 1 Tbsp sugar (optional)
- 1 tsp salt (omit if using salted butter)

DIRECTIONS:

1. **Combine dry ingredients:** In a food processor, pulse together the flour, sugar, and salt (if using) until well mixed.
2. **Prepare liquid mixture:** In a small bowl, whisk the cold water and sour cream or plain yogurt together.
3. **Incorporate butter:** Add the frozen butter cubes to a food processor. Pulse until the butter has broken down into pea-sized chunks.

4. **Form the dough:** Gradually add the water mixture to the flour, pulsing until the mixture comes together. If the dough feels too dry, add one or two additional tablespoons of cold water, one tablespoon at a time, pulsing after each addition.

5. **Check the dough consistency:** The dough is ready when you can squeeze it into a clump of dough with your hands, and it holds together without crumbling apart.

6. **Shape the dough:** Turn the dough onto a clean, lightly floured countertop. Divide it into two equal portions and press each into a flattened disk.

7. **Chill the dough:** Wrap each disk in parchment paper and refrigerate for at least 30 minutes. If the dough becomes too firm after chilling, let it sit at room temperature for 10 to 15 minutes before rolling it out.

HELPFUL TIPS:

- *Keep the water and butter cold to achieve a flaky crust.*
- *Handle the dough as little as possible to keep it from getting tough.*

Strawberry-Rhubarb Pie

Makes one 12-inch pie

Note: This recipe is designed for a 12-inch pie plate. I like big pies! If using a standard 9-inch pie plate, reduce the filling to 4 cups strawberries and 4 cups rhubarb.

INGREDIENTS

- 1 recipe of all-butter pie dough (see above)
- 6 cups strawberries, washed, hulled, and quartered
- 6 cups rhubarb, washed and chopped into 1-inch pieces
- 1 to 1 ½ cup sugar + 2 Tbsp sugar (for sprinkling on top)
- 1 Tbsp cornstarch

- 2 tsp finely grated orange zest (optional, but recommended)
- 1 tsp vanilla (optional)
- 1 egg white, slightly whisked

DIRECTIONS

1. **Preheat oven:** Preheat your oven to 425°F (220°C). Place a cookie sheet on the bottom rack to catch any potential drips.
2. **Macerate the fruit:** In a large bowl, combine the strawberries, rhubarb, and one cup of sugar. Cover and refrigerate the mixture for at least one hour, or overnight. This allows the sugar to draw out the juices from the fruit.
3. **Prepare the bottom crust:** While the fruit is macerating, roll out one disk of pie dough on a lightly floured surface to fit a 12-inch (or 9-inch) pie plate. Put the prepared pie shell in the refrigerator to keep it cool until ready to fill.
4. **Strain the fruit:** Remove the fruit mixture from the refrigerator. Using a fine mesh sieve, strain the fruit from the liquid. Reserve ¼ to ⅓ cup of juice for the filling. Store the remaining juice in a clean jar to make homemade strawberry-rhubarb soda by mixing the syrup with carbonated water.
5. **Prepare the filling:** In a small bowl, combine the reserved juice, cornstarch, orange zest, and vanilla extract. Mix until the cornstarch is fully dissolved.
6. **Combine filling ingredients:** Pour the juice mixture back into the macerated strawberry rhubarb. Stir to thoroughly combine. Taste the mixture. If it's too tart, you can add the additional ½ cup of sugar.
7. **Add filling to crust:** Remove the prepared pie shell from the refrigerator. Spoon the strawberry-rhubarb mixture into the bottom crust, mounding it slightly in the center.
8. **Prepare top crust:** Roll out the second disk of pie dough on a lightly floured surface. Carefully place the top crust over the filling. Trim any

excess dough from the edges of the side, leaving about ½ inch (1 cm) overhang.

9. **Finish the pie:** Press the edge of the top and bottom of the crust together using your fingers or a fork. Make a hole or several slits in the top crust to allow steam to escape. Brush the top crust with the slightly whisked egg white and sprinkle one to two tablespoons sugar over the top.

10. **Bake the pie:** Place the pie on the middle rack of the oven and bake at 425°F (220°C) for 20 to 25 minutes. Reduce the temperature to 375°F (190°C). Continue baking until the pie juices are bubbling and the crust is golden brown, about 30 to 40 minutes. If your crust is browning too quickly, tent the pie loosely with aluminum foil while the filling continues to cook.

11. **Cool the pie:** Remove the pie from the oven and allow to cool on a wire rack for two to three hours, until fully set. Serve with a scoop of vanilla ice cream or dollop of whipped cream. Store the pie in a sealed container on the counter for two days or in the fridge for up to a week.

HELPFUL TIPS:

- *If you don't have a food processer, use a pastry cutter or a couple of butter knives and large mixing bowl to incorporate butter.*

CHAPTER 6

Raising a Nature-Connected Baby

MY FIRSTBORN, FELIX, arrived on a bitter, cold evening near the end of January 2008. On the morning of our hospital discharge, a fine dust of flurries fell from the sky. This winter scene should have filled me with wonder; instead it filled me with worry.

"Will he be alright out there?" I asked the nurse while pointing to the winter scene.

"Oh sure," she said, "it'll only be a minute or two. Just make sure to warm your car so he doesn't get too cold."

For the first three months I kept Felix mostly indoors, safe from the cold. When spring arrived and the towering snow piles at the end of our driveway shrank, I nervously ventured out with Felix safely strapped into a stroller and bundled in blankets. I still wasn't convinced that nature was a safe place for my baby. By late spring, however, he hated being restrained in his stroller. He wanted to lay on the ground and grab all the "yucky" things—grass, sticks, rocks, and, worst of all, dirt. It stressed me out to no end, so I opted to stay in the safety of our home as much as possible.

Fast-forward to the spring of 2023. Felix was sprawled on the front lawn with his younger brother, six-month-old Loïc, handing him sticks, grass, and rocks to play with. When I spotted them there, my heart filled with joy.

Being a new parent is wonderfully overwhelming, especially with the constant barrage of advice that comes from well-meaning family, friends, online forums, and social media. Strangely, when I think back to myself as a new mother, I wish someone would have given me gentle guidance for getting outside with my baby. Even though my parents had taken me and my siblings out as babies, it didn't occur to me to ask them for advice on this topic, and they didn't offer. None of my friends offered advice either. I concluded that babies didn't belong in nature—something that took me years to unlearn. Babies belong outside, just as much as children, and their journey toward a greater connection with nature can begin while they sleep!

NATURE-INFUSED NAPS

The first time I learned that Scandinavian parents placed babies outdoors to nap, regardless of cold weather, I was surprised. I remember looking at a photograph of babies sleeping peacefully in strollers lined up outside of a Norwegian café, snow covering the ground, no parents in sight. Were Scandinavian parents being reckless, or did they know something I didn't?

In Scandinavian countries, placing babies outdoors to nap has evolved into a deeply ingrained parenting practice, one originally born out of necessity that continues to this very day. In the 1920s, Finnish pediatrician Arvo Ylppö encouraged mothers to place their babies outside for naps, believing fresh air and sunshine could reduce Finland's high infant mortality.[1] Ylppö observed that poor indoor air quality and lack of sunlight were contributing to infant diseases and death—he was on to something!

Air pollution, both indoors and outdoors, is a significant risk factor to infant diseases such as preterm birth, low birth weight, asthma, and Sudden Infant Death Syndrome (SIDS)—a devastating, sudden, and unexplained loss of an infant under one year of age.

While outdoor air pollution can be a big problem, two-thirds (64 percent) of worldwide neonatal deaths caused by air pollution were due to household (indoor) air pollution.[2]

Lack of sunlight, and its related vitamin D, also negatively impact infant health. Babies are typically born with low vitamin D—a crucial vitamin for bone growth and immune function. They depend on sunlight exposure, breast milk or formula, and/or Vitamin D supplementation to boost their vitamin D levels.[3] If babies don't get enough vitamin D, it puts them at risk for developing rickets, respiratory infections, asthma, and even type 1 diabetes, multiple sclerosis, and autism later in life.[4]

To combat poor air quality and lack of vitamin D, parents started bringing Nordic babies as young as two weeks outside to nap in temperatures as cold as 5°F (-15°C), a practice that continues in Scandinavian countries where the infant mortality rate is now among the lowest in the world.[5]

I didn't dare attempt outdoor naps with my first three children. My motherhood anxieties were unhinged at that point. Plus, though many Indigenous families once, and some still, welcomed fresh-air naps, this parenting practice was practically unheard of in most Canadian cities.

Then, in 2017, I read *There's No Such Thing as Bad Weather: A Scandinavian Mom's Secrets for Raising Healthy, Resilient, and Confident Kids* by Swedish American writer Linda Åkeson McGurk. Her stories of outdoor napping on American soil piqued my curiosity.

Although the research on outdoor napping is limited, there is evidence that babies sleep longer outside in cooler weather.[6] Scandinavian parents also report that their babies have better appetites after outdoor naps, are more energetic, and catch fewer colds.[7] The more I learned about outdoor napping, the more I mourned the lost opportunity with my first three children. I wondered if outdoor napping would have helped my fussy babies and "bad" nappers. I would soon get the chance to test it out.

When Alice, my fourth child, was born in December of 2020, I quickly discovered that my "terrible napper" turned into a blissful sleeper when she napped outdoors. From about four weeks of age, Alice napped outside at least once a day in daytime temperatures that ranged between 32°F (0°C) to 14°F (-10°C)—the ideal temperature for outdoor naps is around 21°F (-6°C).[8] I often began by taking Alice for a walk in her stroller, then parked it on our porch, allowing her to nap while I meandered around nearby. I used the same strategy with my fifth child, also born in December.

As my two youngest grew older and were able to sit independently, I began taking them on strolls along nearby trails in carriers, where they would often nod off. Instead of feeling trapped indoors by my babies' nap schedules, like I did for my first three children, my fourth and fifth children showed me that better naps can be found outdoors.

There's something magical about the shushing sounds of nature, fresh air, and the gentle movement of a stroller or carrier that soothes a baby to sleep. Plus, outdoor naps freed me from my self-imposed indoor captivity.

Tips for Outdoors Naps

- **Choose a safe location:** Always place your baby in a safe, secure, and sheltered location where you can always see, hear, and monitor your baby.
- **Supervision is key:** Never leave your baby unattended during outdoor naps. Make sure you see and hear your baby.
- **Proper sleeping position:** Lay your baby to sleep flat on her back in a stroller that lays flat or a crib, following the "back to sleep" principle to keep her airway clear. Avoid outdoor napping in a car seat or upright in a stroller.
- **Dress for the weather:** Dress your baby in weather-appropriate clothing, adding layers for cold weather and removing layers for warmer weather. Avoid over-bundling even in cold weather to prevent overheating.

- **Monitor baby's temperature:** Check your baby's temperature regularly to make sure he isn't too hot or too cold. Use your hand to feel the back of your baby's neck and upper back for sweat (overheating) or their hands and feet for chilliness.
- **Protect from elements:** Shield your baby from wind, rain, snow, and direct sunlight by pulling down the stroller shade and placing your baby in a sheltered napping spot.
- **Be mindful of wildlife:** Be aware of curious squirrels, feral cats, roaming dogs, and bugs. Use insect netting to protect your baby from mosquitoes and other bugs.
- **Avoid covering the stroller:** Never cover your baby's stroller with a blanket or towel as this can cause overheating.
- **Check air quality:** Avoid outdoor naps when the air quality is poor because of high pollution or forest fire smoke.

BEYOND NAPS: FOSTERING BABIES' CONNECTION WITH NATURE

Imagine seeing vibrant green leaves silhouetted against a blue sky, listening to raindrops splattering on the ground, or feeling prickly grass on your hands for the very first time. We often take these experiences for granted. However, not only do these magical moments stimulate a baby's nervous system in ways indoor environments cannot but they also lay the foundation for a growing connection to the natural world in the years to come.[9]

Conversations about the importance of babies being connected with nature are surprisingly rare. Books for new parents rarely mention it and health care professionals like doctors, midwives, and nurses often overlook the topic. It isn't covered in prenatal classes or during well-baby assessment. Even in childcare settings, caregivers don't bring babies outside because of safety concerns and infants' limited mobility.[10] Babies are even excluded from "leave no child inside" campaigns. Some outdoor enthusiasts go as far as suggesting that babies don't belong outdoors at all, but babies *need* nature!

From birth to twelve months of age, babies go through incredible growth and development. To truly thrive during that period, they need a loving parent or caregiver to feed, bathe, change, cuddle, play, *and bring them outside*. While studies on babies in nature are limited, recent research shows that babies benefit from simply *being* outside, whether that's a walk around the city block, a stroller ride past urban greenery, or a stroll in a local park. Being outdoors soothes a fussy baby, improves parent-baby bonding—especially if the baby is being carried—and helps with infant development.[11]

CONFIDENTLY BRINGING BABY OUTSIDE

Bringing baby outside can feel intimidating at first, especially in the colder seasons of the year. If you're feeling anxious about exploring the natural world with your baby, know that you aren't alone—I felt this way too. It took me many years to know that it is safe to bring babies outside even in colder weather, but there are many resources available if you want to learn more about this process. A great place to start is my blog, *Backwoods Mama*.

CHAPTER 7

Discovering Dirt Isn't *Dirty*

AS A NEW MOTHER, my nightmares were filled with images of bacteria, viruses, and protozoa. Medical knowledge from my nursing degree and motherhood anxiety mixed to create the perfect protagonist: an obsessive over-sanitizing mother.

I sterilized everything: pacifiers, toys, even board books from the library. The moment my firstborn's soother fell on the living room floor, I rushed into the kitchen to boil it to oblivion.

"It's probably fine," my husband said, trying to reassure me.

I glared at him in reply. Didn't he know that the world was crawling with microscopic ruffians waiting to take down my precious baby boy?

When Felix started to crawl, I hated that his hands touched the floor, but that wasn't the worst of it. I caught him playing in the toilet as soon as he could pull himself to standing.

"No Felix, that's yucky!" I said firmly while extricating his hands from the toilet bowl. He looked up and laughed, giving the toilet bowl a final swish with his chubby fingers before being pulled away.

LETTING KIDS EAT DIRT

"Why don't you go play in the backyard," I shouted over the din of my children's playful hollers.

"Can we play in the mud?" eight-year-old Felix asked, mischief gleaming in his eyes.

"Sure, that's fine," I said, desperate to get them outdoors even if it meant dealing with a bit of mud cleanup.

A short time later, I peeked out the back door to discover three children caked in thick brown mud, from head to boot.

"What in the world?!" I gasped, trying to figure out what happened. That's when I saw the huge mud puddle at the end of the slide. "Oh Felix," I groaned, realizing what I had inadvertently agreed to.

Making the shift from "over-sanitized" parent to "puddle" parent, a term used to describe parents that embrace and encourage outdoor messy play, wasn't easy for me. Initially, I wanted my children to stay clean when playing outside, which meant no digging in the dirt, playing in mud, touching "dirty" things, or splashing in puddles. I would veer them away from puddles and snatch them from dirt piles. If they did happen to get messy, I would give them a hard time: "What did you do? Look at how filthy you are!"

Their smiling faces furrowed and sometimes tears gushed forth—not my proudest parenting era. I soon discovered that "clean" and outdoor play rarely coexist, especially when kids take the lead. Children seem naturally drawn to dirt. Their inner programming instructs them to dig, scoop, squish, roll, and play in dirt. From an early age, kids have an instinctual knowing that dirt is good for them, so good most try to *eat* it—to the horror of their parents. Toddlers quickly learn that a mouthful of gritty soil isn't tasty.

Thankfully, kids don't need to eat handfuls of dirt to boost their microbiome. They do, however, need plenty of time outside getting dirty. Expert microbiologists and authors of *Let Them Eat Dirt: Saving Our Children from an Oversanitized World*, B. Brett Finlay and Marie-

Claire Arrieta encourage parents to get their kids outside often and let them "touch anything they want (except animal waste), including dirt, mud, trees, plants, insects, etc."[1]

Here are some practical tips for letting kids get dirty based on *Let Them Eat Dirt*:[2]

- Let children touch nature, including dirt, mud, sand, trees, plants, insects, and animals.
- Don't let children touch animal waste, unsafe plants, venomous insects, and dangerous animals.
- Encourage children to dig, scoop, and sculpt dirt, mud, and sand with their hands and feet.
- Allow children to be barefoot in mud, dirt, and sand.
- Let kids stay dirty for as long as possible while playing outside.
- Check sandboxes for animal feces and remove them, along with a generous amount of surrounding sand, before children play in them.
- Wash hands with regular soap and water (avoid antibacterial soap) before eating and/or returning indoors.
- If your baby's pacifier or child's snack falls in the dirt or nature trail, give it a dusting off or a quick rinse with water before returning it.
- Harvest or forage fruits, vegetables, and greens from nature, u-picks, or a garden. Only rinse them if they have been exposed to agricultural chemicals, pollution, or are visibly covered in dirt, otherwise they can be eaten right away.
- Continue to wash fruits and veggies from the store.

DIGGING IN THE DIRT: ACTIVITIES AND IDEAS

In the back field of my parents' small acreage, a miniature mountain of soft black soil sat beckoning. Although a sandbox filled with toys, a playset, and trampoline were nearby, they were all but forgotten when my children saw the pile of dirt. Little legs ran up the dusty slope and jumped back down sending puffs of earth into the air. Hands pressed deep into the rich organic matter reaching into the heart of the hill. Hoots and hollers filled the air as they jumped, tumbled, and rolled in nature's gold.

Most children don't need instructions to play with dirt, mud, and sand, they just need an adult to enthusiastically say, "Go for it!" or, at the very least, look the other way. While most children don't have enormous dirt piles to roll in, "dirty" play can still happen close to home or in nearby parks with these fun ideas.

CREATING A MUD KITCHEN

"What are you making, Alice?" I asked, peering over my toddler's shoulder into a pail filled with murky water, bits of grass, marigold petals, and pine cones.

"Pine cone soup . . . for you," she mumbled, focused on stirring the concoction.

"Mmmmm," I said, "looks nutritious!"

She nodded and continued working in her rustic mud kitchen.

Mud kitchens have gained popularity since the early 2010s thanks to muddy play advocates from around the world, such as Professor Jan White, co-founder of Early Childhood Outdoors, and Liz Edwards, founder of Muddy Faces, who together launched *Making a Mud Kitchen* for International Mud Day in June 2012. This free digital booklet popularized mud kitchens around the world. What makes mud kitchens so wonderful, and popular, is that they're simple, cost-effective, and open-ended. They "open up the outdoors," giving children space to play, explore nature, and navigate daily life.[3]

There are plenty of charming mud kitchen designs on the internet, but there's no need to build or buy anything fancy. In fact, the best mud kitchen is the one your child plays in and is often made with things you already have on hand or items found at thrift stores.

GATHER SUPPLIES:

- Dirt and/or sand:
  - Buckets filled with dirt and/or sand
  - A patch of sand/dirt/mud in a yard
  - A sandbox

- Water:
  - Access to running water (a hose)
  - Shallow containers of water
  - A child-sized watering can filled with water
- Nature "ingredients":
  - Rocks, shells, pine cones, sticks, non-toxic berries, leaves, grass, and other things collected from nature for decorating and mixing mud creations.
- Work area:
  - Work surface: A sturdy board placed on supports such as inverted milk crates, large planting pots, logs, bricks, and even old cable spools and set at the right height (about elbow height) for your child to work at.
  - Vertical wall: A fence, wall, or board for adding hooks for pots and utensils.
  - Storage: An old shelf for storing and displaying mud kitchen tools and/or some weatherproof bins for storing supplies when not in use.
- Kitchenware:
  - Pots and pans
  - Measuring cups and spoons

  - Pie plates, muffin tins, cookie cutters
  - Mixing bowls and sieve
  - Cutting board
  - Kitchen utensils (mixing spoon, ladle, whisk, rolling pin)
  - Fun extras: Small teapot, funnel, ice cube tray, mortar and pestle

DIRECTIONS:

1. **Set up mud kitchen:** Choose a spot in your yard or on your deck that's easy to access and safe for your child. Using the gathered items, arrange the work surface and organize the kitchenware and nature ingredients with your child.

2. **Encourage independent muddy play:** Allow your child to explore their mud kitchen, freely offering to be the "taste tester" to make the experience interactive.

3. **Refresh supplies:** Periodically restock the mud kitchen with seasonal ingredients or unique tools, involving your child in this process.

MAKING SEED "BOMB" ORNAMENTS

When clay, soil, and seeds are mixed and shaped into a ball, a seed "bomb" is born. Seed bombs can be left as balls or rolled into ornaments, which are perfect for gifting to others during celebrations and holidays.

MATERIALS:

- 10 oz (280 g) air-dry clay
- ½ cup potting soil
- 1 tsp wildflower seeds (native to your area)
- Water

EQUIPMENT:

- Drying rack
- Rolling pin (for ornaments only)
- Cutting board (for ornaments only)
- Cookie cutters (for ornaments only)
- Chopstick or pencil (for ornaments only)
- Twine or cotton string (for ornaments only)

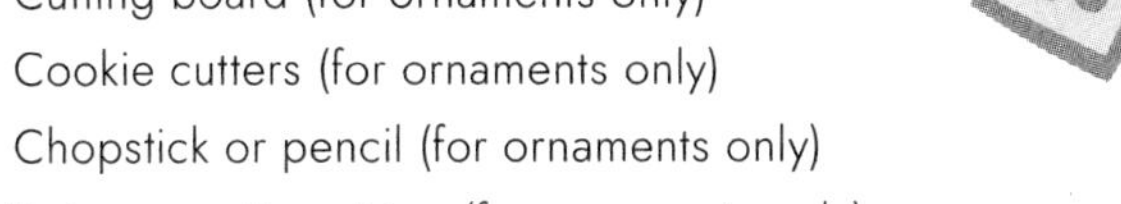

INSTRUCTIONS:

1. **Prepare the seed mixture:** In a large bowl, combine the air-dry clay, potting soil, and wildflower seeds. Knead the mixture thoroughly with your hands until well blended. This is a great task for kids to assist with. If the mixture feels too dry, add a sprinkle of water. If it's too wet, incorporate a bit more soil until the desired consistency is achieved.

2. **To create seed "bombs":** Pinch off two tablespoons of mixed clay and roll into a ball. Place the balls on a drying rack and let them air-dry until firm. Drying time typically takes about two to three days.

3. **To create seed ornament cutouts:**

   a. Place a large ball of mixed clay on a cutting board and roll it out to about ¼ inch (0.6 cm) thick using a rolling pin. To prevent sticking, roll the clay onto parchment paper or a silicone mat, or sprinkle some soil under the clay.

   b. Use a cookie cutter to cut out various shapes.

   c. Carefully lift the cutouts and reshape them with your fingers as needed.

   d. Use a chopstick or pencil to make a hole in the ornament so that you can attach a string to it.

   e. Place the cutouts on a cooling rack and let them air-dry until firm, which takes about two to three days.

   f. Once dry, put twine or cotton string through the hole of the seed bomb ornament.

4. **Planting:** Plant seed "bombs" or ornaments outside in a garden or pot of soil.

Responsible seed bombing: Traditionally, seed bombs are dispersed on vacant lots or neglected urban spaces, an act called guerilla gardening. While rewilding urban spaces sounds like a worthy act of rebellion, it can be problematic when seed bombs spread aggressive non-native seeds. So, to be on the safe side, stick to using seeds native to your area, and plant seed bombs in your own yard or ask permission before spreading them in other areas.

PLANTING A TINY VEGETABLE GARDEN

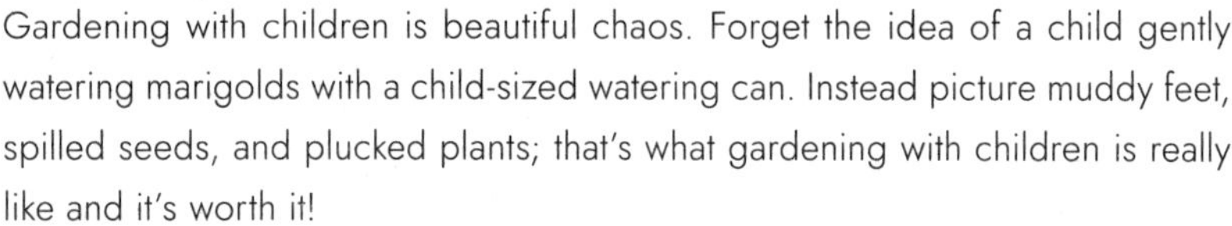

Gardening with children is beautiful chaos. Forget the idea of a child gently watering marigolds with a child-sized watering can. Instead picture muddy feet, spilled seeds, and plucked plants; that's what gardening with children is really like and it's worth it!

Whether it's a sprawling urban garden or a few pots on a balcony, I firmly believe that every child should have a garden. From the perspective of connecting with nature, gardening activates all five pathways of nature-connectedness, it also encourages healthier eating—even the pickiest of children are willing to try eating the fruits and vegetables they grow. This project will guide you and your child in making a tiny vegetable garden inside your home.

MATERIALS:

- Small seedling pots (small yogurt containers, milk cartons cut in half, cardboard egg cartons, single-use water bottles cut in half—poke a few holes in the bottom of plastic containers for water drainage)
- Potting soil (for growing vegetables)
- Water
- Large bowl or container (for mixing soil and water)
- Seeds that are easy to grow indoors (lettuce, radish, spinach, peas, microgreens, carrots, cilantro, cherry/grape tomatoes)
- Tray (for holding the seedling pots)

DIRECTIONS:

1. **Prepare the seedling pots:** Dump soil into a large bowl or container and slowly mix in water until the soil is damp. If you squeeze a handful of soil, water should not come pouring out. If it does, mix in more soil to absorb the water.

2. **Fill the pots:** Fill your small seedling pots 3/4 of the way to the top with the soil.

3. **Plant the seeds:** Following the instructions on the back of the seed packet, poke a hole into the soil. Big seeds need bigger and deeper holes and small seeds need smaller and shallower holes. Place one or two seeds in the hole and cover it with soil.

4. **Find a sunny spot:** Set the seedling pots on a tray and place the tray near a bright window, if possible.

5. **Wait, watch, and water:** Check on the seed pots daily and water when the soil looks and feels dry.

6. **Transplanting time:** Once the seedlings are getting too big for their seedling pots, transplant them into bigger pots to keep growing.

7. **Moving your microgarden outside:** If you have a patio, deck, or outdoor space, bring your tiny vegetable garden outside to continue

growing. Just make sure the weather is warm enough (above freezing at night). When bringing indoor seedlings outside for the first time, place them in the shade to "harden them off." Placing seedlings in the bright sun will scorch their leaves. Over about a week, slowly introduce your seedlings to more and more sunshine.

More Ways to Embrace "Dirty Play"

There are many ways to embrace "dirty play" no matter where you live. Here are a few more ideas:

- **Play in a sandbox:** Set up or visit a community sandbox. Bring along a sand pail and shovel for digging and building in the sand.
- **Build a sandcastle:** Gather some pails, shovels, nature bits, and find a shore or sandbox to build a sandcastle."
- **Paint with mud:** Make nature paintbrushes using sticks and greenery and use mud to paint recycled cardboard from cereal boxes or shipping boxes, the fence, or big rocks.
- **Draw in mud:** Draw pictures in the mud with sticks, stones, or other objects. Drawing in the mud is a great sensory way to learn letters and numbers.
- **Make a mud tree face:** Plaster some mud on a tree trunk and decorate the mud with sticks, rocks, shells, and other nature bits to create a face on the tree!
- **Celebrate International Mud Day June 29:** Take part in a Mud Pie Bake-Off or make a mud pile in your yard.

CHAPTER 8

Rewilding Playtime

"CAN WE PLAY, pleeeease?" my eleven-year-old son begged, giving me his best puppy eyes. I looked over his shoulder to see his two friends flanking him.

"It's a hard no," I answered.

"Just this one time, because my friends are here . . . only for an hour," Theo persisted.

"Don't even try," my teenage son Felix chimed in. "She won't budge on this one."

I hoped he was right. At the start of spring break, our family decided to take a break from screens. I knew without a doubt that too much screen time and not enough *green* time had been having a negative impact on our family.

"Why don't you go play outside instead," I encouraged my son and his friends. "It's a beautiful day. I'm sure you'll find something to do."

Defeat furrowed on their faces, they slipped on shoes and reluctantly stepped outside. A few moments later hooting and hollering seeped through the open window like a fresh spring breeze.

WHAT IS PLAY?

We often hear that "play is the work of childhood," a quote attributed to renowned Swiss psychologist Jean Piaget and sometimes to the Italian educator Maria Montessori. I often see this quote shared on social media, but I'm not sure they ever said it. I can't find evidence they did. In fact, I hope they didn't because for children, play is *not* work.

For children, play is a field of *opportunities*, a mountain of *adventure*, an ocean of *discoveries*, a space of *imaginings.* Play is a child's way of *being*—it's the *heart* of a child.[1] That's why in 1989, the United Nations included Article 31 in the Convention on the Rights of the Child, which states that children have the right "to rest and leisure, to engage in play and recreational activities appropriate to the age of the child."[2]

Play is children's birthright. It's how children learn about the world, about themselves, and about others. It's how they develop all the important skills they will need as adults.[3] Play helps children learn how to regulate emotions, develop social skills, build healthy bodies, and grow creativity, problem-solving skills, and so much more.[4] That's why children need plenty of time to play.

But what is play, exactly? I like to think of play as a shape-shifter. It takes on many forms and continuously evolves throughout childhood and beyond. We know play when we see it, but it balks when we try to put it in a box. Play doesn't like being restrained or limited. That's why a universal definition of play doesn't exist. However, there are characteristics of play that many researchers and educators agree upon. I like to think of these characteries as way finders, bright stars that guide us toward play that is pure, free, and unrestrained.

Peter Gray, research professor at Boston College and author of *Free to Learn*, describes the characteristic of play as being:[5]

1. Self-chosen and self-directed
2. Intrinsically motivated—not forced
3. Guided by children's own mental rules—adults don't make the rules
4. Imaginative—anything is possible!

In other words, children engaged in play must be free to choose *when*, *what*, and *how* they play. Most importantly, play must be fun![6]

THREE WAYS TO MAKE PLAY MORE FUN

Since my first forays into motherhood, I've discovered a few things about myself, my children, and play. First, I really enjoy being with my children, but I never liked *playing* with them. That might seem strange and ironic, but I found that when I stepped in, it changed the dynamic of their play. Invertedly, I would make up rules and nudge the direction of their play. My intentions were good, but I restrained their play and they didn't like it.

Initially, I felt guilty that I was not the perfect playful mom. Then I came to realize that I could make their play fun in different ways. For starters, I could get them outside.

Bring Play Outdoors

Yes, it's true, great play can happen indoors, but in the arms of nature I've noticed that children play differently. There's an unrestrained joyfulness in outdoor play. Children move more, speak louder, and create mess—and it's OK! The natural world, with its ever-changing landscape, is filled with open-ended materials, elements that challenge and stimulate the senses.[7] All this helps to promote physical activity, cognitive development, and creativity.[8]

If there's one characteristic of play that I would add to Gray's list, it would be this:

5. Connected to nature

I realize that nature might seem like more of a location, or backdrop, instead of a characteristic, but if we look at nature from a relational perspective—in terms of nature-connectedness—then perhaps it makes more sense.

Unlike parents, children have a natural tendency to see nature as "friend" and "home." I've noticed that play, when connected to nature, gives children more space and freedom to experience all the characteristics of play to their fullest. The natural world supports play in its wildest form.

Allow "Risky Play"

Watching my eighteen-month-old run at increasing speeds down a small ramp while simultaneously watching my sixteen-year-old climb high into a willow tree made me break out into a cold sweat. If there's one thing that kids love that causes parents, caregivers, and educators to feel uncomfortable, including myself, it's taking risks in play.

Risky play is defined as a thrilling and exciting play where kids encounter unknowns and possible hazards that carry a risk of physical injury or of feeling afraid.[9] The word "risky" is often seen as something negative in our society, so much that some parents don't like the term "risky play." Risk can lead to loss or injury. Something best avoided, especially for children. However, risk can be positive too. Learning, innovation, problem-solving, and discovery only happen by taking risks.

In fact, children use risky play to manage their fears and build confidence. Children climb up trees to quell fear of heights, sled down snow hills to feel confident with speed, or catch spiders to feel brave around insects. Some parents worry that if their child gets injured while engaging in risky play they will develop fears and phobias, but the opposite seems true—children that *don't* engage in risky play are more likely to develop fears and phobias and even get injured.[10]

So how do we parents make play more fun by allowing risky play, while still staying sane? A great guiding mantra is *as safe as necessary, not as safe as possible.*[11] Unless the risk for significant injury is real, give your child space to take risks and watch how proud they are when they do accomplish something challenging.

It's true that sometimes children need help to better understand a risky situation. If this is the case, you can help your child foster awareness or develop problem-solving skills by prompting them with a question or statement such as:

- Notice how . . . these rocks are slippery, the log is rotten, that branch bends.
- Do you see . . . the poison ivy, your friends nearby before throwing that rock?
- Try moving . . . your feet slowly, carefully, quickly, strongly.
- Try using your . . . hands, feet, arms, legs.
- Can you hear . . . the rushing water, the wind whistling, the fire crackling?
- What's your plan . . . if you climb that boulder, cross that log?

Add Loose Parts

"If you could design your dream playscape, what would it look like?" I asked my eldest daughter.

"Well, there would be some nice trees to climb, for sure. A nature kitchen with jars filled with leaves, herbs, berries, pebbles, shells, and honey for making things. I would also like a place to swim. Not a swimming pool but a place with water, sand, shells, and a big waterfall. Oh! Don't forget a trampoline too," she replied with twinkling eyes.

A group of Australian children, between the ages of three and nine, were asked a similar question. The study took place at a shopping mall in Sydney, Australia, where 110 children were asked to design their dream playground for an area of the mall undergoing renovations.[12] Every single picture focused on nature elements like rocks, sticks, sand, and leaves. Other than nature, the two most commonly drawn things were play equipment that encouraged risky play and "active play" elements like props for imaginary or creative play. In other words, children dream of playscapes that are outdoors, have risky play elements, and include loose parts.

I've noticed that most children are naturally drawn to loose parts when they play. Whether it's things like rocks, sticks, shells, or buttons, loose parts fill kids with a sense of curiosity and imagination. Playing with loose parts has also been shown to encourage physical activity and movement; foster problem-solving skills, creativity, and exploration of the environments; and stimulate social interaction, language use, risk taking, and inclusivity.[13]

If you're not sure where to find loose parts for your child, I'm here to help. While it is possible to buy loose parts, it's not necessary at all. You'll be able to find many loose parts in or around your home.

A List of Loose Parts for Play

Natural materials:

- Rocks (stones, pebbles, gravel)
- Wood (sticks, stumps, boards, coins, branches, wood chips, cinnamon sticks, pegs, beads, logs, driftwood)
- Shells
- Dirt (mud, sand, clay)
- Water (ice, snow, slush)
- Seeds (acorns, nuts, dried beans, seed pods)
- Pine cones
- Leaves
- Grasses (hay, straw)
- Mosses
- Flowers (petals)
- Textiles (hemp, cotton, wool, felt, silk)
- Corks
- Sea sponges

Manufactured materials:

- Paper (newspaper, shredded, cardboard, paper tubes)
- Containers (milk jugs, yogurt containers, metal can, buckets, laundry baskets, plant pots, bottles)
- Textiles (sheets, shower curtains, blankets, towels, pillows)
- Ropes (used climbing ropes)
- Tires (inner tubes)
- Gutters
- PVC pipes
- Buckets
- Nuts and bolts
- Traffic cones
- Tarps

EMBRACING THE WILD SIDE OF PLAY

Rewilding play needs to be a movement beyond front doors, one rooted outdoors where children can have the freedom to be children. While play can happen indoors, sending play outdoors allows play to unfold in ways that can't be replicated indoors, all the while depending on our children's bond with the natural world.

CHAPTER 9

Picking Pockets Full of Posies

"MAMAN, LOOK WHAT I found!" four-year-old Claire exclaimed, carefully cupping a treasure in her small hands.

She sidled up to my hunched-up frame as I furiously pulled weeds from the flower bed. Thrusting her hands into my face, she proceeded to unfurl her slim fingers to reveal the gem within. I watched with anticipation, expecting to see the swirl of a snail shell or the sparkle of a shiny rock cradled in her palm. Instead, a pink hyacinth lay within, snapped from its base and crumpled.

"Oh!" I blurted out. Not a happy "oh!" but one filled with disappointment.

Together, Claire and I had watched this single hyacinth push vibrant green leaves through the cold spring soil, stretch out a strong flowering stem, and prepare to burst forth sweet-smelling pink blooms. Now, the recently bloomed flower lay shriveled in her hands.

Within moments, Claire's joy-filled face changed. Confusion and disappointment arrived in rapid blinks, a desperate attempt to hold back the tide of tears from her ocean blue eyes. She had picked this flower to share with me, a gift I had rejected because flowers were *not* for picking. If every child picked a flower, there would be none left for anyone else to appreciate. That's what I was told, by someone at some point. That's what I believed.

Looking into my young daughter's eyes, and the pain and sadness held within, I realized something. Not once had I been scolded by my parents for picking flowers. Whether it was an armful of lilac blooms, pockets filled with dandelions, or tulips plucked from our garden, these gifts were appreciated by them.

"Let's put the flower into a cup with water," I said, trying to backpedal. She nodded solemnly.

IF EVERY CHILD PICKED A FLOWER . . .

Flowers are important parts of ecosystems, giving food and shelter to insects and animals, which are part of the great web of life. Scientists believe there are approximately 350,000 to 370,000 species of flowering plants (angiosperms) on Earth and that a large number of these plant species (36.5 percent) are rare.[1] The rarity of flowers has to do with where they grow and how sensitive they are. Unfortunately, and unsurprisingly, flower biodiversity is reducing around our planet. Certain flowers are even going extinct.

Interestingly, humans have been growing and harvesting flowers for more than five thousand years. It's a strange thing really. Flowers don't fill our bellies, not directly, but we love to cultivate them because they make us feel happy. A study of men and women receiving flowers found that flowers have a positive effect, immediate and long-term, on emotions, mood, behavior, and even memory.[2]

Flowers have another superpower; they draw us to nature. Flowers *demand* us to move toward, stoop over, smell, and tend to them. We can't blame children for doing exactly these things. For many years, I didn't let my young children pick flowers from fields, forests, and even our gardens. When my child reached out to pluck a dandelion from the lawn, I ran interference, reminding them about those starving honeybees. However, that singular pink hyacinth plucked those beliefs right from their roots.

Flowers are important, and the mass destruction of floral ecosystems is problematic. However, preventing children from picking common flowers pulls them away from nature. Ryan Lumber, the father of the Five Pathways framework for nature connection, shared with me how in the UK "bluebells are endangered and should be admired without being picked. But most flowers aren't [and] denying our natural, sensory engagement with nature only deepens our disconnect."[3]

LET CHILDREN PICK FLOWERS

If you are envisioning feral children scooping up tulips from city parks, plucking prized dahlias from the neighbors' yard, and razing wildflowers from protected parks, then let me explain. There are situations when it's not socially or environmentally appropriate to pick flowers, but I would argue that there are more situations when picking a pocket full of posies is perfectly alright.

In the spring, a meadow of dandelions covers my yard. I'm partial to these yellow "weed" flowers and their sunshiny scent, and don't make any effort to restrain them. During peak bloom, my children and I fill a basket of dandelion blossoms to transform into various baked treats and dandelion playdough. I've had people shame me for this act, claiming I'm depriving bees of their first spring food. To set the record straight, bees prefer to gorge on willow blossoms, Oregon grape blossoms, maple blossoms, wild violets, chickweed blossoms, and nettle blossoms in the early spring instead of dandelions. In short, it is perfectly alright to let children gather a bouquet or basketful of dandelions from your yard.

Letting children harvest flowers is not an "always yes" or "never no" situation. It's better to ask if picking *this flower* in *this place* at *this moment* is reasonable, proportional, and ethical, instead of banning children from picking flowers.[4] Ultimately, each situation is different.

When my children want to harvest flowers from a forest, field, yard, or garden, here are the questions I ask to help us.

What Kind of Flower Is It?

Weed flowers, cultivated flowers, and wildflowers—which can be harvested? All the above, if they aren't rare, poisonous, or scarce. For starters, weed flowers, non-native (alien) weed species that outcompete native species are fair game for picking. In North America, flowers like yellow dandelions, blue chicory (can also be white or purple), oxeye daisy, or common tansy fall into that category. Typically, these flowers grow in abundance in yards or along roadsides, and letting kids pick them should cause no problems. Learn about the weed flowers in your area to know which are good for picking.

Wildflowers can also be harvested. It's important to learn about what grows in your area and which flowers can be harvested. Avoid picking sensitive, rare, or poisonous flowers and opt for wildflowers that grow in abundance.

Cultivated flowers, flowers that you or a farmer grow, are a great option for picking. Every year I plant tulips, daffodils, sunflowers, and more so that my children and I can pick them. If you don't have a yard to grow flowers, try growing flowers in pots indoors or on a porch, joining a community garden or visiting a u-pick flower farm.

Where Is the Flower Growing?

Location is important! Avoid harvesting flowers from private property and land, public parks and gardens, or protected lands without getting permission to do so first. Instead, harvest flowers grown in your garden, lawn, public (crown) land, and along roadways. If in doubt, ask before picking.

How Many Flowers Are There?

Quantity matters, especially for wildflowers. Whether there's a single wildflower or a field of them impacts how many flowers, if any at all, can be picked. A common recommendation is that only 2 to 10 percent of wildflowers should be harvested over a single season. Those percentages depend on how fast wildflowers grow and how they spread.

Who or What Else Might Need These Flowers?

Whether it's insects or small mammals like squirrels and birds, encourage your child to consider which other critters need flowers to survive. Milkweed is a great example of this. Monarch butterflies rely on milkweed to reproduce, so we generally only collect and disperse its seeds come the fall.

If your child happens to pick a flower that perhaps they shouldn't have, see it as an invitation for learning and discovery. Show them how to care for that beautiful flower and gently point out why it may have been better to leave that flower behind. Nature is amazing and we should delight in our children's sense of wonder.

FLOWER CRAFTS AND ACTIVITIES

Maria Montessori (1870–1952), an educator who promoted child-led learning and founded the Casa dei Bambini, noticed that children enjoyed touching flowers. Instead of dissuading this behavior, she began teaching toddlers and preschoolers how to arrange flowers, a skill that continues to be taught in Montessori school to this day. The activities in the next pages offer our children plenty of opportunities to connect with flowers through planting, playing, crafting, and cooking.

DANDELION FLOWER BUTTER COOKIES

These delicate butter cookies, with a gentle, honey-like note from dandelion petals, celebrate the gift of spring. A couple of safety notes before you bake: Use only common dandelion (*Taraxacum officinale*). If you're not 100 percent sure of the identification, skip it and cross-check with a reliable field guide. Avoid look-alikes like cat's ear or hawkweed. Harvest dandelion blossoms from clean, unsprayed places, well away from roads or treated lawns. Use only the yellow petals (the green bits taste bitter). Rinse and pat dry before folding them into the dough.

Prep Time: 1 hr 15 mins

Cook Time: 12 mins

Servings: 48 cookies

INGREDIENTS:

- 1 cup unsalted butter
- ½ tsp salt (omit if using salted butter)
- ½ cup sugar
- 2 egg yolks
- 2 tsp vanilla extract
- 1 cup dandelion flower petals
- 2 cups all-purpose flour
- ¼ cup sugar
- 2 Tbsp dandelion flower petals, washed and dried

INSTRUCTIONS:

1. **Cream the butter mixture:** In a large bowl or stand mixer fitted with a paddle attachment, cream together the butter, ½ cup sugar, and salt (if using) until the mixture is light in color and fluffy.
2. **Incorporate eggs and flavorings:** Add the egg yolks one at a time, beating thoroughly after each addition. Then stir in the vanilla extract and 1 cup dandelion flower petals.
3. **Combine dry ingredients:** Add the all-purpose flour to the mixture. Mix until the dough is well combined and smooth.
4. **Shape the dough:** Remove the dough from the bowl and roll it into a log.
5. **Roll in dandelion petal coating**: In a small bowl, mix together the remaining ¼ cup of sugar and 2 Tbsp of dandelion flower petals. Sprinkle this mixture onto a clean work surface (counter or cutting board) and roll the dough log over the sugar-petal mixture until it's evenly coated.
6. **Chill the dough:** Wrap the log in parchment paper or plastic wrap and place it in the refrigerator for a least one hour or overnight.

7. **Slice and prepare for baking:** Preheat the oven to 350°F (180°C). Using a sharp knife, cut the log into ¼ inch (0.6 cm) slices. Place the slices on a baking sheet lined with parchment paper.

8. **Bake the cookies:** Bake the cookies for 10 to 12 minutes, or until the edges begin to turn light brown.

9. **Cool and enjoy:** Allow the cookies to cool on a cooling rack and enjoy!

LILAC-INFUSED HONEY

In the spring, lilac blossoms fill the air with an intoxicating fragrance. As a child, I longed to bottle that spring scent until I discovered that I could do just that—by infusing the blooms in honey. Lilac-infused honey is delicious in tea, on toast, or made into lilac honey ice cream. A quick safety note: Use flowers from the common lilac (*Syringa vulgaris*), avoid look-alikes like privet or butterfly bush, and never serve honey to infants under one.

INGREDIENTS:

- 2 cups lilac flowers
- 1 ½ cups honey, liquid

EQUIPMENT:

- 1 pint-sized (2 cup) jar

INSTRUCTIONS:

1. **Harvest the blooms:** Collect about 2 cups of fresh lilac blossoms during peak bloom for the best fragrance and flavor.

2. **Rinse and dry the blooms:** Gently rinse the lilacs under cold water. Place them in a salad spinner to remove excess water or gently pat dry between clean dishcloths and then lay them out in a single layer to air-dry for about an hour. This step is important to avoid diluting the honey with extra moisture.

3. **Fill the jar:** Once dry, carefully pluck the lilac flowers from their stems. Place the flowers into a clean pint-sized (2 cup) jar. Pour the liquid honey over the flowers, filling the jar to the top. Stir gently to combine the flowers and honey.
4. **Infuse the honey:** Seal the jar with a lid and ring, and leave the mixture to infuse in a cool, dark place for at least 24 hours or up to three days.
5. **Strain and enjoy:** After infusing the honey, strain out the lilac flowers using a fine meshed sieve. Transfer the infused honey into a clear, pint-sized jar and enjoy in a cup of tea of over buttered toast.

YELLOW DANDELION PLAYDOUGH

Bright, naturally dyed yellow dandelion playdough is a lovely way to celebrate dandelion season. The secret to a vibrant yellow dye is blending dandelion flowers with hot water and lemon juice, ensuring the beautiful yellow dye doesn't brown during the processing.

EQUIPMENT:

- Blender or food processor
- Medium pot

MATERIALS:

- 2 cups dandelion flowers, plucked
- 1 cup hot water
- ¼ cup lemon juice
- 1 ¼ cup all-purpose flour
- ⅔ cup fine salt
- 2 ½ Tbsp oil (vegetable or other neutral oil)
- 2 ¼ tsp cream of tartar
- 2 Tbsp dandelion flowers, plucked (optional but pretty)

INSTRUCTIONS:

1. **Prepare the dandelion mixture:** In a blender or food processor, place the 2 cups of plucked dandelion flower petals, lemon juice, and hot water. Blend on high for 30 seconds (or longer if needed) or until thoroughly blended.

2. **Combine dry ingredients:** In a medium-sized pot, whisk the flour, salt, oil, and cream of tartar until evenly combined.

3. **Add dandelion dye and cook:** Pour the blended dandelion flower mixture and additional dandelion flower petals (optional but pretty) into the pot and stir with a wooden spoon. The mixture will look lumpy and gooey—that's perfectly fine. Place the pot on the stovetop on medium heat and stir continuously with a wooden spoon until the mixture thickens and comes together into a smooth ball.

4. **Cool and knead the dough:** Remove the dough from the pot to a counter or cutting board and let cool for a few minutes. Once cool enough to handle, knead the dough until smooth. If the dough feels dry add a splash of water. If the dough seems sticky add a splash of oil.

5. **Store for play:** Place the play dough in an airtight container of reusable plastic. It can be stored at room temperature for about a month, or longer in the refrigerator.

WEAVING A WILLOW FLOWER CROWN

Weaving a willow flower crown is a delightful way to connect with the beauty of nature by creating a wearable work of art. Traditionally, weeping willows are ideal for making nature crowns because of their long and flexible branches. If you don't have access to weeping willows, feel free to use grapevines or other long, pliable branches.

MATERIALS:

- 2–3 long weeping willow branches (or other long pliable branches)
- Bits of nature (flowers, leaves, berries, feathers)
- Ribbon (optional)

EQUIPMENT:

- Scissors

INSTRUCTIONS:

1. **Measure for the crown:** Take one long willow branch and wrap it around your child's head to determine how big the crown should be. For extra space to weave in bits of nature, allow for a slightly loose fit.
2. **Create the base:** Form the willow branch into a circlet by weaving the branch around itself into a continuous circle. Tuck in the ends.
3. **Weave in nature:** Have your child weave bits of nature into the willow base or help them as needed.
4. **Finish and wear:** Once your child is happy with the crown, finish it with a piece of ribbon (optional) then enjoy!

FLOWER POUNDING ART

Flower pounding art is a technique that transfers the natural dyes in fresh flowers onto paper or fabric using a hammer. This project works best with flat flowers—violets are my favorite!

MATERIALS:

- Watercolor paper or natural fabric (cotton or linen, white or off-white)
- Flowers (violets, dandelions, petunias, geraniums, and rose petals)
- Leaves

EQUIPMENT:

- Hammer or mallet
- Paper towel or parchment paper
- Scissors
- Cutting board or flat surface

INSTRUCTIONS:

1. **Prepare your surface:** Lay the watercolor paper or fabric on a flat surface such as a cutting board.
2. **Arrange the flowers and leaves:** Lay flowers and leaves face down onto the paper or fabric, arranging them in a pattern you like.
3. **Cover the flowers:** Place a piece of paper towel or parchment paper onto the back of the flower.
4. **Pound the flowers:** Use a hammer to firmly pound the covered flowers so that the natural dyes imprint onto the fabric or paper below.
5. **Reveal your art:** Carefully lift the cover to reveal your creation. Remove any remaining bits of flowers and leaves and let the plant inks dry.

PRESSING FLOWERS

Pressing flowers is an age-old craft that preserves nature's beauty—one seeing a resurgence thanks to creative wildcrafters.

EQUIPMENT:

- Flower press or large, thick book (a dictionary or encyclopedia)
- Wax paper, parchment paper, or newspaper
- Scissors

MATERIALS:

- Fresh flowers (harvest from nearby nature)

INSTRUCTIONS:

1. **Harvest and prepare:** Collect fresh flowers from nearby nature. Remove the stem close to the base of the flower.
2. **Set up your flower press:** Place flowers face down in a dedicated flower press following the press's instructions. Alternatively, line the pages of a thick book with wax paper, parchment paper, or newspaper and place flowers in between. If you don't have a thick book, use a regular-sized book and then pile books on top to weigh down flowers.
3. **Allow the flowers to dry:** Leave the flowers in the press or book for three to four weeks or until fully flattened and dried.
4. **Store and use:** Once dried, store the pressed flowers in a cool, dry, dark place until you are ready to use them.

Ideas for using pressed flowers:

- **Bookmark or card:** Glue a pressed flower onto a piece of thick paper to make a card or bookmark.
- **Lantern:** Use clear glue to attach pressed flowers to the side of a canning jar. Place a tea light inside to create a magical luminary.
- **Stickers:** Place a pressed flower onto a piece of parchment paper. Place a piece of clear packing tape on top. Cut around the flower. When you are ready to use your flower sticker, remove the parchment paper backing.
- **Eggs:** Decorate eggs (real or wooden) with pressed flowers.
- **Candles:** Place a pressed flower along the side of a large candle and place a piece of wax paper over top. Use an iron to transfer the wax from the paper to the candle, which will stick the flower to the candle.
- **Rocks:** Glue pressed flowers onto small rocks for loose parts play.

Part Three

SUMMER

CHAPTER 10

Celebrating Summertime

THE SUN BARED down on field and forest, forcing soft pink flowers and delicate greens to be overtaken by thick vines, leathery leaves, and heavy fruit. As nature creeped and climbed, breaking away any restraints to run freely, my children did the same. No longer trapped by school schedules and extracurricular activities, they relished in summer's freedom.

At the beginning of summer, I had made the decision not to register my children for summer camps. Truthfully, this decision was difficult. I worried that they would miss out on important opportunities for learning and growth, but once the decision was made, they seemed relieved, even grateful. They filled their days by lounging under trees, splashing in water, snacking on homegrown vegetables, and playing with one another and their friends.

As my children fully embraced their newfound freedom, I did the same. It felt wonderfully daring to enjoy a "90s summer"—one marked by carefree days and plenty of sunshine. Time flowed abundantly, allowing me to root myself more deeply into the natural world alongside my children. While I can't remember every single detail of that summer—there were no grand adventures or travel—I remember feeling a calm strength, one that I hadn't felt in a long time.

Summer is a season of freedom, light, growth, and strength—one that offers our families the opportunity to step away from overpacked schedules to embrace simpler living and a deeper connection with nature.

WHEN DOES SUMMER BEGIN?

Summer officially begins on the *summer solstice*, a specific moment when the sun is at its highest point in the sky. In the Northern Hemisphere, the summer solstice happens on June 20, 21, or 22 when the sun reaches the line of latitude 23.5 degrees north of the equator (Tropic of Cancer) and the Northern Hemisphere is most tilted toward the sun.[1] In the Southern Hemisphere, the summer solstice happens on December 21 or 22 when the sun reaches the line of latitude 23.5 degrees south of the Equator (Tropic of Capricorn) and the Southern Hemisphere is most tilted toward the sun. On this first day of summer, the amount of daylight is at its longest and darkness its shortest. From this day onward the daylight will begin to shorten, and the days will feel warmer.

SUMMERTIME CELEBRATIONS AND TRADITIONS FOR FAMILIES

Ancient celebrations of the sun are etched in the very landscape of our planet. A wonderful example of this etching is Stonehenge. Located on Salisbury Plain in Wiltshire, United Kingdom, sits an ancient stone circle built at the same time as the Great Pyramids in Egypt.[2] Many mysteries surround Stonehenge, but it stands in alignment with the movements of the sun, particularly the solstices, and was a place of gathering for over one hundred generations.[3] The Bighorn Medicine Wheel in Wyoming, USA, is another example of architecture tied to the sun. According to Ponca chief, John Bull, the Medicine Wheel "represents a sun dance circle" with points that align with the rising and setting of the sun on the summer solstice.[4]

Solar celebrations and traditions are deeply embedded throughout human history, and they continue to permeate our every day. It makes sense. Our very existence depends on the sun. Our bodily rhythms listen to the sun. Our age increases every time we make a full journey around the sun.

Like other seasons, summer celebrations are also intertwined with religious rituals and beliefs; however, they often share similar elements. St. John's Day, the Catholic celebration of the birth of Saint John the Baptist on June 24, and Midsummer, the Swedish celebration of summer and fertility, for instance, both include feasting and bonfires.

In our home, summertime celebrations and rituals unfold in micro-moments. We chase the sun, gorge on fresh fruits, play in water, cook food over a fire (and BBQ), and allow the abundance of the season to guide our wildcrafting. These micro-moments might not seem like much on their own, but they coalesce to provide connection and meaning to our summer.

Like other seasonal celebrations, I encourage you to root summer rituals and traditions to *your* family values, cultural heritage, and *Land* you live on. If you're unsure how to go about celebrating summer, here are a few prompts:

- What summer celebrations and traditions were part of my childhood? Do I want to pass down these traditions to my child?
- What is my cultural background? Are there specific summer traditions associated with my culture that I would like to adopt?
- How has summer been celebrated by the Indigenous peoples living on the *Land* I call home? Are there any opportunities to take part in these celebrations?
- How does the *Land* I call home respond to summer? What kind of flowers are in bloom? What are the animals doing? How can I take part in these summer changes?

Summer Solstice / Midsummer (June 20–22)

The summer solstice marks the longest day of the year and the official start of summer. My children and I celebrate this day with making tie-dyed shirts and chasing the sun! Other families enjoy making sun bread, collecting herbs, doing sun art, or gathering around a bonfire with family and friends.

Lammas / Lughnasadh (August 1)

One of the four ancient Celtic fire festivals, Lughnasadh celebrates the first grain harvest. Traditionally, communities baked the first loaves of the season and carried sheaves in procession. Today families bake fresh bread (sun bread!), visit local farms, and give thanks for summer's abundance.

EXPLORING SUMMER

Through the summer season, nature enters a steady crescendo. Berries ripen, nestlings fledge their nests, tadpoles transform into froglets, and insect chirps and buzzes fill the air. The sultry summer air slows animal movement in the peak of the day while pushing plants to production.

Summer provides ample opportunities for exploring and connection with nature because of the sheer abundance of animals, insects, and plants and the relative ease in getting outside—no need for multiple layers of clothing! Depending on the *Land* you live on, you will discover different signs of summer, but here are some common ones to look out for:

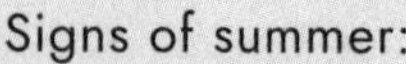

Signs of summer:

- Deciduous (leafy) trees are fully covered in leaves.
- Wildflowers like yarrow, asters, goldenrod, and red columbine are in bloom.

- Honeybees are collecting nectar and pollen, along with plenty of water if the temperature is high.
- Baby birds are learning how to fly.
- A kaleidoscope of butterflies fills the air.
- Baby deer, foxes, raccoons, and bears are wandering through forest and fields.
- Insects are chirping, buzzing, and glowing (fireflies), replacing the spring song of birds.
- Damselflies and dragonflies are flitting around ponds and streams.
- Turtles nest and hatchlings will emerge.
- Bats give birth to live pups.
- Strawberries, blueberries, blackberries, and raspberries are ripening.

Setting Up a Summer Nature Table

Our summer nature table often brims with treasures from days spent outdoors: shells, stones, and flowers gathered by curious hands, picture books of mermaids and beach days tucked between them. Below I've listed ideas to fill your own summer nature table:

- **Posies of flowers:** A small vase or cup filled with a handful of harvested wild or cultivated flowers. To learn more about ethically harvesting flowers with your child, refer to Chapter 9: Picking Pockets Full of Posies.
- **Small potted cactus or succulent:** Cacti and succulents can live without much water, which is perfect for the summer when indoor plants can sometimes get forgotten. Just watch out for little fingers that can get poked with spines.

- **Bug terrarium:** Build a miniature bug habitat in a quart jar or large plastic container to observe bugs and insects more closely. Snails, slugs, and beetles work well for this project.
- **Fossils, crystals, and other unique rocks:** Look for rocks in nearby nature or visit a local rock store for unique stones.
- **Dried seaweed, grass, herbs, or flowers:** Air-dry plants to preserve them throughout the summer. Flowers can be dried upside down to maintain their bloom shape.
- **Shells and sea glass:** Collect and display shells and sea glass from beaches.
- **Summer picture books:** A few beautifully illustrated summer picture books welcome children to step into summer stories.
- **Play silks:** Waldorf schools drape colorful play silks on their nature tables or use them as backgrounds.

OUR DAYSTAR

The sun, our steadfast companion, has been revered throughout history. Ancient people placed the sun in a prominent position within their stories and beliefs, even worshipping it as a god.

Re, sun god of the ancient Egyptians, sailed through the sky each day and through the underworld at night.[5] Helios, strong sun god of the ancient Greeks, drove his four-horse chariot across the sky from sunrise to sunset.[6] Huitzilopochtli, sun and war god of the ancient Aztecs, required the daily nourishment of human sacrifice![7]

Not all stories and beliefs portray the sun as masculine. Amaterasu, the glowing sun goddess of the ancient Japanese, continues to be honored to this day,[8] and Malina, the sun goddess of the Kalaallit (Inuit of Greenland), constantly flees from her evil moon brother Anningan, causing a never-ending chase across the sky.[9]

From a present-day scientific perspective, the sun, our yellow dwarf daystar, is a hot ball of hydrogen and helium that sits as the centerpiece of our solar system, estimated to be 4.5 billion years old, about halfway through its life.[10] The surface of the sun is a steamy 10,000°F (5,500°C) that gurgles, burbles, and spurts. The sun even has its own cycle and when it reaches its peak, called the solar maximus, it can be so violent that disruptions to satellites, energy grids, and radios occur.[11]

Although the sun is far away, it's a crucial part of nature. The sun is feeding the Earth a constant supply of light, heat, and solar energy; helping plants grow; driving weather and ocean currents; and even helping us see. Without the sun the Earth couldn't thrive.

RESPECTING THE SUN (DON'T GET BURNED!)

When my family moved from the northern interior of British Columbia to the sunny Okanagan Valley, I learned several important lessons around respecting the sun. Overexposure to the sun can happen up north, but cooler summers and a plethora of bugs mean we tend to cover up more. In the Okanagan Valley, however, the intense summer heat pulled us toward refreshing lakes, and my children and I arrived unprepared. It didn't take long for us to experience sunburns.

The sun is a powerful force of nature, one that we should respect. Its ultraviolet (UV) rays help our bodies produce Vitamin D, boost our mood, and even treat certain skin conditions.[12] However, those same UV rays can also cause sunburns, skin damage, and increase the risk of skin cancer. Fortunately, Earth has its very own "natural sunscreen"—the ozone layer. This special layer up in the Earth's atmosphere absorbs some of the sun's harmful UV radiation, but not all. In areas where pollution has thinned the ozone, more UV rays reach the ground, increasing the risk for overexposure and the need for sun protection.

Overexposure to direct sunlight can cause burns that can be incredibly painful and last several days. When infants, children, and teens get burned repeatedly it unfortunately increases their risk of skin cancer in later life.[13] To best protect our children from getting overexposure to the sun (sunburned), here are some commonly shared recommendations:

- Avoid direct sun exposure during midday (10 am to 4 pm).
- Wear a wide-brimmed hat and UV protective clothing.
- Apply sunscreen (SPF 30+) to exposed skin at least 15–30 minutes before going outside. Reapply every two hours or after water play.
- Wear sunglasses to protect eyes.
- Seek out shady areas for outdoor play.[14]
- Keep babies under six months of age out of direct sunlight and avoid using sunscreen on their sensitive skin. If sunscreen is necessary, opt for a mineral based sunscreen.

DEVELOPING YOUR SUN SENSE

Weather patterns, seasons, and location all impact how strong the sun's UV radiation will be. Slathering sunscreen on a dark, cloudy morning in late October isn't as crucial as when playing on the beach on a summer afternoon. That's why developing a good *sun sense* helps us parents and caregivers protect our children from harmful sun exposure while still allowing sensible and safe sun exposure.

Here are questions to ask when deciding on the type and amount of sun protection your child may need:[15]

- **What is the UV Index and UV Forecast?** Low UV Index requires less protection compared to higher UV Indexes. You can learn more about the UV Index in your area through a quick internet search.
- **What time of day is it?** UV radiation peaks from 10 am to 4 pm and is less in the morning and evening.
- **Are there clouds in the sky? What kind?** Thick clouds can block UV radiation while fluffy clouds can increase radiation.
- **What elevation are you at?** The higher up you go, the worse the UV radiation. Hiking in the mountains? Sunscreen and a hat are a must!

- **What season is it?** UV radiation is at its highest from April to August (spring and summer) in the Northern Hemisphere.
- **Where do you live?** UV radiation is higher close to the equator and weaker close to the poles.
- **What's on the ground?** Snow, sand, and water can reflect UV radiation.

By taking the time to understand how UV radiation fluctuates throughout the day and year, we can approach sun exposure more confidently, enjoying the sun's benefits while avoiding its risks.

CHOCOLATE ZUCCHINI CAKE

If you happen to have too many zucchinis, this chocolate zucchini cake is the solution. Moist, chocolatey, with a hint of orange, it's guaranteed to disappear from your countertop in no time.

INGREDIENTS:

- Butter for greasing pan
- 2 ½ cups all-purpose flour
- 3/4 cup unsweetened cocoa powder
- 2 ½ tsp baking powder
- 1 ½ tsp baking soda
- 1 tsp espresso powder (optional)
- 1 tsp salt
- 1 tsp cinnamon
- 1 cup vegetable oil
- 1 cup white granulated sugar
- 1 cup brown sugar
- 4 eggs (room temperature)
- ⅓ cup sour cream or plain yogurt
- 2 tsp vanilla extract

- 2 tsp orange zest (optional but highly recommended)
- 3 cups coarsely shredded zucchini*
- 1 cup chopped walnuts or pecans (optional)
- 1 cup chocolate chips

* **Note:** For extra-large zucchini, cut the zucchini in half lengthwise then scrape out the large seeds in the center before grating to avoid chewy bits of seeds in the cake.

INSTRUCTIONS:

1. **Preheat oven and prep pan:** Preheat the oven to 350°F (177°C). Grease a tube or Bundt pan thoroughly with butter.
2. **Combine dry ingredients:** In a large mixing bowl, whisk together the flour, cocoa powder, baking powder, baking soda, salt, cinnamon, and espresso powder (if using). Set aside.
3. **Mix wet ingredients:** In another large bowl, mix the vegetable oil, white sugar, brown sugar, eggs, sour cream, vanilla extract, and orange zest.
4. **Add zucchini:** Stir the grated zucchini into the wet ingredients.
5. **Combine the dry and wet ingredients:** Add the dry ingredients into the wet ingredients and mix until just combined. Avoid overmixing, which can make the cake dense. Fold in the nuts and chocolate chips.
6. **Fill the pan and bake:** Transfer the batter into the prepared cake pan (Bundt or angel food cake), spreading it evenly. Bake the cake for 60 to 75+ minutes, or until an inserted toothpick comes out clean, or with a few crumbs attached.
7. **Cool and enjoy:** Let the pan cool on a cooling rack for 15 to 20 minutes. Place the cooling rack on the top of the pan and gently invert to release the cake from the pan. The cake can be enjoyed warm or fully cooled.

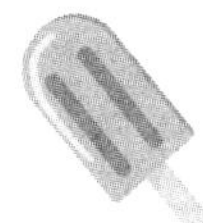

MELON ICE POPS

Homemade ice pops using seasonal fruit make a delicious summer treat—a favorite for kids and parents! This basic recipe can be easily adapted for peaches, berries, and all types of melons.

INGREDIENTS:

- ½ cup sugar
- ½ cup water
- 1 melon, bowling ball sized
- A sprig of mint leaves, lemongrass, basil, or lavender (optional)

INSTRUCTIONS:

1. **Make the simple syrup:** In a small saucepan, mix the water and sugar together. Add the mint, lemongrass, basil, or lavender to the syrup if using. Over medium-high heat, stir the syrup until the sugar has fully dissolved. Set the syrup aside to cool.

   Note: If you want to make several ice pop recipes, you can double or triple the simple syrup and store it in a sealed container in the fridge for up to two weeks.

2. **Blend the fruit:** Deseed, peel, and cut the melon into chunks and toss them into your blender. Blend the melon until smooth.
3. **Add the simple syrup:** Add ¾ cup simple syrup to the fruit puree and blend to mix together. Taste the puree and add more simple syrup if needed.
4. **Pour into ice pop molds:** Pour the pureed fruit into ice pop molds and freeze until solid.

Watermelon pops: Replace the cantaloupe with a bowling ball–sized piece of watermelon (half to one-quarter of a watermelon depending on the size).

Peach pops: Replace the cantaloupe with five peaches, peeled, pitted, and cut into quarters, plus the juice from half a lemon.

Raspberry pops: Replace the cantaloupe with a pound (about four cups) of raspberries.

MAKING A SUNDIAL

Humans have been making sundials for thousands of years. Using a simple stick (gnomon) and a set of labeled rocks (dial), you and your child can watch the sun's shadow as it marches across the sky.[16]

MATERIALS:

- A stick, wooden dowel, or pencil, with a pointed end (gnomon)
- Twelve rocks or shells (dial)
- Acrylic paint marker, permanent marker, or paint and paintbrush

INSTRUCTIONS:

1. **Make the dial:** Write the numbers 1 through 12 on rocks using an acrylic or permanent marker. If you don't have markers, use paint and a paintbrush.
2. **Choose a sunny spot:** Find a location in your yard or nearby nature that gets full and direct sunlight.
3. **Place the gnomon:** Push one end of the wooden stick, dowel, or pencil into the ground so that it stands upright.
4. **Place the first rock:** Note the current time (e.g. 10 am) and place the corresponding rock (labeled 10) where the stick's shadow falls on the ground. Morning hours will be on the left side of the dial and afternoon hours will be on the right.

5. **Arrange the remaining rocks:** Position the remaining rocks in a rough circle leaving about 5 inches (10 cm) between the stick and circle. Don't worry if the spacing isn't perfect.

6. **Adjust the rocks throughout the day:** Check your sundial every hour, if possible, and adjust the rocks to match the time.

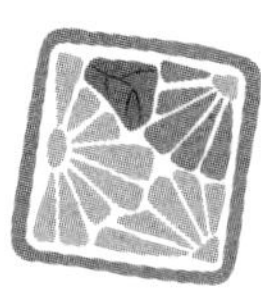

CONSTRUCTION PAPER SUN PRINTS

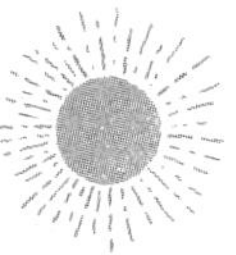

Create art with the power of the sun! Create art prints on colored construction paper or photosensitive (cyanotype) blueprinting (sun print) paper with this simple nature craft.

MATERIALS:

- Colorful construction paper or sun print paper
- Nature bits: leaves, flowers, sticks, feathers
- Piece of sturdy cardboard (a collapsed box)
- Rocks to weigh down items or piece of acrylic sheet
- Basin of water (for sun print paper)

INSTRUCTIONS:

1. **Prepare a sunny work area:** Place the study cardboard in a sunny location and lay pieces of colored construction paper or sun print paper on top of the cardboard.

2. **Arrange nature bits:** Create designs by placing bits of nature onto the paper. Weigh down any bits of nature with rocks or acrylic sheet.

3. **Expose to sunlight:** Allow the art piece to sit in the sun for about four hours, longer if it's cloudy outside.

4. **Reveal your art:** Carefully remove the bits of nature to display your art pieces! If using sun print paper, follow the product instructions as it may need to be rinsed in water for the full effect.

More Sun Activities

- **Face the sun:** Step outside, close your eyes, and lift your face to the sun. Breath in and out slowly, and absorb the sun's radiant warmth for a few minutes. Notice how the sun feels on other parts of your body like arms, hands, and bare feet.
- **Explore shadows:** It seems we are rather "attached" to our own shadow. Take a moment to notice the way the sun changes your shadows during different times of the day. In the summer, shadows are at their shortest midday.
- **Create a suncatcher.** Make a suncatcher out of recycled materials like clear plastic lids and pressed flowers or paint. Hang the suncatcher in a sunny window and see how the sunlight splashes color into your home.
- **Build a solar oven:** Use the power of the sun to make sun s'mores—yum!
- **Watch the sunrise or sunset:** Wake up early to watch the sunrise or stay up late and enjoy the beauty of the sunset together.
- **Sit by a bonfire:** Build a bonfire outside or set up a propane firepit if you aren't allowed open fires, and enjoy some snacks, stories, and snuggles by the fire.

CHAPTER 11

Finding a Favorite Tree

I CAN MAP my life in trees. The trees of my childhood—crab apple, birch, spruce, and pine. The trees of my early adulthood—cedar and rhododendron. The trees of my thirties—maple, cherry, and larch. All these trees, like different friends, have impacted my life in different ways, but there is one that I hold close to my heart.

The year I turned four, my parents bought their first home, a split-level suburban house with white vinyl siding and walnut-brown trimmed windows. The house felt expansive with its three bedrooms and big backyard. My favorite thing about this home, however, was the tree in our front yard. It was a crab apple tree, one that could withstand the cold climate and short growing season of northern Canada. It had perfectly formed limbs for climbing and a low canopy that hung to one side.

In the fourteen years that I lived in that home, I became attuned to the tree's seasonal rhythms, embracing each one—the cloud of cotton candy pink flowers filling the air in the spring, the growth of lip-puckering apples in the summer, and the sweet crab apple jelly that filled jars in the autumn. The tree and I grew alongside each other, getting taller and stronger. The year I graduated from high school my parents sold my childhood home, but I never forgot about my tree friend.

TREES GIVE TO US

When the topic of favorite trees comes up with family, friends, and even strangers, I see a shift in their demeanor. Eyes soften with remembering and shoulders relax.

"There was a tree . . ." their stories begin.

We are deeply interconnected to trees. They are the lungs of our planet. Their leaves "breathe" in carbon dioxide and water, a process known as photosynthesis, and "exhale" oxygen into the troposphere, while our lungs breathe in oxygen and exhale carbon dioxide—perfect synergy. Trees also hold incredible power to make our world a better place. Not only do trees provide oxygen for supporting life, but their roots hold the earth, preventing flooding and erosion. They moderate climate and capture carbon. They provide food, shelter, and medicine. All these superpowers hold incredible power to make families healthier and happier.

Trees have other specific benefits that are worth mentioning. For starters, trees remove a massive amount of pollution from the air, preventing heart and lung diseases in adults and in kids, as well as brain development problems for young children—trees save lives, especially in cities![1]

When it comes to choosing a city, neighborhood, or home to live in, we almost never base our decision on the surrounding trees, or lack thereof, but we should! Neighborhoods with lots of trees have less crime, gun violence, and tighter-knit communities, and families in those neighborhoods tend to be healthier and happier.[2] In a large population-based birth cohort study of children in Canada's third-largest metropolis, Metro Vancouver, researchers also found that when young children lived close to trees and grass, they were more likely to meet developmental milestones, especially so if there were trees.[3]

Trees also impact our children's academic performance. Researchers from the faculty of Forestry at University of Toronto, Canada, found that when controlling for socioeconomic status (how much money a family makes), the presence of trees on school properties has a significant positive impact on children's academic performance.[4] In another study of 318 public elementary schools in Chicago, USA, that serve high-poverty children in urban neighborhoods, school tree cover contributed to improvements in academics, mostly in math but a bit in reading too.[5] A 2024 study showed that leafy trees in schoolyards, especially those that have colorful fall foliage, have a restorative effect on children helping to reduce stress, improve attention, and increase well-being.[6]

DO YOU HAVE A TREE FRIEND?

On September 28, 2023, a tree made international news.[7] Shortly after the autumn equinox, an old sycamore tree was cut down near Hadrian's Wall in the Northumberland County of the United Kingdom. This tree was known as Robin Hood's tree after making an appearance in the 1991 movie *Robin Hood: Prince of Thieves*. The lone sycamore sat perfectly situated in Sycamore Gap, a low-lying area of Hadrian's Wall. It was a photographer's muse, a local's guidepost, a tourist's calling—a tree loved by many.

Severed from its roots under the cover of night, its untimely demise was met with guttural cries.

"Why would someone cut this iconic tree?"

"Who would do such a thing?"

"What were they thinking?"

Others didn't care.

As the incident unfolded, two people were arrested on suspicions of causing the act of vandalism but were later released. Seven months later, on April 30, 2024, two men in their thirties were charged and eventually found guilty of the "mindless destruction."[8] Like many, I felt saddened by the loss of such an iconic tree. I wondered if those involved ever had a tree friend, or perhaps that friend was long forgotten, an artifact of their childhood.

One thing that makes connection with trees different than many other plants, insects, and animals is a tree's lifespan. Trees can live a long time, so long that love for a tree can span generations. The sycamore tree at Hadrian's Gap was about 200 years old but the oldest living tree in the world, the Methuselah, a Great Basin bristlecone pine, is said to be 4,855 years old—incredible![9] The long lifespan of trees might explain why trees can hold such a deep symbolic, cultural, and even spiritual meaning for us adults, but what about children?

CHILDREN LOVE TREES EVEN MORE

When we lived in Okanagan Falls, British Columbia, my three older children were deeply attached to the big Crimson King Maple that stood in our backyard. The tree had been planted by previous owners, years ago, a bit too close to the back of the home. Its branches reached toward our windows, providing dappled shade against the heat of the afternoon sun. Its trunk stretched from our backyard to the upper deck and beyond, probably thirty or forty feet tall. Its well-placed branches provided a perfect ladder to the sky. It didn't take long for my children to master the climb from the backyard to the upper deck, often preferring it to the stairs.

In the eight years we lived in that home, Felix, Claire, and Theodore bonded with the maple tree. They didn't just climb it. They read books in crooks of its branches. They spied on the neighbors. They set up picnics in the shade of its canopy. They made wands and swords out of its branches. They collected, pressed, and played in its fallen foliage. Five years after we moved from Okanagan Falls, I asked my older children what they missed most about our old home. Without hesitation they answered in one voice, "The maple tree."

When children talk about nature and their relationship with it, trees are often mentioned. Children are drawn to trees. Even at playgrounds where there might be slides and swings, children prefer to play in and around trees. In 2017, two Finnish researchers wanted to learn more about how children living in urban environments relate to trees. Over the course of three years, they observed children between the ages of seven and twelve play in and explore the Kumpula School Garden, a 4.3-hectare green space with trees of various kinds, in the city of Helsinki, Finland. To their surprise, they discovered that children's relationships with trees was beautifully complex.[10]

From a practical perspective the study found that trees provide children with materials and space for open-ended play. Sticks, leaves, bark, stumps, and pine cones are the perfect loose parts for engaging children's creativity and problem-solving skills. In the study children used tree leaves as pretend food, branches for tools, cones to decorate, and bark as a vessel. I've noticed the same attraction to the loose parts of trees with my own children. From toddler to teen, at any given point during a tree encounter, they will discover a stick, pine cone, nut, leaf, or intriguing piece of shed bark that makes its way into pockets.

Trees also hold physical space and shelter for children. In the backyard of my childhood home, there were three spruce trees that grew together in the middle of the lawn. They were in such proximity that I could climb up one tree, reach over to the next trunk, and climb down the other tree. Watching me climb up and down those trees gave my father an idea—a tree fort! As far as tree forts go it was basic, a small wooden platform surrounded by helicopter cargo netting to prevent falls. It had no roof, but it didn't need one. The crisscrossing evergreen branches provided shelter from the rain and sun.

Different types of trees provide different opportunities for connection. A large, sturdy tree can provide space to climb, hide, and rest. A group of trees, a forest, can allow for exploration and creative play. A young tree can invite observation. A fruit and nut tree can give and sustain.

GETTING TO KNOW A TREE

Moving to a bigger city and leaving that wonderful Crimson King Maple behind wasn't easy. In the years that followed, my children struggled with the loss of friends, the disconnection from nature, and the downward spiral of my well-being, all without the comforting steadiness of their favorite tree. With time, however, my children have made new tree friends: an old cherry tree, a weeping willow, and several young apple trees planted with their own hands.

If your family has moved away from a favorite tree, or perhaps you or your child have never had a tree friend, know that making tree friends can happen, sometimes more easily than making human friends! In this section, I'm going to break down a few ways to help you and your child get to know a tree based on the three different types of tree relationships that researchers have observed: the admiring relationship, nurturing relationship, and nostalgic relationship.[11]

The Admiring Relationship

On a recent trip to the Big Island of Hawaii to see Rainbow Falls, an eighty-foot cascade of water flowing over a lava cave said to be the home of ancient Hawaiian moon goddess Hina, my children noticed something impressive in the forest nearby—an enormous banyan tree.

The Banyan tree was king of the grove; in fact, the entire grove was one tree. For my children, Rainbow Falls paled in comparison with the majesty of the banyan tree. They circled and touched the giant, grasping hold of a thick branch, allowing the tree to swallow them into its depths. This moment would be one of their favorite experiences on the Big Island of Hawaii.

One type of relationship we can have with trees is an *admiring relationship*. This type of relationship happens with trees that overwhelm us in awe, "Wow! Look at that amazing tree!" Trees that welcome us and our children into an admiring relationship are those that are older and/or have unique characteristics, gnarled trunks, rainbow bark, sweet flowing sap, sprawling canopies, and trembling leaves, to name a few.

Here are some ideas for fostering an admiring relationship with a tree:

- Notice the shape, size, and color of trees growing nearby.
- Look for trees with unique features close to home.

- Take pictures of favorite trees.
- Appreciate how deciduous trees change through the seasons.
- Notice how different leaves make different sounds (trembling aspen are my favorite).
- Feel the textures of tree bark on hands, cheeks, or forearms.
- Make a bark rubbing using a piece of paper and wax crayons.
- Taste edible sap from trees (maple, birch, and walnut).
- Press a piece of evergreen between your fingers to release heady scent of pine, cedar, or spruce.
- Walk, jump, and sashay through fallen leaves.
- Use leaves, sticks, seeds, and nuts that have fallen off trees to make arts and crafts.
- Notice how different trees make you and your child feel (happy, calm, excited).
- Encourage your child to play under, around, or in a tree.
- Have a tree-hugging contest for the longest, funniest, or most unique tree hug.
- Express gratitude for trees and all that they give us.

The Nurturing Relationship

The second most common type of relationship with trees is the *nurturing relationship.* Trees that welcome us and our children into a nurturing relationship are often younger trees in our yards and/or in community gardens.

In the spring of 2024, my family had vastly outgrown the 1,200-square-foot log home we'd been living in. It was time to move.

One of the first priorities after moving in to our new home in the city was rewilding our yard with trees. Unfortunately, we quickly discovered that the urban deer were decimating our saplings by eating their tender leaves. So, we fenced, fertilized, and watered the trees to help them thrive, entering a relationship with each one.

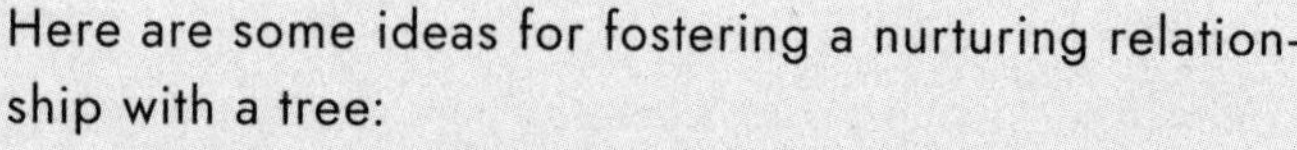

Here are some ideas for fostering a nurturing relationship with a tree:

- Plant a young tree in your yard or in a pot indoors (citrus, fig, olive, banana, and Norfolk pine are child-friendly).
- Protect your tree from damaging insects or animals.
- Fertilize and water your young tree to help it establish a strong root system.
- Prune your tree's branches for optimal canopy growth.
- Harvest fruits and nuts from your tree, from a community tree, or from a u-pick orchard.
- Provide food or shelter for beneficial wildlife that can help your tree thrive by setting up a bird feeder and building a bat home or mason bee home in or near your tree.
- Volunteer to help plant trees in your neighborhood, at your child's school, in city parks, or at community gardens.
- If you cannot have a tree of your own (in a yard, balcony, or home), offer to help to care for trees that belong to family members or close friends.

The Nostalgic Relationship

When I think back on the crab apple tree of my childhood, I'm filled with feelings of nostalgia. The fragrant blooms, the sour-tasting apples, and the sweetest of jelly fill my mind and link me to the past. My feelings have been so strong that after purchasing our new home, one of the first trees I planted was a crab apple tree.

Another common type of relationship with trees is the *nostalgic relationship*. Trees that welcome us into a nostalgic relationship are trees that we no longer have contact with, but we were close to at some point. These trees are locked into our memories, often acting as a bridge to the past.[12] This type of relationship is more common for adults than children; however, older children and teenagers who had a tree friend but moved away or the tree died might have a nostalgic relationship.

Here are a few ideas for using a nostalgic relationship with a tree to connect with trees:

- Share a story with your child about a tree from your own childhood. What did you admire about this tree? How did you play with this tree? How did you care for it?
- Talk about past relationships with trees that your older children and teenagers have had. What do they miss most about those trees? How can they connect with new trees?
- Learn about important trees in your local area. What makes a tree important for a community?
- Discover indigenous stories about trees such as *The Giving Tree: A Retelling of a Traditional Métis Story* by Leah Dorion.
- Attend a tree lighting event and talk about this community tradition.
- Explore the symbolism of trees in spirituality and religion.

SIMPLE ACTIVITIES FOR CONNECTING WITH TREES

There are many wonderful ways to connect with trees. Below you will find several of my family's favorite tree-connected recipes and activities.

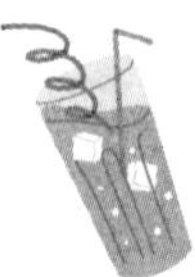

FIZZY PEACH SODA

Bright, bubbly, and perfect for hot summer afternoons, this peach soda celebrates the sweet, sun-kissed flavor of ripe peaches in every sip. Inspired by Emma Christensen's *True Brews*, the original version relies on champagne yeast, whereas this kid-friendly take swaps in fizzy water so you can serve it freely to little wildlings.

INGREDIENTS:

- 2 lbs ripe peaches
- 2 Tbsp lemon juice, freshly squeezed
- ½ cup of sugar, more if needed
- 1 cup water, or enough to fill the bottle
- Pinch of salt
- 4 cups (about 1 L) of carbonated water (club soda or seltzer)
- Ice cubes (optional)

EQUIPMENT:

- Food processor or blender
- Fine mesh sieve (or strainer)
- Large mixing bowl
- Small saucepan
- Airtight bottles or jars for storing the peach syrup
- Glasses for serving

DIRECTIONS:

1. **Prepare the peaches:** Remove the peel of the peaches with a paring knife or by blanching the peaches in boiling water for 30 seconds to one minute. Cut the peaches in half, remove the pits, and chop the peaches coarsely. Toss the peaches, lemon juice, and pinch of salt in a mixing bowl.
2. **Make the simple syrup:** In a small saucepan, mix the water and sugar over medium to high heat until the sugar is dissolved. Remove the simple syrup from the heat and let it cool.

3. **Blend the peaches and syrup:** Place the peaches and simple syrup in a food processor or blender and blend until smooth.

4. **Strain the puree:** Set the fine mesh sieve over the mixing bowl and strain the puree in batches. Try to squeeze through as much liquid as possible.

5. **Assemble and serve:** To serve, fill each glass about one-third full with chilled peach syrup (approximately 3–4 Tbsp, depending on your sweetness preference) and top off with about ¾ cup to 1 cup of carbonated water, adjusting to taste. Stir gently and enjoy.

6. **Store or chill the peach syrup:** Transfer any remaining peach syrup to airtight bottles or jars. Store in the refrigerator for up to five days.

AN INTRODUCTION TO WHITTLING: MAKING A GARDEN GNOME

Most folks think of whittling as an "adult only" hobby. After all, who would willingly hand over a sharp knife to a child? It seems dangerous and outright foolish. However, this age-old skill is how elders taught generations of children to use a knife skillfully. These whittled garden gnomes are a perfect introductory project for children. The cuts are simple, but the result is magical. You can even use these garden gnomes as markers in your vegetable or flower gardens or potted plants indoors.

SAFETY FIRST

With some basic knowledge, tools, and supervision, children as young as five years old can be introduced to the art of whittling. The first step to safe whittling is finding an appropriate whittling knife for your child:

- **Right size:** The handle of the whittling knife should fit comfortably in your child's hands. Your child should be able to wrap their fingers around the handle and hold it easily.
- **Fixed blade:** A whittling knife should not fold like a Swiss Army knife; rather, the blade should be fixed.

- **Sharp blade:** A sharp knife is easier to use and control, making it safer.

Consider for younger children:

- **Rounded tip:** A whittling knife with a rounded tip is a good option for younger children.
- **Finger guards:** Guards near the top of the blade prevent little fingers from creeping down to the blade and can prevent cuts. Finger guards are a good choice for young children, but they can get in the way of more intricate whittling when children become more skilled and confident whittlers.

The second step to safe whittling is the setup. "Sitting while whittling" is an important rule in our home. To help prevent any mishaps, your child should be seated in a calm and comfortable space while whittling. This can be indoors or outdoors, although cleanup is much easier outdoors.

The third step to safe whittling is supervision. For young children and for children new to whittling, I always recommend supervision. Proper supervision and good teaching will ensure that your child learns good whittling and knife skills and habits.

BASIC WHITTLING CUTS

In this project, children will use two basic whittling cuts.

- **The Push Cut:** To perform this cut, have your child hold the wood in their nondominant hand and the knife in the dominant hand. Your child can grip the knife handle fully or place their thumb along the back of the blade for better control of the knife. Have your child push the blade of the whittling knife along the wood surface away from their body in long cuts.
- **The Thumb Push Cut:** To perform this cut, follow the instructions for the push cut except place the thumb from the

nondominant hand along the back of the whittling knife for more power and control while cutting.

TOOLS AND MATERIALS:

- Wood sticks, about ½–1 inch in diameter and 10 inches long
- Whittling knife, fixed blade
- Stump, wood board, or old cutting board (optional)
- Sandpaper
- Permanent marker, black with a fine tip
- Acrylic paint, white and various colors
- Paintbrushes

DIRECTIONS:

1. **Set up a safe whittling space:** Gather up all the tools and materials in the list above and set up a comfortable whittling space indoors or outdoors.

2. **Show your child how to whittle safely:** Have your child sit on a chair or sturdy stump with their feet firmly planted on the ground. Get your child to rest their forearms on their knees so that the knife will clear their legs when whittling. Alternatively, have your child whittle toward a wood stump, an old wood board, or sturdy wood cutting board. Have your child hold the base of the stick in the nondominant hand. Show your child how to hold the whittling knife by firmly gripping the handle in their dominant hand. Placing the thumb on the back of the blade is optional but it can help control the knife more effectively.

3. **Whittle the gnome's hat:** Have your child whittle away the bark and wood about one inch down from the top of the stick using the **push cut**. Coach your child to slowly turn the stick in their nondominant hand and whittle until a point at the end of the stick is formed. Older children might wish to use the **thumb push cut** to create a bevel at the base of the hat to make it more apparent.

4. **Peel the bark to make a beard:** Starting about two inches from the base of that hat, have your child use a **push cut** to peel a section of bark away from the stick to form the beard.

5. **Remove a section of bark to make a label:** This step is optional but handy if you plan on using the garden gnomes as plant markers in your garden, or to write a child's name onto the gnome. Have your child turn the stick 180 degrees and hold it where the hat and beard were just carved. Starting about two inches from the base of the stick, instruct your child to peel a section of bark away from the stick using the **push cut**. This will be the area for the garden label (peas, carrots, potatoes, etc.).
6. **Let the sticks dry overnight:** Before the gnome can be sanded and painted, it needs to be placed in a warm, dry spot overnight or until the surface of the wood is dry to the touch. If your child is impatient, skip the drying and sanding steps and go right to painting the gnome.
7. **Sand the exposed wood:** Sanding the wood will create a smoother surface for painting, and sanding is a good skill for kids to learn too!
8. **Paint the gnome:** Have your child paint the gnome's beard with white paint. The gnome's hat can be painted in any color your child prefers.
9. **Add the eyes and label:** Using a fine-tip permanent marker, invite your child to make two little eyes and to write the label on the lower part of the stick. It might be helpful for you or your child to write the label in pencil first to make sure it will fit in the space.

Sit Spotting Among the Trees

Sit spotting is a simple activity that invites us and our children to slow down and connect with nature. We often move through nature quickly and distractedly, missing much along the way. Sit spotting offers an antidote for this tendency and is very doable in the backyards of suburban and urban neighborhoods—just find a tree or a bush.

In its authentic form, no special supplies are needed for sit spotting. It can be spontaneous or planned, and works well for all ages, especially for teenagers. I like to spontaneously sit spot while exploring nature with my teens by saying, "Let's just sit here for a minute." Sometimes they resist, but afterward they always appreciate the opportunity to stop, look, and listen.

DIRECTIONS:

1. **Dress for the weather:** Wear appropriate clothing for the weather. If it's wet or snowy outside, rain or snow pants are needed.
2. **Go outside with your child:** Find a safe place to sit in nature, whether this is a rural forest or a city park. Somewhere close to home that is relatively quiet with trees works best.
3. **Sit quietly in nature for a few minutes:** Try to sit quietly in one spot for five minutes and look, listen, smell, and feel the surrounding nature.
4. **Share your discoveries:** Ask your child, tween, or teen to share their discoveries and emotions.

Sit spotting can feel uncomfortable at first. We aren't used to sitting quietly. That's why I recommend starting with a short amount of time and slowly building up the length. For teens and older children, twenty to thirty minutes is an ideal length for the body to fully settle into nature. For younger children, five to ten minutes is more realistic. Also, returning to a sit spot throughout the seasons allows for deeper connections to form with nature.

While sit spotting, there's no need to "do" anything, but I *do* find that children and teens find it easier to sit spot with some guidance. Here are a few sit spotting prompts to try:

- **5-4-3-2-1:** Search for 5 things you can SEE, 4 things you can TOUCH, 3 things you can HEAR, 2 things you can SMELL, and 1 thing you can TASTE.
- **Three good things:** Name three (or more) good things in nature that you are thankful for. This practice is shown to boost your sense of well-being.
- **Moving and grooving:** Look for nature that is moving. Ants crawling on the ground, trees swaying in the breeze, or birds flitting through the forest canopy.

- **Eco-artist:** Use bits of nature within your reach to create a piece of nature art on the ground.
- **Sound mapping:** Start by noticing the sounds of nature, then map them out on a piece of paper or on the ground with a stick.
- **Patterns in nature:** Search for patterns in the nature that surrounds you.
- **Close up:** Get close to nature. Pick up and look at a rock, pine cone, or other bit of nature closely.

More Simple Activities for Connecting with Trees

- **Interview a tree:** Imagine trees could talk and share the stories that they hold within their trunks. What kind of stories would they tell? What have they seen in their lifetime? Grab paper and pencil and ask a nearby tree these questions and discover the answers.
- **Go back in tree time:** Trees are some of the longest-living plants on our planet. Learn about trees in your neighborhood and try to find out how old they might be. Wonder about what life was like when that tree was just a sapling.
- **Bathe in the forest:** Forest bathing, or *shinrin yoku*, is the Japanese practice of being quiet and calm in a forest and noticing the forest with all your senses. It's like sit spotting but has certain traditions such as tea drinking that make it unique.
- **Take part in a national or international tree day:**
    - National Forest Week (Canada last week of September/USA second week of July)
    - National Tree Day (Canada last Wednesday of September/USA last Sunday in July)
    - Arbor Day (April 26)

CHAPTER 12

Delighting in Water Play

"C'MON MAMAN, LET'S jump in," said Felix, putting his arm around me and pulling me toward a deep pool of water carved by a slow-flowing creek.

Rays of late-morning sun plunged through the cedar trees, heating up the forest floor and thickening the air with dust. Sweat dripped down my back, doubly heated by the baby I was carrying. The flowing water tempted me, but I knew where this water came from. Even though the sun scorched the valley floor, this water came from snow melt high up in the mountains. Its icy waters shocked those brave enough to plunge in.

I looked at my teenager, towering over me, a huge grin on his face and eyes glinting.

"I'll go if you go," said Theo, never keen on risky activities even at twelve.

"But we don't have bathing suits . . . and what about the littles?" I tried, knowing that my excuses wouldn't work.

"Just jump in with your shorts and sports bra. We can take turns watching Alice and Loïc," volunteered Claire.

I gritted my teeth and nodded. "Let's do it!"

We clambered down smooth rocks toward the creek bed, each taking a turn dipping into a pocket of water etched into a large rock. Felix counted down the seconds to see how long we could stay in. I barely lasted thirty seconds. Felix lasted ninety. Our bodies balked at the cold-water plunge, muscles seizing, skin turning pink, and breath coming in short bursts.

Two-year-old Alice dipped her toes into the shallow side of the creek tentatively and shouted a deafening "Cold cold cold!," which was mixed with adrenaline-filled teenage hoots and hollers.

Given opportunities to play in and with water, most toddlers, children, and teens jump into the fun. We parents, well, sometimes we can be *wet blankets* when it comes to water play, especially with rain, puddles, and cold water.

Children's fascination with water has always interested me, along with their propensity to find it no matter where they are, but I shouldn't be surprised. Water, after all, is the life force of our planet, one that draws us in and fills us up.

BECOMING WATER STEWARDS

Despite our natural love for water, we've become disconnected from water in many ways. We embrace comfortable illusions about freshwater. We assume water flows endlessly from taps and believe that an infinite cache of freshwater lays hidden deep within the Earth. While it's true that freshwater won't disappear from our planet, it can be polluted or depleted to a point where it takes years to be restored. Fresh, clean drinking water is a *gift*, one worth protecting.

One of the most popular posts on my website, Backwoods Mama, is a simple list of twenty-two actions children can take to help conserve water. It isn't a perfect list, and there are a few silly things in there. For instance, have you ever heard the pithy saying "If it's yellow, let it mellow. It it's brown, flush it down"? I used to be adamant about this water conserving strategy until my kids got bigger, along with their bladders. Thankfully, dual flush toilets have come a long way. Nevertheless, the point of the article was that our children are never too young to learn about where their freshwater comes from and to help be stewards of their local freshwater sources.

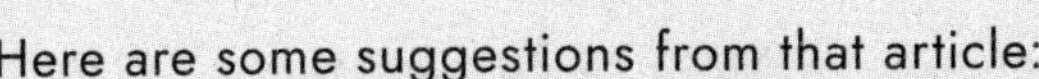

Here are some suggestions from that article:

- **Get cold water from the fridge:** Fill a dedicated jug with water to keep cool in the fridge.
- **Have a special water cup or bottle:** Don't grab a new cup every time you feel thirsty, instead have a special water cup or bottle that you can refill throughout the day. This way there will be fewer dishes to wash.
- **Fill a cup halfway:** When filling up a cup of water, only fill it halfway to avoid wasting water. Another option is to use a reusable water bottle.
- **Don't throw out old water:** Don't waste old water from cups, water bottles, or baths! Instead of pouring this water down the drain, use it to water plants instead.
- **Don't bathe so much:** Most kids can get behind this water conservation strategy! Did you know that you only need a bath once or twice a week, unless you're really dirty (think: covered in mud). I don't know about you, but my kids would rather not bathe at all.
- **Take speedy showers:** Showers use way less water than baths. Learn how to take a speedy shower. Parents: Teaching younger kids to take showers can be tricky, but it can be done.
- **Reuse towels:** Use the same towel for at least a week. Remember you should be clean after your shower and if you hang your towel to dry, it will be ready and waiting.

- **Re-wear clothes:** Clothing gets washed far too often. While I wouldn't recommend turning those undies inside out, let your clothes get nice and dirty before throwing them in the wash.
- **Turn off the water while brushing your teeth:** Don't let the water run while you're brushing your teeth. Turning off the tap saves a lot of water.
- **Be a leak detective:** Train those ears to pick up the sound of dripping water and become water saving superheroes by tightening up leaky taps.
- **Fill the dishwasher:** Dishwashers use less water than washing dishes by hand. Help scrape dishes and fill the dishwasher . . . and empty it too!

WATER PLAY AND CHILD DEVELOPMENT

Water is a *magical* material. This curious substance, made up of one oxygen molecule and two hydrogen molecules, also known as H_2O, has no color, no smell, and no flavor in its pure form. It has three unique states: solid, liquid, and gas, and infinite play possibilities. Another wonderful thing about playing in and with water is that it's inclusive. All ages, abilities, living situations, and cultures can enjoy water play in some capacity. A baby splashing water in the bath, a toddler jumping into a puddle, a child playing with a garden hose, a teen jumping into a deep lake—these are all forms of water play.

Water play has been championed as an important part of holistic child development for some time. Early childhood educators often incorporate elements of water play in preschools and day cares to help young children develop foundational skills and knowledge relating to movement, science, mathematics, and language. I couldn't agree more!

Science and Mathematics

Water play helps children develop a foundation in science and math in the best kind of way.[1] Why best? Science isn't just about knowing things, but about exploring, investigating, and connecting with the world.

I've seen this firsthand, especially with puddles. When my children jump into puddles, they discover that water moves (displacement). When they throw a rock or leaf into a puddle, they notice that some objects float, and others sink (buoyancy). When they sit in a puddle without waterproof pants, they realize that some materials absorb water, and others don't (porosity)—not their favorite lesson!

When they pour, scoop, funnel, and ladle water from one container to another, they learn about measurement and flow. Add some dirt, leaves, petals, and sticks and now they've made a mixture, or even better—a potion! Pour in some dish soap and now there are bubbles and surface tension.

I give the example of puddles, which tend to be more common in the spring and fall seasons, but these discoveries can be made in a small inflatable pool, a water table, a mud kitchen, a shallow container of water, a pool, a bathtub, or a lake—basically, anywhere, inside or outside, where there's water. And while I don't hover over my children throwing around scientific terms when they play in water, I think it's helpful to know that beneath the surface of water play, a whole world of learning is happening.

A NOTE ABOUT WATER SAFETY

When I was a young mother, a blogger I followed had a drowning scare with her toddler. Not in a pool, lake, or creek, but in a five-gallon bucket. Her toddler fell into the bucket headfirst, and although it wasn't full, the water level was high enough to cause drowning. Thankfully the toddler was resuscitated, and I believe made a full recovery, but I will never forget that story.

Forget movie scenes with children screaming and flailing in water. Drowning is silent and fast, taking a mere twenty to sixty seconds to happen. According to the World Health Organization, drowning is the fourth most common cause of death in children between one and four and the third most common cause of death in children aged five to fourteen years old globally.[2] Home swimming pools (for children between one and four) and bathtubs (for children under one) are where most little ones drown, typically when an adult is in the vicinity.

I don't mean to cause panic with this information, nor do I think we should ban children from water play, but losing a child or loved one to drowning is a tragedy. If you or your family have been touched by such a loss my heart mourns with you. For us parents and caregivers, the most important thing we can do while encouraging water play is take water safety seriously.

Research shows that to significantly reduce the risk of drowning, several things need to happen: drowning hazards need to be barriered, controlled, and supervised, and children need to learn swimming skills and water safety skills.[3] That means little ones need constant supervision in the bath, pools should be properly fenced, and play around kiddie pools, ponds, lakes, creeks, and any other body of water needs to be monitored. Swimming lessons are important too.

My children have grown up near water—lakes, ponds, and pools—and because of that we have made community swimming lessons and water safety skills a priority. Some of their swimming lessons have even taken place in the lake—fully clothed! They've also learned about where and when it's safe to swim, not diving in shallow areas, avoiding swift moving currents, wearing a life jacket on a boat, and knowing how and when to call for help. Swimming skills and water safety lessons are also important for teens to learn or review. Teens tend to take on riskier forms of water play, especially males, so it doesn't hurt to review the basics with them.

SPLASH-TASTIC OUTDOOR WATER ACTIVITIES

There are many wonderful ways to play and connect with water. In this section I've included some simple and fun activities that have been favorites for my children over the years.

FROZEN PAINT-CICLES

These frozen paint-cicles are so easy to make and perfect for hot summery weather. All you need are some watercolor paints, liquid or tube, an ice cube tray, and popsicle sticks.

MATERIALS:

- Ice cube tray
- Watercolor paint (liquid watercolor paint or tubes)
- Popsicle sticks or twigs
- Painting paper

DIRECTIONS:

1. **Make the paint-cicles:** Using liquid watercolor paint or watercolor tubes, add one color in each ice cube tray cell. If you are using watercolor tubes, add enough paint to make vibrant colors. Test the colors out on a piece of paper if needed. Place a popsicle stick in each ice cube cell. Freeze until solid.
2. **Paint with the paint-cicles:** Set up a piece of painting paper on a flat surface outdoors, in the shade, and let your child discover the magic of paint-cicles.

POND DIPPING WITH CHILDREN

Pond dipping is a wonderful way to explore the magical world of pond minibeasts that lie hidden just beneath the surface of ponds. This simple activity, a kid favorite, works well in ponds and slow-moving creeks. Urban and city ponds work great for this activity; just be sure this activity is allowed in public parks before setting out.

EQUIPMENT:

- Long-handled net (fine-meshed aquarium or pond net)
- Bucket or shallow container (white or light colored)
- Magnifying glass (optional)
- Ladles, pipettes, turkey baster, or ice cube trays (fun extras but optional)
- Field guide or identification chart (handy but optional)
- Rubber boots or water sandals
- Notebook and pencil (optional, for sketching observations)
- Camera or phone (optional, for identification)

DIRECTIONS:

1. **Gather and clean equipment:** Rinse any equipment that will go into the pond with clean water *before* going pond dipping to prevent accidental introduction of contamination or diseases into ponds.

2. **Choose a safe and accessible pond:** Pick a shallow pond or slow-moving stream that has a bank or area children can stand on.

3. **Prepare your gear:** On the edge of the pond or stream, fill a bucket or container with a few inches of water directly from the pond. This will be a temporary home for any minibeasts your child wants to look at more closely.

4. **Dip the net into the pond:** Lower the pond net into the water and sweep the net through the water in a circle or figure eight. If you don't catch critters, try sweeping through plants near the bottom of the pond to help dislodge hidden minibeasts.

5. **Transfer pond minibeasts to the bucket:** Gently but quickly place the net into the water-filled bucket or container and turn the netting inside out into the water.

6. **Observe and wonder:** Allow the water to settle for a minute then look for little friends wiggling and swimming around—water beetles, dragonfly larvae, snails, tadpoles, and many more! Use a magnifying glass to get a closer look.

7. **Record your findings:** This step is completely optional, but if your child is keen, take some pictures or make notes or a drawing in the journal. See if you and your child can identify the pond minibeasts.

8. **Release and rinse:** Gently release all pond minibeasts back into the pond before leaving. If it's warm outside, return the minibeasts back into the water after about ten to fifteen minutes, or sooner, so that they don't get too warm. Rinse your nets and buckets in the water and let them fully dry when you return home.

MAKING BIG BUBBLES

Making giant bubbles and setting them free is one of the most quintessential childhood summer activities. There are many recipes for making big bubbles, some with long lists of ingredients. This recipe, my go-to, has five ingredients that are all easy to find at the grocery store—look for glycerin in the pharmacy section. If you don't have a bubble wand, I've included the steps to making one with a couple of sticks, string, and a heavy washer.

MATERIALS:

For Big Bubbles

- 14 cups water
- 1 cup Dawn dishwashing liquid
- ½ cup cornstarch
- 1 Tbsp glycerin
- 1 Tbsp baking powder (not baking soda)

For a Bubble Wand

- 2 long sticks or dowels, about ½ inch thick and 3 feet (1 meter) long
- Thick cotton string (¼ inch thick), 6 to 8 feet (2 to 2.5 meters) long
- Heavy washer
- Eyelets (optional)

DIRECTIONS:

1. **Make the bubble solution:** Add the water, reserving one cup, to a deep tray or container, gently stir in the dishwashing liquid, and then add the glycerin and baking powder. Mix the reserved water with the cornstarch to make a slurry and mix into the solution. Use the bubble solution right away, or let it sit for several hours.
2. **Make the bubble wand:** Take two long sticks or dowels. If you are using eyelets, screw an eyelet at the end of each stick. Tie one end of the thick cotton string to one end of a stick, or thread it through into an eyelet. Thread the washer through the string and then tie the other end of the string to the other stick, or thread it through the eyelet, making sure there is about three feet of string between the sticks. Tie the string ends together.
3. **Make BIG bubbles:** Set the bubble solution in a shaded area with minimal wind. Dip the bubble wand into the bubble solution to thoroughly soak the string. Keeping the stick close together, lift them out of the solution, gently open the wand, and move backward to make big bubbles!

LAVENDER LEMONADE

After spending time playing outside in the summer sun, the zesty sweetness of this lavender lemonade is the perfect thirst quencher. It's so popular in our home that I make a batch of it every few days during the summer months. Our family prefers lightly sweetened lemonade, so feel free to adjust the sweetness to your liking. If you don't have fresh lavender (*Lavandula angustifolia*), feel free to substitute with mint or toss some strawberries or raspberries into the lemonade for a nice fruity punch.

INGREDIENTS:

- 6 fresh lemons, about 1 cup of juice
- 5 to 6 cups of water

- ½ to 1 cup sugar
- 2 to 3 fresh lavender sprigs
- Ice cubes (for serving)

EQUIPMENT:

- Citrus juicer
- Small saucepan
- Mixing spoon
- Pitcher

DIRECTIONS:

1. **Extract lemon juice:** Use a citrus juicer to squeeze out the lemon juice from the six lemons. It should yield about 1 cup of lemon juice.
2. **Make a simple syrup:** Combine 1 cup of sugar with 1 cup of water in a small saucepan. Warm the mixture over medium heat until the sugar has fully dissolved. Remove from heat and add the sprigs of lavender. Let the lavender infuse into the syrup for 5 to 10 minutes.
3. **Finish the lemonade:** In a pitcher, combine the lemon juice, simple syrup, and 4 to 5 cups of cold water. Taste the lemonade and adjust the sweetness to your liking. You can also remove or leave in the lavender sprigs.
4. **Serve over ice cubes:** Fill glasses with a generous amount of ice and pour the lemonade over the ice. Garnish with a lavender sprig or lemon slice if you'd like.

More Simple Activities for Connecting with Water

- **Discover your water source:** Learn where your tap water comes from. Check local utility maps or websites to see which river, lake, or aquifer supplies your home. If possible, plan a short visit (even just a drive or walk) and talk through each step of how water travels from its source all the way to your faucet.

- **Set up a water play station:** Fill a shallow tub or kiddie pool with clean water. Scatter in measuring cups, funnels, droppers, basters, small plastic bottles, and floating/sinking objects (e.g. pebbles, leaves, and pine cones). Encourage kids to pour, scoop, measure, and experiment.
- **Build a simple rain gauge:**
  1. Take a clean, clear plastic bottle (a 2-liter soda bottle works well).
  2. Cut off the top third and invert it like a funnel, taping it securely in place.
  3. Use a permanent marker (or stick-on labels) to draw measurement lines on the bottle's side (in millimeters or inches).
  4. Set it outside in an open spot, away from overhanging eaves. After each rainfall, check how many inches (or millimeters) of rain collected. Record daily or weekly totals and compare how much rain falls from one storm to the next.
- **Explore rain sounds:** Bring a variety of everyday containers (metal cans, plastic tubs, etc.) outside into the rain. Have kids listen to the way raindrops sound on each object and notice differences in pitch and volume. Then encourage them to listen to rain on different natural surfaces (leaves, grass, rocks) and compare how each surface "sings" its own rain song.

CHAPTER 13

Turning Bug Fear into Curiosity

"EEEEK! A BLACK WIDOW spider crawling up the stairs!" (me, age 28)

"Mamaaaan! There's a wasp in the house—help!" (Alice, age 3)

"Get it off, get it OFF! I hate ticks—they're so gross." (Claire, age 10)

"If *these* mosquitoes have diseases, I don't want to go outside!" (Theo, age 8, while visiting Bali)

I might be Backwoods Mama, but my kids, like most, are leery of insects and even fearful. While I don't fear most insects, there are a few bugs I don't like. Wasp stings give me huge welts. Disease-carrying mosquitoes and ticks make me cautious. Venomous spiders demand my respect. I give those bugs a wide berth, but I don't mind small spiders scurrying across the floor, holding a grasshopper in my hands, or working with hives of honeybees. I'm not typical. . . .

Most children and adults don't like bugs, and many even fear them. Fear of insects tends to be so common that spiders rank in the top list of most feared animals while ticks rank high in the disgusting factor.[1] Evolutionary psychologists believe our dislike of bugs is something we are born with, to avoid getting injured or sick. Strangely, our fear of bugs is getting worse, especially for those of us living in urban and suburban areas, and it's having an impact on insects.[2]

NOT ALL BUGS ARE BAD

Our planet is crawling with bugs. According to latest estimates, there are about 1.5 million species of beetles, 5.5 million species of insects, and 7 million species of terrestrial arthropods on our planet.[3] That's a lot of bugs!

Just so we are clear, even though I've been using *bugs* and *insects* interchangeably, entomologists, people that study bugs, would say they are different. *True,* bugs have part-hardened wing cases and tubular sucking mouth parts like aphids, cicadas, leafhoppers, boatmen, bedbugs, and water skaters.[4] Lately, though, people use *bugs* to refer to insects, like I am doing in this chapter.

Back to bugs. Truthfully, some bugs *can* harm us. Mosquitoes, ticks, fleas, and flies can carry diseases that make us very sick.[5] Wasps, bees, scorpions, spiders, and ants can sting and bite. It's important to take precautions with these creatures. Thankfully, harmful bugs only make up a small percentage of all the bug species in the world. Most bugs are neutral or beneficial.

Bugs weave together life here on Earth and play a crucial role in our planet's ecosystems.[6] They decompose plants and animals, cycle nutrients in the soil, pollinate plants, act as food for other animals (and humans!), and even help control populations of problematic insects. Without bugs of all types and sizes, we would be in a heap of trouble and right now that's where we are heading. Insects are declining around the world.[7]

EMBRACING NATURE'S TINY WONDERS

Shortly after moving to the Okanagan Valley of British Columbia, my children and I had our first encounter with a black widow spider. Felix, only four at that time, spotted the spider climbing up the basement stairs. Her polished black body and angular legs sent warning bells in my brain. As I tried to relocate her, the flash of a red hourglass on her underbelly shouted "danger!" My reaction to this dangerous beauty was *fear* and the hard smack of a shoe.

As my children and I learned more about the black widow spider, which is not typically aggressive, a new appreciation grew. I still didn't want her in my home, but when another black widow happened to creep in, I caught and released her with a jar. When we found her sticky, messy webs in our yard, we let them be. We no longer feared her; in fact, we learned to love her.

I'll be the first to admit that bugs look otherworldly. Their exoskeletons, plethora of legs and eyes, and odd appendages seem alien to us. Learning to love a creature that looks and behaves so differently doesn't come as naturally as loving kittens and ducklings. While it's tempting to swat away the call to love bugs, it's important to try. When we learn to love the unloved thing—encouraging our children to do the same—we're more likely to help bugs out, which is exactly what they need right now.

Learning Away the Fear of Bugs

Studies show that learning about insects makes them less scary for children, and I've seen this firsthand not only with the black widow spider but even with ticks. When my children and I approach bugs with curiosity and learn more about them, fear dissipates. No, we don't love ticks, but our knowledge of them gives us an important awareness of them when exploring nature where ticks hang out.

To start loving bugs, I invite you and your child to learn about a bug that lives close to home, preferably ones that can't sting or bite—a butterfly, moth, ladybug, praying mantis, or beetle. Start by observing these critters in their natural habitat and wondering about them. What do they eat? Where do they live? How do they behave? Bring bug curiosity home by reading books about these bugs or even making a bug terrarium to place on your nature table.

Learning about bugs can also happen at a local insectarium, community museum, science center, or environmental education center. Reading books about bugs can help us relate to them most, especially picture books with bug heroes.

Modeling Calm Curiosity with Bugs

Do you screech and hide at the sight of a bug crawling up the wall? Or do you calmly shoo bugs back outside? Modeling calm and curious behavior around bugs has a very significant impact on the way your child reacts to bugs. I know it's not always easy to stay calm when faced with an angry wasp in the home, but children look up to us and copy the way we act and behave, and yes, even around bugs.

BUZZ OFF: STAYING SAFE FROM DISEASE-CARRYING BUGS

One year, my family of five joined two other families to explore Thailand for one month. We arrived in Bangkok at the end of January, flew up to Chiang Mai, then traveled by passenger van through picturesque towns until our destination of Phuket.

Although Felix, Claire, and Theo have few memories of this trip—they were eight, five, and three at the time—it remains one of my most memorable family adventures. Not only because of the friendly locals, soft sandy beaches, mouthwatering street food, and great company, but also because a friend of ours contracted dengue fever, a mosquito-borne disease, while we were there.

I vividly remember the concern etched on my friend's face when her partner began showing symptoms—fever and severe achiness. The jovial cheer of our travels quickly took on a somber tone when doctors revealed the diagnosis. Thankfully our friend made a full and healthy recovery, but it opened my eyes to the danger of disease-carrying bugs.

Mosquitoes carry diseases that infect hundreds of millions of people every year.[8] Ticks can also carry bacteria and viruses that cause illnesses, as can fleas, flies, and other insects.

It's important to know that not all mosquito and tick species carry the same diseases, and some don't carry diseases at all. In Canada, for example, there are about eighty species of mosquitoes. Only a few carry diseases, so the risk of getting sick from a mosquito bite in Canada is very low, although that may change in the future.[9]

Ticks are similar. Different tick species can carry different illnesses. In my home province of British Columbia there are more than twenty species of ticks, and only a few of those species bite humans and can carry diseases. The Western blacklegged tick (deer tick) can carry a bacteria called *Borrelia burgdorferi*, which causes Lyme disease, and the Rocky Mountain wood tick can carry Colorado tick fever virus and Rocky Mountain spotted fever.

Here's an important lesson I've learned about disease-carrying bugs: Knowing about the *types of insects* that can cause illnesses *in your area* empowers you to go outside with your child confidently. When we know what's out there, we can act accordingly. When bad bugs are buzzing about, it doesn't mean you have to stay indoors, it just means taking steps to safeguard your child and yourself. Here are some important ways to stay safe from disease-carrying insects:

- **Cover up:** Dress your child in light-colored pants, a long-sleeved shirt, socks, and shoes when exploring nature that has lots of biting insects. If ticks are bad, tuck pant legs into socks.
- **Use insect repellent:** Spray child-safe insect repellant that is formulated to keep mosquitoes and ticks away.
- **Apply sunscreen first:** If your child needs sunscreen, lather the sunscreen first and then insect repellant.
- **Stay on the trail:** When ticks are out in full force, walk on trails and avoid walking through tall grassy or brushy areas.
- **Grab a bug net:** Cover up strollers and outdoor hangout or sleeping areas with bug nets.

- **Avoid peak bug times and areas:** Mosquitoes are ravenous at dusk and dawn when it's cooler. Ticks like tall grass and shade.
- **Check for ticks and bugs before going inside:** Look for ticks on clothing and in hair after playing outside in nature. Check around the hairline, behind ears, and the groin area. If ticks are particularly bad, place all clothing in the washing machine and family members in a shower.
- **See a tick—don't panic!** If a tick is roaming free, pick it up with tissue paper, put it in a plastic zip baggie, and figure out what kind of tick it is (for fun!) before tossing it out. If a tick has attached to your child's skin, grab a pair of tweezers, grab hold of the tick as close to the skin as possible, and pull slowly but firmly out. Don't twist the tick, light it on fire, or try other random things. Wash the bite wound with soap and water. Keep the tick in a plastic zip baggie and monitor the bite wound for signs of infection. If you have concerns about the tick carrying diseases, contact your doctor within twenty-four hours of removing the tick.

SPECIAL ACTIVITIES FOR CONNECTING WITH BUGS

Reconnecting with bugs is an important part of reconnecting with nature. Here are some fun, simple, and not-so-scary ways to get a bit more comfortable with our buggy friends.

BUILD A BUG HOTEL (THE RIGHT WAY)

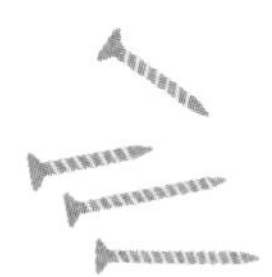

Bug hotels are little havens for bugs, but if a bug hotel doesn't have the right "rooms," beneficial (good) bugs won't check in. A well-designed bug hotel should have no pine cones, chunks of bark, wood shavings, random sticks, seed heads, moss or lichen, grass, feathers, rocks, large holes (over 10 mm or 3/8 inch), glass, or plastic.[10] This might be surprising since almost all bug hotels sold in-store and online are built with these items. However, when bug hotels are poorly designed, they attract wasps, flies, and parasites that can hurt or destroy beneficial bugs.[11]

This activity will guide you and your child in designing a simple bug hotel the right way and is a great activity whether you live in the city, suburbs, or the country.

SAFETY FIRST:

- **Readiness check (for kids):** There is no set age for when children can start using a cordless drill. However, a child should be able to follow instructions as well as hold and control the drill safely and steadily. If fatigue sets in, a parent should take over.
- **Protective gear and setup:** Safety glasses for drilling and a dust mask for sanding are a must. Clamp the wood to a stable surface. Set the drill to low speed. Remove the battery when changing bits or when not in use. Ensure that hair is tied up, close-toed shoes are worn, and there are no loose clothes that could get caught in the drill.
- **Supervision:** A parent must stay within arm's reach when a child uses the drill. Also, be sure that other children or bystanders stand back.
- **Safe technique:** Be sure to keep hands well away from the bit and mark a depth stop with a piece of tape.

MATERIALS:

- A piece of hardwood, untreated seasoned (dried) poplar, ash, beech, or oak that is 4 to 8 inches (10 to 20 cm) wide, 8 to 12 inches (20 to 30 cm) tall, and 2 or more inches (5 cm) thick
- Power drill
- Drill bits, sizes ⅛ to ¼ inch (3 to 6 mm)

- Electric sander or sandpaper
- Something for a roof: scrap wood, recycled plastic, scrap metal, aluminum pie plate
- Screws, for attaching the roof
- Pencil

DIRECTIONS:

1. **Set up:** Gather all the tools and materials in the list above, read through the instructions from beginning to end, and set up a comfortable workspace indoors or outdoors.
2. **Teach power drill use and safety:** Show your child how to use a power drill safely: how to hold the drill, turn it on and off, and drill a hole. I recommend getting your child to drill some practice holes in a piece of scrap wood. It's important to supervise and guide your child closely through this learning process.
3. **Draw a design on the wood (optional):** Draw a simple design or outline on the face of the wood. It could be a simple flower, bee, bug, or rocket ship. Drawing a design is completely optional. It's perfectly fine to drill a bunch of random holes.
4. **Drill holes into the wood:** Use a drill bit to drill a hole into the face of the wood along the picture outline or randomly placed. Drill just short of 2 inches (5 cm) deep. This is very important: **Do not drill holes all the way through the piece of wood**. Bugs only like having one door to their rooms. **Tip:** To prevent holes from being drilled all the way through, place a piece of tape on the drill bit as an easy reminder to stop at a certain depth. If your child accidentally drills through the wood, that's OK. You can plug up the hole with a piece of wool or cotton ball afterward.
5. **Drill many more holes:** Continue drilling holes along the picture outline or randomly in the wood. Make sure the holes are about ¼ to ⅜ inch (6 to 10 mm) apart. Wider holes should be placed farther apart from each other than smaller holes. Also, be sure to drill a variety of hole sizes to attract different types of beneficial bugs.

6. **Sand the surface of the wood:** Smooth and clean splinters away from each tunnel entrance. Beneficial bugs won't use tunnels with splinters or sawdust in the entrances.
7. **Attach a roof:** To prevent rain from getting into the tunnels, attach a roof to the top. Nail or screw on a piece of scrap wood, recycled plastic, metal, or an aluminum pie plate so that it overhangs the wood piece.
8. **Hang the bug hotel:** Place the bug hotel at least 3 feet (1 meter) off the ground with the tunnel entrances facing south or east. If you notice birds poking into the holes, wrap a piece of chicken wire around the front of the bug hotel. This will discourage birds from eating the bug larvae, and beneficial bugs don't seem to mind the wire.
9. **Clean and care for your bug hotel:** Wait, you're not done! At the end of summer inspect the tunnels and clean out any dead and dirty stuff from the rooms. Tunnels that are sealed closed most likely have solitary bee larvae. To protect the bee larvae, place the bug hotel in a cold, dry place, like a garden shed, during the winter months. Bring the bug hotel back out in the early spring, which is when the larvae will hatch.

Go on a Bug Hunt

Going on a bug hunt in nearby nature helps your child get to know insects close to home. While all you need for this activity is access to the outdoors and a keen sense of observation, some optional materials can help you observe bugs more closely.

OPTIONAL MATERIALS:

- Magnifying glass
- Insect net
- Observation container
- Insect field guide

When hunting for bugs outside, look under rocks, logs, and fallen leaves and search around flowers, ponds, creeks, and puddles. Check out cracks in concrete, around rain downspouts, and under trees. Many bugs are safe to touch and handle, and some are not. When in doubt, take a picture instead.

Bugs that are safe to handle:

- Fireflies
- Ladybugs and beetles
- Crickets and grasshoppers (can bite, but rarely do)
- Pill/roly-poly bugs (terrestrial crustaceans, not insects)
- Butterflies and moths (avoid touching the wings)
- Mantises

Bugs that shouldn't be handled:

- Wasps
- Honeybees, solitary bees, bumblebees
- Spiders (some spiders are safe to touch)
- Ticks

More Simple Activities for Connecting with Bugs

- **Set up an ant farm indoors:** Ants are amazing insects. They search for food, care for eggs, and protect their queen in a highly organized way. Children can watch ants indoors by setting up an indoor ant farm.
- **Visit an apiary with a beekeeper:** Going on an apiary tour is a fun way to learn about honeybees in a safe way. Children will be given proper gear to protect them from

stings and may even get to taste some honey too! Of course, you may want to skip this activity if your child is severely allergic to beestings.

- **Set up a butterfly water station:** Set up a shallow dish or saucer and fill it with small pebbles or gravel so butterflies have a safe place to land. Place it in a sunny spot near flowers, then pour in just enough water to reach the top of the stones. Add a few slices of orange or watermelon to provide extra sugar and minerals. Watch patiently from a short distance, and notice which butterflies visit.
- **Create a pitfall trap:** Bury a small, clear container (like a yogurt cup) so its rim is level with the ground. Add a bit of leaf litter as cover. Check every hour or so to see which ground-dwelling insects (ground beetles, ants, rove beetles) have wandered in. Identify them, then release them back into the yard.
- **Let your yard "go wild":** Mow your lawn less frequently, plant flowers, and avoid using pesticides and herbicides.

CHAPTER 14

Navigating the Teenage Dip in Nature Connection

"CAN I STAY HOME?" fourteen-year-old Claire asked.

Her question broke my frenzy of packing bathing suits, towels, water, and snacks for our impromptu post-supper trip to the beach. With one week of summer vacation remaining, I wanted to capture every moment of summer's goodness with my children.

"You don't want to come?" I asked, perplexed. "You love the beach."

"I don't really feel like going," she said, casually flipping her long blonde hair over her shoulder.

Ever since Claire turned thirteen, I noticed a shift in her relationship with nature. As a child, she loved being outdoors. I would often find her perched in a tree listening to birds or whittling wands in the front yard. She penned poems about friendly spiders, pressed flowers for crafts, and ran barefoot throughout the summer months. By fourteen, however, she declared she "*hates*" spiders along with most creepy-crawlies and actively resisted my many attempts to bring her outdoors, often being the first to ask, "when are we going home?"

I noticed a shift in Felix as well, although differently. While he didn't balk at our outdoor excursions, when I asked him about his relationship with *Land* at the age of sixteen, he answered, "Uh, well, I guess I feel weird just being outside with nothing to do, like there has to be a purpose to going out. I have to be *doing* something. When I was younger, I would just play outside or sit in a tree, I don't really do that anymore. It feels weird. I guess I don't have time. Nature isn't easy to get to . . . you know."

At first, I dismissed their subtle shift away from nature, but as the fissure grew, I began to worry. Soon, I found myself wallowing in self-blame wondering how I had failed them, figuring I must have done something wrong. Whether you have a teenager now or are watching them approach those years, knowing that teens naturally shift away from nature helps you find ways to keep them connected to the outdoors as their interests and priorities change.

THE TEENAGE DIP IN NATURE-CONNECTEDNESS

Teenagers and tweens are generally overlooked when it comes to their relationship with nature. This oversight might stem from an unspoken belief that children age out of nature by twelve, that teens don't have time for nature because of academic and extracurricular pressures, or that teenagers don't seem all that interested in nature. The truth is, teenagers need to be in and with nature as much as children and adults, but something happens during the tween and teenage years that changes the way they relate with the natural world.

In 2022, 1,872 children between seven and eighteen years were surveyed about their connection with nature.[1] Researchers noticed with some surprise that around seven to eight years of age, children start to disconnect from nature, and this disconnection gets worse until thirteen or fourteen years, before leveling off throughout the rest of adolescence. This dip in nature-connectedness earned the name "teenage dip" in an earlier 2019 survey.[2]

The first time I learned about the "teenage dip" a weight lifted from my shoulders. Until then I worried that I had pushed my teens away from their love of nature. Knowing that this disconnection happened to tweens and teens on a broader level shifted my approach. Instead of asking, "Where did I go wrong?" I wondered, "How can I best support my teens?"

During the tween and teen years, there's a lot going on physically, mentally, emotionally, and socially. New identities conflict with old identities. Truths held in childhood are challenged. Social connections change and mature.[3] As tweens and teens navigate through these changes, they move away from nature and closer to their peers. Sean Blenkinsop, professor in the Faculty of Education and codirector of the Imaginative Education Research Group at Simon Fraser University, suggests that a pre-adolescent psychological split happens where "youth realize that a relational way of being with nature is *weird*" in our culture.[4] Suddenly, tweens and teens must choose to belong to nature or belong with their peers—the tribe usually wins.

This tribal orientation makes sense from an evolutionary perspective. Our ancestors depended on each other for survival, and being rejected from the tribe meant not only ostracization but likely death. Teenagers become increasingly aware of being part of *the tribe*, or not. If today's adolescents find spiders "scary" and backcountry adventures "boring," no matter how much nature they were steeped in during childhood, a disconnection from nature will likely occur.[5]

WHY TEENS NEED NATURE FOR HEALTH AND WELL-BEING

Despite their shift away from nature, teens' favorite places are often outside, close to nature, and many report that spending time outside makes them feel happier and healthier. Not only are studies showing that being in nature helps teens thrive, but this nature isn't in far-off places. Urban nature green spaces are shown to reduce stress and anxiety in teens, giving them a place to escape where they feel at peace, accepted, and cared for.[6]

Knowing that time in nature can help reduce mental health issues in teens, a growing health concern among youth, connecting teens to nature is gaining more attention.[7] Even short amounts of time outdoors can have a significant positive impact on teens. An analysis of 29,784 Canadian adolescents found that enjoying time outside for a mere thirty minutes per week decreased negative psychological symptoms in females by 24 percent and that feeling connected to nature helped both males and females experience better mental health.[8] A 2023 systematic review of studies from the last two decades also found that nature-connectedness has a positive effect on the well-being of youth.[9]

Although studies are showing that teens need more time outside, connecting with the natural world, often educators and even us parents try to force this connection in all the wrong ways.

WHY KNOWLEDGE ALONE PUSHES YOUTH AWAY FROM NATURE

"You see this here," the high school teacher pointed to a shrub, its glossy spiny-edged leaves and clusters of bright yellow flowers begging to be appreciated, "this is Oregon grape, and that over there," he waved his arm in the general direction of a tall shrub engulfed in delicate white flowers, scenting the air with a sweet almond-like fragrance, "is a saskatoon bush."

The teenagers looked blankly at the shrubs in front of them.

"This is nature guys, pay attention," the teacher insisted, trying to elicit a flicker of enthusiasm from the group of teens.

I remember doing a similar thing when my kids were younger. As they traipsed through heady ponderosa forests kicking up fine dust with their small feet, pocketing rocks and getting sticky pine resin on their hands, I would stop their explorations to share nature facts.

"Do you know what this is?" I would quiz them, waiting for a reply. When none came forth, I would answer the question, "It's Oregon grape."

"Can we go now, Maman?" they would wiggle and beg.

"Alright, go ahead," I conceded, releasing them back to the forest and wondering why they seemed so uninterested in the knowledge

I wished to impart. I didn't want my kids to know more Pokémon creatures than the floral and fauna that surrounded them, a reality for most children.[10] Years later, however, I discovered why my children, and those teenagers, didn't seem all that interested in Oregon grape plants—learning facts about nature in the absence of connection with the natural world doesn't interest youth, nor does it draw them closer to nature.[11]

This may explain why many environmental education classes and programs struggle to create positive pro-environmental behavioral changes in tweens and teens. Facts and knowledge about nature in the vacuum of indoor classrooms, without consistent opportunities to connect with nature in positive ways, fail to move hearts and elicit action.

If we truly want to reconnect tweens and teens with nature, to have them care for their *home*, it's crucial that we—parents, caregivers, educators—move beyond knowledge and facts toward a more holistic approach, one that leans into nature as teacher and friend.[12] In the words of David Sobel, environmental educator and author, "If we want children [tween and teens] to flourish, to become truly empowered, let us allow them to love the earth before we ask them to save it."[13]

BEYOND FACTS: FOSTERING NATURE CONNECTION IN YOUTH

The fall of 2024, my three eldest children made the switch from being homeschooled to going into a brick-and-mortar school. It was their first foray into a typical Canadian classroom. On their tour through the high school, we walked through brightly lit hallways lined with identical lockers, punctuated by doors that opened to sterile classrooms with rows of desks and chairs.

As the principal highlighted the unique features of the school, I gazed out a small rectangular window over the expanse of the neatly trimmed lawn of the sports field. A line of evergreen trees edged the property. When I asked about the school's outdoor education programs, the principal shook his head in the negative. No program existed. My teens were already pulling away from *Land* and now for more than thirty hours a week, they would be trapped within walls, literally and figuratively. My heart sank with despair as I signed their admissions papers.

When I advocate for a shift away from focusing solely on nature knowledge and facts toward a relational way of being with and in nature, there is often a knee-jerk response from parents and educators. I understand. Learning about nature from textbooks feels safe. Dissecting animals in a school classroom offers control and domination over nature. Categorizing species according to binominal nomenclature provides structure. But if these strategies aren't helping our teens truly *know* and love nature, what's the point?

Anna Botsford Comstock, American writer and the first woman professor at Cornell University, felt similarly. In her 1911 book, *Handbook of Nature-Study for Teachers and Parents*, she wrote, "If nature-study as taught does not make the child love nature and the out-of-doors, then it should cease. Let us not inflict permanent injury on the child by turning him away from nature instead of toward it."[14]

Now, it's clear that new paths are being walked. Forest preschools and kindergartens are multiplying, especially throughout North America, giving young children regular opportunities to connect with nature. Outdoor education, place-based education, nature-based environmental education (NBEE), living environmental education, and sustainability education are becoming more well-known and provide environmental education in a more holistic way, making positive differences in children's lives.[15] However, when it comes to our tweens and teens, very few have access to this type of education in typical school settings. That's why, as parents, as the key to fostering nature connection in our teens, we must support them in reconnecting to nature.

If encountering an angry skunk seems less scary than trying to get your teen outside, then read on. Yes, it can be incredibly challenging getting teens outside when their connection with nature has plummeted, their lives are overscheduled, their eyes are glued to screens, and their tribes do the same, but it's worth the effort for their health and well-being. Getting teens outdoors can also be an amazing opportunity for family reconnection.

Role Modeling Nature Connection

Adolescents are constantly on the lookout for hypocrisy. If we want our teens to reconnect with nature, we as parents must role model the way authentically. We need to nurture our own relationship with nature, making time to explore the pathways and allow our tweens and teens to see how it helps us thrive. Then, we need to do the same thing *with* our teens—explore the natural world together as much as possible and notice how this time together in nature feels.

Share Stories About Being in Nature

Stories are powerful ways to reconnect our teens with nature. I'm not referring to stories in the pages of books, although those are great too, but the stories in our hearts. No matter where or how we were raised, we all have moments of connection with nature that have deeply impacted us. As a teen, I loved listening to the adventures that my Métis father went on in the wilderness of Manitoba when he was my own age. It helped me understand how a connection with nature shaped him, and why it mattered that he passed that connection to me.

Foster a Connection to Place

Teens and tweens are drawn to specific places outdoors, places that offer a sense of familiarity, comfort, or adventure. These are places close to home, often in urban and suburban areas. While it might seem "boring" to visit the same place again and again, studies show that returning to specific places over and over again for a long period of time helps youth develop a deep connection to nature.[16]

Felix, at age sixteen, loved to visit a creek that flowed through a canyon flanked by towering crags and hugged by heady western cedars. In the summer, he would wade through the frigid water's moving boulders, observing how it changed the flow of water. As summer came to an end and the weather began to cool, he would scour the creek edges for fruiting mushrooms.

As a parent, supporting a connection to *Land* starts by asking questions and listening. When I notice an opportunity to spend time outdoors with my teens, I start by asking, "Is there a special place you'd like to explore today?" If no answers are forthcoming, I suggest a few places I know they enjoy visiting. If still they seem uninterested, I tie in a motivator (yes, a bribe—trust me it's worth it). Let's pick up a special treat to enjoy along the way.

Sometimes I get stuck believing that tweens and teens need epic adventures outdoors, like multi-day backcountry hikes, to connect with nature. After all, studies on outdoor adventure camps for teens show that these experiences can help teens improve their sense of self and social skills.[17] However, it's everyday nature moments close to home that help our teenagers reconnect with nature.[18]

NO TEEN OR TWEEN LEFT INSIDE

It can be easy to look at the "teenage dip" in nature connection and assume teens don't want nature or need nature, but that's not true. When given the opportunity to spend time outside, most teens feel better afterward. While our youth might not take the initiative to get outdoors on their own, nature helps them in many ways so it's up to us parents to make sure that *no teen or tween is left inside.*

Part Four

AUTUMN

CHAPTER 15

Honoring Autumnal Days

THE OKANAGAN SUMMER recoiled like the exhale of an exhausted yawn, leaving nature heavy with harvest and a bit worn out, ready to give birth to a new season. While no grand adventures had taken place over the summer months, there had been many moments in nature, close to home, and these filled my heart. Like pebbles, their weight felt imperceptible at first but soon my pockets overflowed. Fortified by streams of sunshine and water, my feet stood firmly grounded to *Land*, ready to move with her into the kaleidoscope of change that would soon stretch throughout the landscape of life.

My children noticed the changes that came with the shortening days and slanting sunlight, pointing them out with unrepressed excitement—leaves singed with colors, forlorn geese in flight, and ripe pumpkins in farmers' fields. Sweaters were pulled from the depths of drawers and mismatched socks appeared like fruiting mushrooms everywhere. I gathered them by the bushelful.

Autumn is a time of gathering and preparation for the winter ahead. For our ancestors it was a time when plants and animals were harvested and preserved, and feasts of thanksgiving were celebrated.

WHEN DOES AUTUMN BEGIN?

Autumn officially begins on the *autumnal equinox*, also called the fall equinox, which marks a specific moment when the sun crosses over the Earth's celestial equator. In the Northern Hemisphere, the autumnal equinox happens on September 22 or 23 when the sun moves from north to south over the equatorial line. In the Southern Hemisphere, the autumnal equinox happens on March 20 or 21 when the sun moves from south to north over the equatorial line. On this first day of autumn, the amount of daylight and darkness are *almost* equal, and from this day onward light will slowly fade away.

Nature slows and silences in autumn. At the beginning of autumn, leafy trees parade their showy foliage in a wave from north to south, a cheery farewell to migrating birds and butterflies. As darkness squeezes away daylight, crisp mornings and cool rains beckon mushrooms from the soil and push animals to cache and gorge on food. By late fall, gusts of icy winds streak snowflakes through skeletal trees and ever darkening skies—lulling *Land* to sleep.

AUTUMN CELEBRATIONS AND TRADITIONS FOR FAMILIES

Across continents, cultures, and ages, humans have embraced autumn as a time for harvesting and gathering, celebrating the bounty of the season with harvest festivals. Like other seasonal celebrations, the golden threads of ancient harvest festivals are interwoven into religious as well as modern-day celebrations. Thanksgiving, for instance, a national celebration in North America, was inspired by ancient harvest festivals from Europe. Sukkot, a Jewish holiday, celebrates the fall harvest and is known as "the season of joy."

Once again, I encourage you to root autumnal rituals and traditions to *your* family values, cultural heritage, and *Land* you live on. If you're unsure how to go about celebrating autumn, here are a few prompts:

- What autumnal celebrations and traditions were part of my childhood? Do I want to pass down these traditions to my child?
- What is my cultural background and religious beliefs? Are there specific autumn traditions associated with my culture that I would like to adopt?
- How has autumn been celebrated by the Indigenous peoples living on the *Land* I call home? Are there opportunities to learn about or take part in these celebrations?
- How does the *Land* I call home respond to autumnal changes? What kind of plants are being harvested? What are the animals doing? How can I take part in these autumn changes?

In our home we root ourselves to the unfolding season of autumn through several celebrations.

Autumn Equinox (September 22 or 23)

We celebrate the autumn equinox, the first day of fall, by wandering outside as a family. Because the equinox coincides with children settling into a new school year in the Northern Hemisphere, a simple celebration to acknowledge the season's turning works well for our family. Other families celebrate with a special supper, hauling fall-themed books from the library, or enjoying a warm fall-themed drink together.

Michaelmas (September 29)

Celebrated in Western Europe since the fifth century, Michaelmas marks the end of the harvest and start of autumn, honoring the struggle between darkness and light under Archangel Michael's watch.[1] Traditional customs include eating roasted goose, harvesting blackberries, picking wild carrots, and "borrowing" the neighbor's horse for the night. Our family's twist on this seasonal celebration involves roasting locally raised chicken and root vegetables, enjoying a berry pie for dessert, and leaving the neighbors' mode of transportation, horse or otherwise, untouched.

Halloween (October 31)

Modern-day Halloween traces its roots to the ancient Celtic festival of Samhain, which marked the end of summer and beginning of winter, as well as Hallowtide, observances of All Hallows' Eve, All Saints' Day, and All Souls' Day. Though today's candy collecting feels far removed, the heart of these celebrations—walking bravely through darkness and acknowledging that death is part of life—continues to burn bright.

Samhain (October 31–November 1)

One of the four ancient Gaelic fire festivals, Samhain marks the end of summer and the beginning of winter. Traditionally, it was a time for lighting communal bonfires, leaving offerings for the spirits, and honoring ancestors. Many families today mark Samhain with a small fire, seasonal foods, and a moment of quiet to remember loved ones who have passed.

Martinmas (November 11)

Martinmas, a medieval harvest festival, celebrates autumn harvests and the coming winter while honoring Martin of Tours, a fourth-century Roman soldier who chose kindness and love over the fame and glory of war.

It also coincides with Veterans Day (Remembrance Day or Armistice Day), connecting themes of light in dark times and honoring those who serve. To celebrate, we make lanterns from recycled glass jars. As dusk settles, we take our lanterns outside and let them shine into the encroaching darkness while singing a Martinmas lantern song.

Thanksgiving (October or November, varies depending on country)

Modern Thanksgiving, with its cornucopia of plenty and gathering of loved ones, echoes harvest celebrations over the ages. While stories of the "first" Thanksgiving in North America exist, Indigenous people have given thanks for harvests time immemorial.

Celebrating Thanksgiving is a cherished tradition in our home, much loved by my children. From harvesting vegetables from our garden or sourcing locally grown food for our feast to preparing food together, we do all these things while giving thanks for the bounty we've received.

GOING ON AN AUTUMN NATURE GRATITUDE WALK

Gratitude, noticing and appreciating life and what surrounds us, changes the way we think and feel, improving our well-being. Like a stone thrown into water, when we experience and express gratitude as parents it ripples outward to our children, our community, and *Land*, binding us closer together. Even if the steps are slow and small, walking under the autumn sky hand in hand in gratitude gives our children hope and strength for their future.

Go for a walk around your neighborhood, in a nearby park, or local trail. Find a sit spot under a tree or walk slowly along a trail or in a park and notice the nature surrounding you.

- Give thanks out loud for nature that you see, smell, feel, hear, and taste—big and small things. (e.g. Thank you, sun, for your light and warmth. Thank you, water, for giving life. Thank you, honeybee, for fruit and honey.)
- Give thanks for your relationships with other people and the natural world. (e.g. Thank you for [my child], for her kindness and curiosity. Thank you for busy squirrel preparing for winter.)

- Give thanks for physical things in your life. (e.g. Thank you for my coat that keeps me warm on this cold autumn day.)
- Give thanks for recent experiences. (e.g. Thank you for this time together outside.)

You can continue to cultivate gratitude throughout autumn by reading books about gratitude, starting an autumn family gratitude journal, or expressing thanks when you notice the many signs of autumn.

Signs of Autumn in Nature

- Days getting shorter and shorter
- Leaves of deciduous trees turning yellow, orange, red, and purple
- Birds migrating south to warmer climates
- Squirrels caching nuts and conifer cones
- Bears gorging on berries, nuts, and acorns in preparation for winter hibernation
- Deer, moose, and elk mating
- Bats flying south or finding homes for hibernation
- Beavers cutting down and storing trees and branches near their dams for winter food
- Turtles, frogs, snakes, and salamanders finding snug spots for hibernation
- Monarch butterflies migrating south
- Woolly bear caterpillars searching for winter homes
- Plants releasing seeds into nature for propagation
- Mushrooms fruiting on forest floors, lawns, and trees
- Apples and pumpkins ripe for harvesting

SETTING UP AN AUTUMN NATURE TABLE

Our autumn nature table often overflows with an abundance of pumpkins, leaves, seeds, and nuts that make their way into every nook and cranny of our home in little hands. Below I've listed ideas to fill your own autumn nature table:

- **Pumpkins and squashes:** Squashes and pumpkins were cultivated by the Indigenous peoples in the Americas and come in a delightful array of sizes, colors, and textures.[2] Look for unique squashes at your local farmers' markets.
- **Deciduous leaves:** To extend the life and color of fallen leaves, press them between the pages of a book or dip them in melted beeswax.
- **Nuts, seeds, and pine cones:** Look for walnuts, chestnuts (conkers), and acorns beneath trees, white fluffy milkweed pod, or delicate lunaria (honesty, money plant) along roadways or grass or poppy seed heads in fields.
- **Ornamental corn:** Scour your local farmers' market or grocery store for jeweled ornamental corn. When stored in a cool, dry place these can last for many years.
- **Lanterns and candles:** Homemade lanterns using recycled glass jars with electric tea lights or natural wax candles to light up the darkness of the shortening days.
- **Mushrooms:** Dried mushrooms, mushroom spore prints, wooden mushrooms, felt mushrooms, or a mushroom grow kit—perfect for the budding mycologist!
- **Sprigs of herbs:** A bundle of thyme, rosemary, or lavender or small potted plant for smelling.

- **Variety of apples:** A basket of apples for snacking on.
- **Bouquet of fall flowers:** Gather sunflowers, purple asters, black-eyed Susans, rudbeckia, goldenrod, or any other flowers growing in your yard, nearby nature (if picking is permitted), or your local farmers' market.
- **Autumn-themed books:** A few beautifully illustrated picture books invite children to fall into the magic of autumn.
- **Play silks:** Autumn-colored play silks or fabrics.

RECYCLED GLASS JAR AUTUMN LANTERNS

Every autumn my children and I create homemade lanterns from recycled glass jars. From little to big hands, this project delights all ages and requires only a few materials, many of which can be rescued from recycling bins or gathered from nature.

MATERIALS:

- Recycled glass jar (jam jar, pickle jar, mason jar, all sizes work)
- Tissue paper or kite paper or dried flowers and leaves*
- Decoupage medium (i.e. Mod Podge)
- Scissors
- Paintbrush
- Tea light candle (electric or wax)

* **Paper note:** Kite paper, colored wax paper, is much stronger than tissue paper and easier to use. Dried flowers and leaves can be made using a flower press or purchased from local sellers.

INSTRUCTIONS:

1. **Set up your workspace:** Start by gathering your materials and covering a surface with recycled paper to catch glue drips.

2. **Using kite or tissue paper:** To create a lovely stained glass lantern effect. Cut pieces of tissue paper or kite paper into squares, strips, or shapes like trees, leaves, mushrooms. Paint decoupage medium onto the glass jar, stick the paper to the jar, and cover the paper with more medium to secure it to the glass.

   ***Using dried flowers and leaves:** To create a botanical lantern, paint decoupage medium on a glass jar and place dried flowers and leaves onto the jar. Paint decoupage medium over the dried flowers and leaves to secure them to the glass.

3. **Let the jar dry:** Set the glass jar aside until it has dried completely.

4. **Illuminate your jar:** Place an electric or wax candle in the jar and enjoy the lovely glow.

BODACIOUS BEET AND CABBAGE HARVEST SOUP

This hearty bowl of fall comfort is packed with freshly harvested root vegetables. It's wonderfully forgiving, no need to fuss over exact measurements, so use what you have on hand. It also dehydrates and rehydrates beautifully for backcountry trips. Quick note: If using Italian sausage, remember some spicy varieties pack a serious punch.

Prep Time: 30 mins

Cook Time: stovetop—45 mins,

slow cooker—2 to 3 hours on high, 4 to 6 hours on low

Servings: 10–12

INGREDIENTS:

- 1 lb (500 g) Italian sausage casing removed* (mild, spicy, or a mix)
- 1 large onion, chopped
- 2–3 garlic cloves, minced
- 1–2 Tbsp olive oil

- 2–3 large carrots, grated
- 2–3 medium potatoes, peeled and cubed
- 2 large beets, peeled and grated
- ¼–½ head of cabbage, thinly sliced
- 2–4 cups stewed tomatoes
- 5 cups chicken stock
- 5 cups beef stock
- 2 Tbsp tomato paste
- salt and freshly ground pepper, to taste
- sour cream, to serve
- fresh marjoram, dill, or oregano, to serve

*__Heat note:__ Spicy Italian sausage varies a lot. For kid-friendly, use mild or go fifty-fifty.

INSTRUCTIONS:

1. **Brown the sausage and onions:** Preheat a frying pan to medium-high, add the sausage and chopped onion. Break the sausage up into smaller pieces and fry until the meat and onions are nicely golden brown.

2. **Add garlic:** Add the garlic and fry until fragrant, about 30–60 seconds.

3. **Deglaze the pan:** Scrape the sausage, onions, and garlic into the slow cooker or into a soup pot. Add two cups of stock (either one) and deglaze the frying pan. Be sure to scrape up all those yummy bottom bits. Add this stock into the slow cooker or pot.

4. **Cook the vegetables:** Add a splash of olive oil to the frying pan and cook the carrots, cabbage, and beets until slightly tender. Work in batches if needed.

5. **Deglaze the pan again:** Scape the vegetables into the slow cooker or soup pot and add two more cups of stock to deglaze the frying pan. Add this stock into the slow cooker too.

6. **Combine the remaining ingredients:** Add the cubed potatoes, stewed tomatoes, tomato paste, and salt and pepper to the slow cooker or soup pot and extra water or stock until you like the consistency of the soup. Season with salt and pepper.

7. **Cook until tender:** Cook in the slow cooker on high heat for 2 to 3 hours or low heat for 4 to 6 hours or simmer on the stovetop for 45 minutes or until all the vegetables are tender.

8. **Season and serve:** When the soup has cooked long enough, taste and adjust the seasoning. Enjoy with sour cream and fresh marjoram or oregano.

CHAPTER 16

Back to School, Back to Nature

"ARE YOU EXCITED to start grade nine?" I asked fourteen-year-old Claire.

"Yes!" she said with honest enthusiasm.

My lips pressed into a tight sad smile and I blinked back tears.

It might seem strange for a teenager to be excited about the start of school, and a mother to mourn sending her teenager back to school, so let me explain.

My three older children were homeschooled from kindergarten until the fall they entered grades seven, nine, and eleven. That fall would mark the first time all three would go into a brick-and-mortar school, a monumental change for our family.

I started homeschooling Felix in kindergarten, wanting to give my curious son the opportunity to learn in ways that best suited him and to have time for plenty of outdoor play. Like most parents new to homeschooling, I felt nervous about being responsible for his education and promised myself that I would take this journey one year at a time.

Eleven years of homeschooling flowed through the river of our family life, at times peaceful, sometimes turbulent, never regretted. As my children grew older, however, academic pressure mounted, and friends seemed fewer, most having made the switch to public school. Eventually, online courses dominated their days, chaining them to screens, lonely prisons of learning, while picturesque images of them frolicking through forests faded into the background.

"What's the point in being homeschooled if all I do is sit in front of a computer all day?" Felix asked one afternoon. "I might as well go to school."

Any suggestion I had added hurdles to his hopes of getting into post-secondary education. I capitulated. My three older children went to a brick-and-mortar school for the first time.

Dropping them off for their first day of school felt surreal. Yes, I worried about how they would fit in socially and academically, but I worried most about their connection with nature. It was a well-founded worry.

SCHOOL: A MAJOR BARRIER TO CHILDREN'S OUTDOOR TIME

Even though time outdoors positively impacts children's academic performance, well-being, and social development, access to the outdoors during school hours has been under threat for some time.[1] Since the early 2000s, schools across North America have reduced the length of recess time from 60 minutes to an average of just 25 minutes per day with many states and provinces having no recess policies or mandates.[2]

Not all schools around the world have followed this trend. Finland takes a different approach, offering two to four recess periods of 10–15 minutes after each 45–90-minute lesson along with one longer recess period of 30 minutes for school lunch and other activities.[3] In China, elementary children have a 10-minute recess time for every 40 minutes of learning, a 30–60-minute lunch break, and a 30-minute "nap" or break right after lunch. In a sample of Shanghai schools, about 40 percent of the school day was spent in free and structured recess for elementary-aged children, and 30 percent for high school students.[4]

In North America, recess is shrinking in the face of growing academic pressure on children. Teachers must meet curriculum mandates to prepare our children for standardized testing. Tight schedules and lack of time mean that even the transition from indoors to outdoors can be seen as a time waster.[5] Added barriers like a lack of knowledge and confidence in outdoor education, limited access to safe outdoor spaces, few resources for outdoor engagement, and students that don't have appropriate outdoor clothing for the weather make it even less likely that teachers will bring their students outside during the day.[6]

While it's easy to point a finger at governments, policymakers, and teachers, three fingers point back at us parents. As parents we want what's best for our children, and many of us have come to believe that more academics will set our children up for a successful life. Ironically, by taking away time outside, and supporting schools to do the same, we stifle our children's ability to succeed academically.[7]

As I watched my teens and tween walking in the cold gaping mouth of the school doors for the first time, I felt like David in the face of Goliath's fortress. *What can I, one parent, do in the face of such an establishment?* The answer: Fill my children's pockets with stones.

HOW MUCH TIME OUTSIDE DO KIDS NEED? NUMBERS THAT HAUNT US

As a child, the moment I got home from school, I threw my school bag through the front door and went right back outside to play with the neighborhood kids. Without doubt, the best part of the day was the hours between school and supper when I ran amuck outdoors.

These days it's said that North American children spend a mere 4 to 7 minutes outside each day. This statistic is repeated on websites, in books, and on social media, but is it true? These numbers come from studies by the University of Michigan's Institute for Social Research, which looked at surveys of how children used their time in 1981, 1997, and 2003.[8] The researchers noticed that participation in "outdoor activities" declined significantly over time, a 37 percent decline for children between ages 6 and 12 from 1997 to 2003.[9] However, these surveys had categories like "outdoor activities" separate from "playing" and "school," but all of these categories can include outside time so the "4 to 7 minutes outside a day" claim has some problems.

Wanting to get a better idea of how much time American kids play outside, the USDA Forest Service conducted a National Kids Survey from 2007 to 2009. They found that during this period American children spent on average at least 120 minutes outdoors daily and more time outside on weekends.[10] A 2021 U.S. national survey found that 40 percent of children ages 3 to 5 spend 60 minutes or less outside on weekdays.[11] So, it seems that many children are getting outside more than 4 to 7 minutes each day, but how much time *should* our children be spending outside?

Ginny Yurich, American educator, mother of five, and founder of 1000 Hours Outside, recommends aiming for 1,000 hours outside in a year—an average of 2.7 hours a day—although she admits that in practice even her own family doesn't achieve this daily average.[12] Angela Hanscom, a pediatric occupational therapist and founder of TimberNook, recommends that children should get at least 3 hours of free play outside every day in her book *Balanced and Barefoot: How Unrestricted Outdoor Play Makes for Strong, Confident, and Capable Children*.[13] Long before them, British educator Charlotte Mason urged families to go outside "not two, but four, five, or six hours [. . .] on every tolerably fine day."[14]

It's tempting to get caught up in numbers. Children *need* time outdoors—no argument there. But connecting with nature isn't just about numbers or tallying minutes, it's about meaningful moments.

MOMENTS NOT MINUTES

At the start of 2022, I committed to taking part in the 1000 Hours Outside challenge. It was a desperate attempt to reconnect with nature. My printer spat out four zentangle trackers, three for my older children and one for myself. I taped them to the kitchen cupboards in plain sight, reminding us to spend two to three hours outside each day. For the first few days my children and I were enthusiastic. One month later I quietly recycled our trackers; no one noticed them gone. I believed *time* in nature would help me escape the dark clouds gathering round, but it wasn't merely minutes that my children and I needed most. We needed moments of reconnection with nature.

Despite what some say, and the recommendations we hear, there isn't a universal, agreed-upon amount of time that every child should spend outside to flourish. A 2024 meta-analysis found that *more* time outside reduces the risk of nearsightedness in children.[15] Another found that physical activity and cardiorespiratory fitness improved with *more* time outside.[16] And still another shows that *more* time in nature reduces stress and improves attention span.[17] The consensus: Children need time outside, the *more* the better, but none of those studies defined *more*.

As a parent, not knowing the specific number of minutes and hours children need to be outside can be frustrating. In a culture obsessed with efficiency and productivity, we want to know exactly how long things will take. How long should my daughter brush her teeth? Two minutes.[18] How long should my son wash his hands? At least twenty seconds.[19] How many minutes of "Vitamin Nature" should I prescribe my child? Maybe we're asking the wrong question.

When I asked Ryan Lumber about how we as parents can foster a connection with nature for our families, his answer had little to do with minutes and everything to do with *moments*.

> I think sometimes people overestimate how much time they need to spend outdoors. Of course, spending a whole day in nature is wonderful, but it's really about small, everyday moments. We've found that everyday encounters—just moments, not necessarily minutes—can be profoundly important. You can do this wherever you are. It doesn't have to be in a pristine, postcard-perfect environment. One of my favorite experiences with nature happened at a

busy tram stop in the city center. I was the only one who noticed a peregrine falcon swooping down to grab a pigeon in midflight. Even a glimpse of urban nature can be powerful. Wherever you are, tiny moments can inspire you to connect.

As a mom of five, I have an incredibly busy life. Although I love nature and aim to spend as much time outside as possible with my children, I often feel like it's never enough. However, when I started to shift my thinking away from getting the correct dose of "Vitamin N" to embracing nature moments to deepen my connection with the natural world, my anxieties began to fade away. Lumber advised:

> Start small and incorporate these "nature moments" into your everyday life. . . . Pause to notice what's around you: birds, trees, even from a window. Observe and stay curious. Then you might find yourself wanting to explore more, touch or smell something new, and build an emotional attachment. This everyday noticing will build confidence. Eventually, you might want to learn more, discover more, or do more. It can become self-sustaining.
>
> We all lead busy lives—there are always chores or responsibilities—but it doesn't take much time. Just two or five minutes a day, to begin with, can have remarkable benefits. Regular, consistent contact with nature matters. Even small but repeated experiences add up significantly.

Instead of asking how much time—the quantity—let's focus instead on the quality of the moments and remember that these meaningful experiences can happen in urban and suburban settings. After all, studies show that a connection with nature isn't fostered through mere minutes outside, knowledge of nature, or even by chasing waterfalls but through simple nature activities and moments, something every parent can help foster, even when it's time to go back to school.[20]

REWILD HEARTS AND HOMES THROUGH SIMPLE NATURE MOMENTS

With children being in school, time is limited, but we can still reorient our children and ourselves "back-to-nature." How is that possible? Think about nature connection as a relationship. Fostering a deep and healthy relationship with a person takes regular effort (time) but the way we spend that time (quality) is even more important. Nature connection isn't a race or competition to see how many minutes we can clock outside, instead it is about making a habit of embracing simple nature moments and noticing how that makes us feel. I want to share a few strategies for doing that with your school-aged child.

NOTICE THREE GOOD THINGS IN NATURE (TGTIN)

We often live in "auto" mode. Our brains' well-trodden pathways act as blinders keeping us on the track ahead. This is especially true for us parents. These pathways help us move through the day more easily, but sometimes they can blind us to the good things that surround us. This is particularly true for the outside world. However, there is a simple activity that can help us and our children build a deeper connection to nature and one another: *notice nature*.

Noticing Three Good Things in Nature (TGTiN) has been the subject of several research studies spearheaded by the University of Derby's Human Factors and Nature Connectedness Professor Miles Richardson. In 2017, 92 students from the University of Derby, England, were recruited to see if noticing nearby nature increases connection with nature. The results showed that simply noticing and writing down three good things in nature each day improves nature connection along with psychological health.[21] Another study of TGTiN found that individuals experiencing depression or anxiety had an improvement in their mood after going for a thirty-minute walk in nature and noticing three good things in nature for five consecutive days.[22]

Noticing nature is a very simple activity that can be done anywhere, and yet it's very effective at fostering nature connection. Most children are more than happy discovering three good things in nature walking to or from school, on a walk around your neighborhood, during commutes, or in between activities. Start this simple activity by saying: "Three good things I'm noticing in nature are . . . [*name three good things*]."

A variation on this activity is the Noticing Nature Intervention (NNI) developed by Holli-Anne Passmore, associate professor and department chair of Psychology at Concordia University of Edmonton (CUE) in Alberta, Canada, and Mark Holder, associate professor at the University of British Columbia. For this activity, notice everyday nature as you go about your day with your family and share with one another how nature moments make you feel. These micro-moment connections to nature can help you and your child feel happier even as the weather begins to cool.[23]

WATCH, WAIT, WONDER, AND WANDER IN NATURE

Watch, Wait, and Wonder is a psychotherapy intervention developed by Nancy Cohen, Mirek Lojkasek, and Elisabeth Muir that helps parents and young children strengthen their attachments with one another.[24]

A typical session invites parents to give their child the freedom to explore while watching, waiting, and wondering. The only rule is the parent cannot initiate or take over any of their child's activities, but the parent is encouraged to respond to their child's interaction. Research on the Watch, Wait, and Wonder intervention shows that this approach helps young children develop secure attachments with parents and improves their cognitive development while also helping to reduce depression and increase satisfaction in parents.[25]

What I love about this activity is how simple, yet effective it is. By being fully present, observing our children carefully, we are truly witnessing them. Adding *Wander* to this list, and taking this approach outdoors, loops in nature, allowing deepening attachments to flow between parent, child, and nature. Watch, Wait, Wonder, and Wander can take place in yards, parks, schoolyards, and park trails. As a parent, it means taking a step back and giving your child space to wonder and wander, while being fully present and supportive of that process.

MAKING TIME IN NATURE: PEBBLE PRACTICES

For many parents, getting outside with our children is one of the biggest challenges we face. Not only are we starved for time, but there are endless distractions keeping us indoors. On top of these challenges, the human brain prefers the path of least resistance.[26] For example, in Canada, one poll showed that even though 87 percent of Canadians agreed that they are happier when they spend time in nature, 74 percent of Canadians found it is *easier* to stay indoors than go outside.[27] I know this feeling all too well—getting my five kids outside should be an Olympic sport!

How, exactly, do we motivate ourselves to get out that front door? It's a question that comes up frequently in online parenting forums and social media platforms. Here's my answer: Make time through small but manageable shifts in habits and routines—I like to call these pebble practices. When it comes to changing behavior, small steps stick.[28]

The idea of tiny habits was popularized by BJ Fogg, a professor of research in behavior science at Stanford University. In his book *Tiny Habits: The Small Changes That Change Everything*, he shares that we need to do three things when making new habits: (1) stop judging yourself, (2) break a big goal into tiny behaviors, and (3) embrace mistakes as part of the journey. Here's how we can apply this strategy to getting outside:

1. **Stop judging yourself:**
   - Throw away the idea of the "outdoorsy parent"—nature is for every parent and child no matter where you live (city, suburban neighborhood, or rural town).

- Let go of the belief that nature time must be an epic adventure far from home. Nature moments are best close to home.
- Stop tracking minutes and hours outside—a moment connected with nature is worth celebrating.
- Don't blame yourself if you or your child doesn't seem excited to go outside—practice self-compassion.

2. Break a big goal into tiny behaviors:

Start small:

- Turn off screens for a bit and look out windows instead (a great one for kids in cars).
- Open your front door and sit on the threshold for a few minutes with your child.
- Live in an apartment? Spend a few minutes on the balcony or the stoop with your children noticing the view and breeze.
- Not ready to go outside? Spend time gathering and organizing outdoor clothing.
- Do a dry run: Practice getting your child dressed for going outside—honestly sometimes this is the biggest hurdle in getting outside.

Incorporate nature moments in your daily routine:

- Collect nature bits for your nature table while walking to the mailbox.
- Sit or meander around your yard for a few minutes after school.
- Read a book to your children on the front steps.
- Take morning snack time outside.
- Eat one meal outside a week.

3. **Embrace mistakes as part of the journey:**
    - If you don't go outside for a day or longer, don't be discouraged. It happens to everyone. Reflect on what's keeping you inside and adjust your strategy or expectations if needed.
    - If something challenging happens while outdoors with your child, see if you can preempt the problem by being better prepared next time—always bring lots of snacks, water, and a change of clothing.

CHAPTER 17

Birding Brings Happiness to Families

I HAD DRIVEN past the pullout countless times, an innocuous strip of gravel that veered off the narrow highway skirting around the blue-gray waters of Vaseux Lake.

"Is this the place?" said Felix, craning his neck to get a better view of the road ahead.

I spotted a lone car tucked into the trees.

"I think this is it," I said cautiously, pushing away images fueled by a recent glut of murder mystery novels.

My three children, then eight, six, and four, tumbled out of the car and together we walked down a short trail encroached upon by red osier dogwood shrubs and filled with the steady chirp of birds whose names I did not know. The trail opened into a small clearing that housed an ancient trailer and a tiny white building on wheels, its door slightly ajar.

"Hello?" I called out, making our presence known.

The door creaked open. Stooped behind the low wooden desk, a wizened man mumbled to himself. His balding head wreathed in wiry ivory hair barely contained by wearable binoculars, gray and dirty with longtime use. He studied his liver-spotted hands, encircled by dirty torn up cuffs, caressing . . .

"Come in," a young man's voice spoke from beside me.

I jumped. I hadn't noticed him until now. He greeted me with a wide smile, his dark eyes crinkling behind his black rimmed glasses.

"Once this bird is tagged and logged, I'll go and check the nets again. Would you like to join me?"

"Look Maman, a bird," Claire said. She pulled me closer to the old man, unfazed by his rough appearance.

A small bird with vivid yellow feathers, a yellow warbler, yielded to the gentle weather-worn hands. He extended one wing, measured it, and wrote numbers on a piece of paper. My three children huddled around the desk, watching as he fitted a tiny metal band onto the bird's leg before setting it free through a chute.

"Can I put the next bird in the chute?" asked Felix.

"First let's see if there are birds to band," said the young man. "Let's go and check the nets."

We followed the bird bander along a narrow mucky trail that was overgrown with wild roses and grass. He pointed to the mist nets that were placed between trees, almost invisible to our eyes.

"Does it hurt the birds?" Claire asked.

"No," said the researcher, "the nets don't hurt the birds. We check on them regularly to make sure birds don't get stuck long and we take the nets down when we aren't here."

We rounded a bend in the trail and ahead of us a small brown bird was tangled upside down in a net. My children pointed excitedly at the bird.

"It's a wren," said the bird bander. He untangled the bird, plopped it into a cloth bag, and looped the bag around his neck for safekeeping. We continued onward.

"What do we have here?" he said with a tone of excitement. "It's a Virginia rail. We don't see many of these. It's our lucky day!"

With two birds safely bagged we returned to the banding station where the old man waited for us. He now wore a blue baseball hat with the words "Force of Nature" emblazoned over the front of it in capital white letters. I didn't doubt that he was exactly that.

"Only two birds, but we caught a Virginia rail!" said the young man as we approached. The old man nodded with approval.

This time my children watched the process from beginning to end—measuring, note-taking, and banding.

"Who wants to release the birds?" the old bird bander asked.

"Me!" Felix and Claire replied in unison. Theo anxiously shook his head no.

The two birds were brought outside and placed into their small hands. Wide smiles pinched their cheeks and glittered their eyes. Felix released the wren and Claire the Virginia rail. My heart soared with the birds into the sky.

My children and I visited the bird banding station at least once or twice a year for several years. Despite it being some time since our last visit, my children hold dear our time spent at the bird banding site on Vaseux Lake, in the South Okanagan of British Columbia. The experience opened their eyes to the world of birds, inviting them to know and love our feathered friends in a way that I will forever be grateful for.

TINY FEATHERS, BIG CONNECTION: THE SCIENCE AND JOY OF BIRD-WATCHING

"Maman! Look, the Stellar's jay is at the bird feeder again," Claire pointed out.

Together we crept through the kitchen to peek out the back window overlooking the bird feeder. There the Stellar's jay scattered seeds all around. It's black mohawk bobbing up and down, picking out the coveted sunflower seeds.

Although most birds had migrated south for the winter, the Stellar's jay, a resident bird, would be staying and had staked his claim to our bird feeder. He gorged on the steady supply of seeds, shooing away smaller birds with his iridescent blue wing feathers.

"He's kind of sassy," Claire said, laughing. "I like watching him."

Birds are marvelous creatures. For starters, they fly, an ability that humans have been fascinated by for ages, and they also come in a wide variety of colors and sizes, each with their own unique behaviors. It's estimated that there's a whopping 10,000 to 18,000 species of birds worldwide depending on how bird species are being counted.[1]

It's no surprise that birding, observing birds in their natural habitat, has been gaining in popularity in many parts of the world. Originally seen as a city gentleman's hobby, today birders are much more diverse and widespread and include children and families.[2] In a 2022 survey done by the U.S. Fish and Wildlife Service, about 96 million Americans ages sixteen and older observed birds around their home and on trips—37 percent of the American population (sixteen and up)! Of those 96 million, 95 percent were backyard birders, which means they enjoyed watching birds from the comfort of their homes.[3]

What makes birds particularly special is that they exist everywhere. From pole to equator, ocean or desert, and everywhere in between, birds make the Earth their homes. In fact, birds are one of the most common types of wildlife in urban areas, making them perfect for urban families to appreciate and connect with.

Other than being relatively easy to spot, watching birds has some unique benefits for children and parents. Recent studies are showing that bird-watching reduces stress and anxiety, increases joy, and improves nature connection even when done close to home and for short periods of time.[4] This is especially true when watching birds is done simply for the "joy of it" instead of counting birds or naming species.

BIRDING MADE EASY FOR BUSY FAMILIES

The fact that birds are everywhere means that no matter where we are, at home, in the car, or wandering outside, there are birds to spot. The most important piece of equipment for noticing birds isn't binoculars, identification books, or apps, although those can be helpful, it's you and your child—your eyes and ears. Once we know birds surround us, it becomes impossible not to spot them.

Setting Up a Bird Feeder

Hands down, my children's favorite way to get to know birds has been setting up a bird feeder near our home. Typically, a bird feeder should be less than three feet (1 meter) from a window to prevent high-speed collisions and five feet (1.5 meters) from the ground to prevent other critters from helping themselves to seeds or birds.[5] Better yet, if you have a domestic cat, keep it indoors or build a "catio," an enclosed outdoor cat patio.

While birders recommend hanging multiple bird feeders with different feeds to attract the greatest variety of birds, one feeder with a birdseed blend seems most manageable for my family. It doesn't take much effort to keep a bird feeder running, but it is important to keep seeds topped up, clean dropped seeds on a regular basis, and clean out the bird feeder twice a year, spring and fall, to prevent the spread of diseases. Overall, setting up a bird feeder is a low effort, high reward activity that brings a deeper connection to the avian world.

On-the-Go Birding Moments

Even with busy schedules, birding can also happen on the go. Noticing birds from vehicles during commutes to and from school can be a fun game—even a handy distraction. My kids have become notorious for shouting out the names of birds as we drive around town, and regularly spot magpies, ravens, crows, and quails, along with bald eagles, red-tailed hawks, great blue herons, and red-winged blackbirds.

Noticing birds can also happen while walking around the city, while visiting parks, or while strolling on nature trails. If you want to bring your child on a specific birding walk, know that there's no need for fancy equipment, just head to a spot birds like to congregate and look around. Ponds, streams, fields, and forests are great locations for bird-watching, and so are city parks. If you want to learn more about the birds you see, get a birding book about local species from your library or download a bird identification app. What's most important, however, is to focus on the joy of seeing birds together.

FEATHER COLLECTING: A CONVERSATION WORTH HAVING

In 1916, Canada and the United States entered into an international agreement to protect migratory birds.[6] At that time, hunting and fashion were decimating bird species, pushing certain species into extinction, including the Labrador ducks, great auks, passenger pigeons, Carolina parakeets, and heath hens.[7] Thanks to growing awareness of these losses, acts were signed making it illegal to take migratory birds, their eggs, and their nests without special permission.[8] These became known as the Migratory Birds Convention Act (MBCA) in Canada and the Migratory Bird Treaty Act (MBTA) in the United States.[9]

What most parents might not realize, however, is that these laws prohibit the collection of naturally molted bird feathers found on the ground. According to these universal laws, a child that collects a fallen feather from forest trail would be considered a felon, as made clear by enthusiastic educators, enthusiasts, and influencers on social media platforms.

"Don't let your child touch feathers!" they preach. "It's against the law."

Technically they're correct; however, a young child collecting a molted American robin feather from their front lawn likely won't be fined. The law was written to prevent the exploitation or harm of migratory birds on a bigger scale and these days it isn't feathered fashion that's the biggest problem.

Ultimately, I believe we need to have conversations around providing allowances for children when it comes to collecting molten feathers for personal use when appropriate. Children have a deep desire to handle and collect nature, which in turn develops a greater understanding of and connection to nature. Lecturing a child for picking up a fallen feather carries more harm than good—it creates disconnection instead of connection—a lack of interest and love for birds.

As we navigate our children's desire to collect fallen feathers and laws prohibiting this act, here are a few helpful tips. First, there are bird feathers that are legal to collect. Feathers from invasive birds, domestic birds, and legally hunted birds can be collected. Each country offers different lists on these birds so it is best to check them before heading out. Second, handling feathers is fine too. Go ahead and let your child pick up a fallen feather and look at it closely. Feel free to take some pictures or draw a sketch. Hold it for a little while and then leave it behind. Third, if your child insists on bringing a molted feather home to display on a nature table, I won't be tattling. You can always bring the feather back to where it was found afterward.

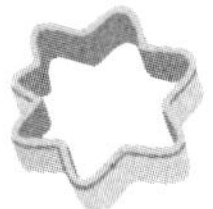

BIRDSEED COOKIE-CUTTER ORNAMENTS

Each autumn, as the days grow colder and food becomes scarce, my kids and I press birdseed into cookie-cutter molds, tie the ornaments with twine, and hang them on a special backyard tree for our feathered friends. These treats not only nourish migrating birds passing through but also sustain the resident birds as they hunker down for the winter.

MATERIALS:

- 3 Tbsp unflavored gelatin (45 mL or 3 pouches)
- ⅓ cup cold water
- ⅓ cup boiling water
- 2 ½ cup birdseed
- ¼ cup raisins or currant (optional)
- ¼ cup walnuts, peanuts, or almonds, chopped (optional)

- 2 Tbsp jam, jelly, or marmalade (optional—grape, berry, apple, cherry, raspberry, red currant, and orange)
- Cookie cutters
- Twine, cotton, or wool string
- Large cookie tray
- Sticks for making holes (2 inches long and as thick as a drinking straw)
- Parchment paper

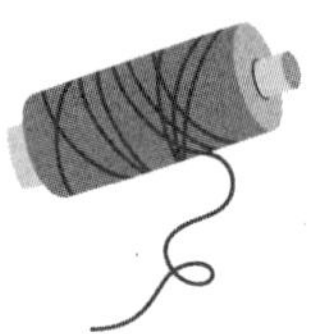

INSTRUCTIONS:

1. **Bloom the gelatin:** Pour ⅓ cup of cold water into a large bowl and sprinkle 3 Tbsps of gelatin over the liquid. Add ⅓ cup of boiling water and stir the mixture constantly until the gelatin has fully dissolved, about 1–2 minutes.
2. **Combine with the birdseed:** Scoop 2 ½ cups of birdseed along with optional add-ins into the gelatin mixture and stir together until all the seeds are well coated. Continue to stir until there is no liquid puddling at the bottom of the bowl. This should only take a few minutes.
3. **Fill the cookie cutters:** Prepare the cookie cutters by placing them on a large cookie sheet lined with parchment paper. Once the mixture is ready, firmly pack the cookie cutters with the birdseed mixture.
4. **Creating a hanging hole:** Make a hole in the ornament using a stick (about the size of a drinking straw) about ½ inch down from the edge of the ornament.
5. **Dry the ornaments:** Leave the ornaments in a warm, dry area for 48 hours, flipping them or propping them on their sides so that the bottom can dry as well. To speed up drying, place the ornaments in a food dehydrator machine on low.
6. **Remove from cookie cutters:** Once the ornaments feel dry, carefully press them out of the cookie cutters and remove the sticks.
7. **Hang and observe:** Pass a string through the hole of the ornaments and hang on a tree outside. Watch our feather friends enjoy their treat.

CHAPTER 18

Preserving the Bounty of Fall

MY FASCINATION WITH preserving the fall bounty started young. In the northern parts of British Columbia, Canada, the gardening season is short and cool. My parents had a small backyard vegetable garden that produced lettuce, peas, and carrots with ease, but heat-loving vegetables like tomatoes languished. Every summer, I willed a few green tomatoes to turn brilliant red without success, but my mother had a practical solution for this problem.

Every fall, when a fruit truck arrived from the sun-soaked Okanagan Valley, she came home with boxes filled with Roma tomatoes and set to work. Our kitchen counter overflowed with glass canning jars, metal lids and bands, sieves, ladles, funnels, paring knives, a stockpot, and a water bath canner, a cauldron so large and black I suspected my mother borrowed it from a witch. Tomatoes were plopped in scalding water to release their skins, crushed by hand, and simmered in the stockpot. The crimson liquid burbled and splattered, permeating our home with the earthy scent of tomatoes.

I didn't think much about preserving tomatoes until the year my eldest came into the world. Whether by an instinct, weaved into my genetic code, or fueled by nostalgic childhood memories, I returned to the original birth site of food preservation in our northern city—the Okanagan fruit truck—and bartered for boxes of peaches, pears, and tomatoes for preserving. It didn't take long for my interest in food preservation to become an obsession, one that fully bloomed after our move to the Okanagan Valley, *Land* of abundance.

HONORING THE SEASON OF GATHERING

Autumn, with its abundance, invites us to gather—to collect food from nature and to come together with friends and family. In the Indigenous Métis tradition, autumn was marked by hunting and trapping bison, elk, deer, rabbits, and grouse; fishing for whitefish; and harvesting ripening wild rice, chokecherries, saskatoon berries, and highbush cranberries.[1] During autumn harvests families often hold picnics and enjoy traditional dancing and fiddle music.[2]

Although more than 80 percent of North America's population lives in urban areas, a recent resurgence in reconnection with food and *Land* has been captivating families.[3] While this trend started well before the pandemic, the disruption of food supply chains and the aftermath of rising food costs amplified this resurgence to the point that canning jars are being swiped from grocery shelves as fast as toilet paper during the pandemic.

It's clear that families, both urban and rural, are in their own ways wanting to return to *Land*, to be more connected to their food sources, and to learn traditional preserving practices. Some families are motivated by eating healthier foods, others by reducing food costs, some both, but what's clear is that there is a desire. When we pair this desire with the realization that all families can return to the *Land*, even those living in cities, a pathway toward a greater connection with nature through the season of gathering opens for all families.

CRAFTING WITH AUTUMN'S ABUNDANCE

As autumn unfolds, the earth receives a shower of colorful leaves, heavy nuts, and prickly pine cones, an abundance of offerings for little and big hands to create with. The moment my children spot these treasures, baskets are hauled outside and filled to overflowing. Soon the sweet warm of melting beeswax fills the air of our home and the kitchen table yields to the important work of autumnal crafting.

These open-ended crafting materials can be transformed in countless ways, but over the years my children have settled on a few favorite fall crafting traditions—the first being preserving fallen leaves in melted beeswax.

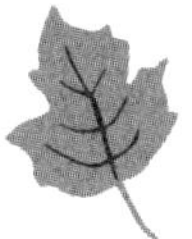

AUTUMN LEAVES PRESERVED IN BEESWAX

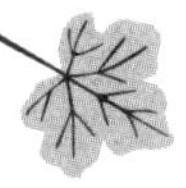

Preserving autumn leaves in beeswax captures and extends the lovely colors of fall. These leaves can be used to decorate a nature table, hang around the home, or make other crafts.

SAFETY FIRST: MELTED BEESWAX

- **Melt slowly over low heat:** Beeswax melts at 144–147°F (62–64°C). If overheated it can discolor and, in extreme cases, ignite! Keep the temperature low and steady. Never leave melting beeswax unattended.
- **Use a double boiler or slow cooker.** Use a dedicated pot or slow cooker for melting beeswax. Avoid open flames when melting beeswax.
- **Supervise your child:** Hot wax can burn. If your child helps with dipping, stay within arm's reach. Let the wax cool slightly before dipping leaves. Dip leaves from the stem and

let excess wax drip off before laying the leaf to dry. If hot wax splashes onto skin, cool underwater.

- **No draining down the sink:** Don't pour wax down the sink. Let leftovers harden and store for next time.

EQUIPMENT:

- Double boiler or mini slow cooker, dedicated for beeswax
- Cutting board
- Knife

MATERIALS:

- Butcher paper, recycled paper, or an old tablecloth
- Beeswax, pellets or block
- Fall leaves

INSTRUCTIONS:

1. **Prepare the beeswax:** Chop beeswax into small pieces, if using blocks or ends of candles, and add them to a dedicated small slow cooker or a double boiler on the stovetop. Slowly melt the beeswax over low heat, monitoring closely. Beeswax has a relatively low melting point of 144–147°F (62–64°C). If melted beeswax gets too hot it will start to change colors and potentially catch fire.
2. **Set up a workspace:** While the beeswax is melting, set up your workspace by covering a table surface with butcher paper, recycled paper, or an old tablecloth to catch drips of beeswax.
3. **Prepare the leaves:** Spread collected leaves over your work surface to allow any moisture to dissipate.
4. **Dip the leaves in beeswax:** When the beeswax has melted, place the slow cooker or pot in the center of the work surface. Carefully dip leaves by holding the stem of a leaf and submerging the leaf into the melted beeswax, lifting it out and holding it over the beeswax for a few seconds to allow the extra wax to drip back into the pot.

5. **Let the beeswax harden:** Gently lay the leaf on your covered surface to harden. This will only take a few minutes.

HELPFUL TIPS:

- *The most affordable and sustainable way of purchasing beeswax is to get it from a local beekeeper. Typically, beekeepers sell natural (yellow) beeswax in blocks by the pound. Another option is to collect the ends and drippings from 100 percent beeswax candles and reuse them for this project.*
- *If you notice that the beeswax is leaving thick drips or streaks on the leaves it means that the wax is getting too cold and needs to be rewarmed.*
- *Red and orange leaves hold their color best, while yellow leaves turn brown over time.*
- *Leaves dipped in beeswax will maintain their color for several months, but they do eventually fade.*
- *These leaves are 100 percent biodegradable and can be added to the compost pile.*

PRESERVING AUTUMN'S FLAVORS

There are many ways to preserve autumn's flavor. Apples, for example, can be stored whole in the fridge, made into applesauce and canned, chopped into pies and frozen, and sliced thinly and dehydrated into apple chips.

In my early days of food preservation, I made all sorts of canned concoctions that collected dust in my basement storage: pickled garlic scapes, Chinese plum sauce, rhubarb relish, and pickled fiddleheads. I discovered that the best foods to preserve are those that my family will eat. It's taken some trial and error to figure out what those foods will be and how to best preserve them.

Typically, when it comes to preserving the bounty of fall, I recommend starting with food preservation strategies that are simple (freezing) and moving to more technical strategies (canning) as you gain confidence.

Freezing

There's one food preservation tool that exists in almost every home: a freezer. Freezing, the most common form of food preservation, is my go-to method for preserving fall foods like pumpkin puree, leafy greens like kale or Swiss chard, premade apple pies, herby pesto, and even tomato sauce. Certain foods, like beans, greens, carrots, or beets require blanching, being boiled in water, to preserve well in the freezer, but other than that this method is simple.

FREEZER PUMPKIN PUREE

Every fall, billions of pounds of pumpkins are thrown away—billions of pounds of *food*! With a bit of time, pumpkins can easily be transformed into puree that can be frozen and then used in soups, breads, muffins, and pies.

EQUIPMENT:

- Food processor, blender, or food mill
- Rimmed baking trays
- Parchment paper or silicone baking mats
- Cutting board
- Sharp knife
- Spoon
- Containers, bags, or wide-mouth jars for storing and freezing

INGREDIENTS:

- Pumpkin, or other winter squash (butternut, acorn, kabocha)

INSTRUCTIONS:

1. **Preheat the oven:** Preheat the oven to 400°F (200°C) and line baking sheets with parchment paper or silicone mats to make cleanup easier.

2. **Prepare the pumpkin:** Using a knife and a sturdy cutting board, cut the pumpkin in half or in quarters, depending on the size. Scrape away seeds and stringy bits with a spoon into a bowl (optional: Save the seeds for roasting!).

3. **Bake the pumpkin:** Place the pumpkin pieces cut side down on the prepared baking sheets. Roast for about 45 to 60 minutes, or until a fork easily pierces the pumpkin flesh. Bigger pumpkins will take closer to an hour.

4. **Blend the pumpkin:** Remove the pumpkin from the oven when soft and let cool so that they are easier to handle. Peel away the pumpkin skin with your fingers or a knife. It should come off easily. Place the flesh into a food processor or blender and blend until a smooth puree forms. Scrape down the sides as needed.

5. **Freeze the pumpkin puree:** Divide the pumpkin puree into containers, freezer bags, or wide-mouth jars and label them with the date. Tip: Storing the puree in one- or two-cup portions makes it easier for using in recipes. Freeze the pumpkin puree and use it within twelve months. Thaw in your refrigerator overnight or in the microwave for several minutes.

DRYING AND DEHYDRATING

After freezing, drying and dehydrating can be done easily at home. This traditional form of food preservation can be done in an oven set at its lowest temperature, in a food dehydrator appliance, in a solar oven, or in warm dry air. Typically, things like cherry tomatoes, pears, peppers, and applesauce dry best in an oven or food dehydrator while woody herbs like rosemary and thyme can be hung to dry.

APPLE FRUIT LEATHER

Homemade fruit leather is an easy and cost-effective way of preserving the abundance of apples that arrive during the early fall months. Use this as a base recipe, one that can be tweaked to suit your family's taste.

Makes a dozen fruit leather pieces

EQUIPMENT:

- Food dehydrator or kitchen oven
- Fruit roll sheets, silicone mat, or lightly oiled parchment paper
- Rimmed baking sheet
- Food processor, immersion blender, or food mill

INGREDIENTS:

- 4 cups apples, chopped and peeled
- ½ cup water
- 1–2 Tbsp lemon juice (optional)
- 1–2 Tbsp honey or maple syrup (optional)
- 1 tsp of cinnamon

DIRECTIONS:

1. **Cook the apples:** Place peeled and chopped apples in a saucepot with ½ cup of water. Bring the water to a boil, cover with a lid, and simmer the apples until they are soft, for about 10 to 15 minutes.
2. **Puree the apples:** Puree the apples using an immersion blender, food blender, or food mill, working in batches if needed.
3. **Add spices and sweetener:** Add the cinnamon and sweetener, if needed, and blend it together. Taste and adjust as needed.
4. **Dehydrate the applesauce:** Place the fruit roll sheets on the dehydrator tray or place the silicone mat or oiled parchment paper on a rimmed baking tray. Pour the pureed apple evenly over the sheets, about ⅛ to ¼ inch thick.
    a. **For food dehydrators:** Set the correct temperature to 135°F to 140°F (57°C to 60°C) for even cooking without scorching. Let the leather dry for 4 to 10 hours.
    b. **For kitchen ovens:** Set the oven to its lowest temperature 140°F to 170°F (60°C to 75°C). If your oven doesn't get to this temperature,

choose the lowest temperature available and prop the door open with a wooden spoon. Bake for 4 to 8 hours.

5. **Check for readiness:** Check the leather regularly for doneness. When done, it should feel pliable and soft, with no stickiness.

6. **Store the apple leather:** Allow the apple leather to cool fully before cutting and storing it in a container.

Have fun with this recipe by adding or substituting ingredients: Add a pinch of nutmeg, ½ cup berries, ½ cup pumpkin puree, 1 banana, substitute 1 cup chopped pear, 1 Tbsp chia seeds (soaked in water for 10 minutes and added after blending apples).

Pickling and Fermenting

Pickling and fermenting are food preservation skills that have been developed over thousands of years. Pickling happens when food is placed in an acidic solution that gives it a sour flavor and keeps it from spoiling (pickles!). Fermentation happens when bacteria feed off food, also resulting in a sour flavor and preservation (sauerkraut, kimchi). These processes are relatively simple but take some learning. One type of pickling that's simple yet satisfying are refrigerator pickles.

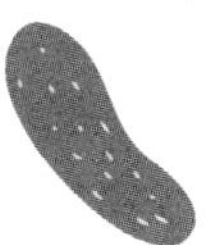

ZESTY REFRIGERATOR DILL PICKLES

Makes 2 pint jars of pickles

EQUIPMENT:

- Saucepot
- Whisk
- 2 pint mason jars, cleaned and sanitized
- Funnel

- Chopping board and knife
- Measuring cups and spoons

INGREDIENTS:

- 4–6 cups (1–1.5 lbs) pickling or small cucumbers, sliced or speared
- 1 cup white vinegar (5 percent acidity)
- 1 cup water
- 2 Tbsp pickling or kosher salt
- 2 Tbsp sugar (optional)
- 1 tsp dried dill seed *or* 2 dill sprigs, per jar
- 2–3 garlic cloves, peeled, per jar
- ¼ tsp whole black peppercorn, per jar
- Pinch of red pepper flakes, per jar (optional)

INSTRUCTIONS:

1. **Prepare the cucumbers:** Wash the cucumbers and slice them into ⅛-inch-thick rounds, long slices, or spears.

2. **Prepare the brine:** In a small saucepan, combine water, vinegar, salt, and sugar (if using). Stir over medium-high heat until the salt and sugar have dissolved. Remove from heat and cool slightly.

3. **Prepare the canning jars:** In each clean, sanitized pint canning jar, add 1 tsp dill seeds (or 1–2 dill sprigs), 2–3 garlic cloves, ¼ tsp black peppercorns, and a pinch of red pepper flakes, if using.

4. **Fill the jars with cucumbers and brine:** Pack the cucumber slices or spears tightly into jars, leaving ½ inch headspace (gap). Using a funnel, pour the brine into the jars, fully submerging the cucumbers. Cover with a lid.

5. **Refrigerate the pickles:** Refrigerate for at least 24 hours before eating. The pickles will develop more flavor over time and keep in the fridge for up to 3 months.

CANNING

Preserving food in jars is a relatively new form of food preservation that came about in the early 1800s thanks to the Frenchman Nicolas Appert. He discovered that when food was placed in jars with lids and heated to a certain temperature for a specific length of time, it stayed shelf-stable.[4] Fifty years later Louis Pasteur discovered that this process worked because it killed harmful bacteria and sealed the food from outside air.

Canning has a steeper learning curve than other preserving techniques and more can go wrong. If canning is a new skill for you, I strongly recommend taking a local canning course or picking up a reputable up-to-date canning book to learn from. Knowing which foods can be canned in a water-bath canner versus pressure canner, and for how long, is crucial to prevent dangerous food poisoning.

Despite the extra care needed, canning is a wonderful skill to learn and can be a wonderful fall family tradition—though my tomato-splattered children might disagree! One bonus to home canning is that properly canned food can last a year or more on the shelf, which is great when freezer space is limited.

Because canning carries real risks if methods aren't tested and current, the recipe below is a refrigerator version of a classic canning recipe. If you'd like a shelf-stable version of this recipe, use reputable sources such as the USDA Complete Guide to Home Canning and the National Center for Home Food Preservation (US). Follow their ingredients, jar sizes, headspace, processing times, and altitude adjustments exactly.

HOMEMADE REFRIGERATOR APPLE BUTTER

Apple butter turns humble applesauce into a thick, caramel-colored spread that begs to be spooned onto warm toast.

EQUIPMENT:

- Food processor or blender
- Large soup pot or slow cooker
- Mixing spoon
- Jars or containers with lids
- Funnel

INGREDIENTS:

- 4 lbs (8 to 10 medium) apples, peeled, cored, and chopped
- 1 cup apple cider or unsweetened apple juice *(not apple cider vinegar)*
- ½–1 cup brown or white sugar, or a combination, packed
- 1–2 Tbsp lemon juice, fresh (optional)
- 1–2 tsp cinnamon
- Pinch of nutmeg and/or cloves (optional)
- ¼ tsp salt
- 1 tsp vanilla extract (optional)

INSTRUCTIONS:

1. **Cook the apples:** Cook the apples: Place the chopped apples, apple cider, or jus into a large pot. Bring the apple mixture to a boil on medium-high heat and then reduce to a simmer. Simmer the apples on low heat for 15 to 30 minutes, until tender.
2. **Blend the apples:** Once the apples are soft, remove the pot from the stovetop and let the apples cool for 15 to 20 minutes. Then, working in batches, puree the apples in a food processor or blender.
3. **Add sugars and spices:** Return the puree to the large pot. Add sugars (start with ½ cup and adjust to taste), lemon juice, spices, and salt. Simmer, uncovered, on low to thicken the puree. This can take anywhere from 30 minutes to more than an hour. Stir occasionally to prevent burning. The apple butter is done when the mixing spoon leaves a trail behind when stirred. Add the vanilla extract at this point, if using.

4. **Cool and store:** Allow the apple butter to cool for about 15 to 20 minutes, then carefully scoop the butter into jars and containers. Refrigerate and use within two to three weeks or freeze for up to 6 months.

PRESERVING A FAMILY TRADITION

If the idea of involving your children in preserving autumn's bounty makes you feel stressed, I completely understand. Often it is easier without little hands getting in the way or without having to nag after older children to help. However, participating in these activities together offers opportunities for learning and connection. Offer your child age-appropriate tasks when helping preserve food, and help guide them with learning new skills, like cutting, safely. The banter that ensues over cutting apples is just as heartwarming as the first few spoonfuls of warm applesauce from the pot.

CHAPTER 19

Into the Hidden World of Fungi

FELIX'S FASCINATION WITH fungi fruited overnight. I can't remember what triggered it. A book from the library? A conversation with a friend? I couldn't tell you. I can say, however, that his budding obsession with the world of mushrooms had little to do with me, at least at first.

At one point, I knew very little about the world of mushrooms. Frankly, fungi terrified me, at least the wild varieties. They sprung up out of nowhere wearing funny little caps that shed spores—messy business. I knew that edible varieties existed, but I didn't have the knowledge to identify mushrooms properly. As a result, I treated most mushrooms with suspicion, cautioning my children to give them a wide berth, especially fairy rings. You never know who and what lurked in those magical places—fairies, elves, or, worse, witches guarded by enormous toads with bulging eyes.

Despite my overly cautious approach with fungi, Felix, at the age of ten, started bringing home thick tomes filled with images of mushrooms.

"Is he actually reading those mushroom textbooks?" my husband asked one evening.

"I think so," I said, "but I can't imagine this obsession will last long."

My husband gave me a knowing look. Clearly, he knew something I didn't.

While walking through the farmers' market one Saturday morning in late September, Felix spotted a vendor I'd never noticed before. Behind a table a man fussed over rows of the prettiest pale pink, blue, yellow, white, and brown mushrooms. They drew Felix in like a dragon slinking toward a chest of shimmering jewels.

"Where did you find these mushrooms?" Felix asked, eyes sparkling with wonder.

"I grew them," said the vendor.

"Grew them . . . in a forest?" asked Felix.

"No, in buildings near my home," he said. "Want to try growing mushrooms?"

Felix nodded vigorously.

Within a week Felix had a mini greenhouse in our dining room, fitted with shallow bins of warm water for humidity, my daughter's lime plant for extra oxygen, and a bag of sawdust inoculated with elm oyster spawn. He fussed over the baby mushrooms, spritzing water, lifting greenhouse flaps, and taking careful notes. Eventually, he proudly presented me with a handful of delicate cream-colored mushrooms to fry up in butter and garlic, winning our hearts and stomachs over to the fascinating world of fungi.

WHY PARENTS FEAR MUSHROOMS: MYTHS AND TRUTHS ABOUT FUNGI

Thanks to folktales and news stories filled with mushroom mishaps, many parents, especially in North America, are afraid of mushrooms, believing these shady shrooms have ill intentions toward our innocent children. At best, parents might enjoy reading picture books filled with colorful mushrooms like the red-capped fly agaric (*Amanita muscaria*) or allow their children to kick puffball mushrooms in the lawn, but most discourage hands-on mushroom encounters in nature.

For many years, I was that parent. "It could be poisonous!" I would warn, wiping invisible dangerous spores off their hands if they poked the cap of a mushroom with a finger.

Truthfully, I would still be afraid of mushrooms had it not been for Felix's keen interest in them. His childlike curiosity and openness to mushrooms dissolved many long-held myths that I believed about fungi and the dangers associated with them.

One of the most common myths about mushrooms is that they're delicious vegetables, but they're *not*, not *vegetables* that is—mushrooms are scrumptious! Mushrooms are not plants. In the world of scientific classification, mushrooms are part of Kingdom Fungi, a kingdom more closely related to animals—to humans!—than plants.[1] Kingdom Fungi has an estimated 1.5 to 12 million species, depending on who you ask, with only about 150,000 of those species being *known* to scientists.[2]

While we often think of fungi and mushrooms as the same thing, mushrooms are the fruiting bodies, the reproductive organs, of certain types of fungi. Not all fungi make mushrooms—most don't. Some fungi like yeast make bread, sauerkraut, and kimchi, without the added mushrooms.

Other than our plates, fungi are everywhere and play a very important role on our planet. Fungi are decomposers. They break down organic matter and make nutrients available in soil. They also interact with plants and animals, sometimes using them as hosts but also helping them.[3] They can even help us fight diseases like cancers, dementia, and heart diseases, which might explain why our ancestors prized wild mushrooms for thousands of years.[4] Indigenous people like the Métis, for instance, have gathered chaga mushrooms (*Inonotus obliquus*), to support immune health. This fungus infects birch trees, producing crusty black masses that can be harvested and made into teas.[5]

Over time, unfortunately, much traditional knowledge of mushrooms has been lost, replaced instead by scary stories of accidental poisonings and folktales linking mushrooms to wickedness. In some parts of the world, entire countries fear mushrooms, but not all.[6] This mushroom fear leads into the second most commonly believed myth that most mushrooms are toxic, even if touched.

The truth is that only about 2 percent of fungi species are poisonous and problematic only if *eaten*.[7] Other than a very few mushrooms that can cause skin irritation, most mushrooms are safe to touch, even toxic ones. That's why David Arora, American mycologist and author, insists that searching for mushrooms, even touching and picking them, is a safe activity for children. Plus, their keen sense of observation and closer proximity to the ground gives them an advantage in finding mushrooms, something I can attest to! My children almost always spot mushrooms before I do.

Arora does caution parents about toddlers in their "grazing phase," the stage when little wildlings put things in their mouths without forethought. Typically, accidental consumption of toxic mushrooms or plants happens when children are very young, and it happened to my youngest with a berry.

At eighteen months of age, while wandering down a creekside trail, my youngest snagged a toxic bittersweet nightshade (*Solanum dulcamara*) berry and quickly popped it into his mouth. I immediately attempted to release the berry from his pudgy lips, but it was long gone, swallowed whole. In a panic, I called poison control, who calmly assured me that one bittersweet nightshade berry, especially the unripe variety, more green than red, would probably not cause much harm. He encouraged us to give my toddler plenty of water.

In the end, my toddler had no symptoms, but it reminded me that our littlest wildlings need careful watching during their grazing phase. It can happen quickly and when least expected. If your little one ever eats an unidentified mushroom, berry, or plant, collect a sample of what was eaten, store it in a bag, and/or take a picture (if possible), and call poison control right away.

On the opposite spectrum is the myth that every mushroom that isn't poisonous is good for eating. The truth is that only about 4 to 5 percent of mushroom species are considered *choice* edible species.[8] These include mushrooms that taste good and are easier to identify. Many mushrooms are too woody, slimy, or bitter to get down, or have toxic look-alikes. Also, even if a mushroom is edible, some people can have allergic reactions to them. A local mushroom expert once cautioned me to "always cook edible mushrooms" and if being eaten for the first time to only "eat a small amount and keep remaining mushrooms in the fridge for at least a week in case of a reaction." Ultimately, when it comes to eating wild mushrooms, caution is crucial.

In the end, we don't need to be afraid to look at, touch, or pick mushrooms, but never eat mushrooms without 100 percent confidence that it is edible—"if in doubt, throw it out!" Also, I do suggest washing hands after handling wild mushrooms, especially before eating food.

HANDS-ON FUN WITH FUNGI

Truthfully, I find the world of fungi wonderfully overwhelming, especially in the autumn months when endless varieties of mushrooms pop up all over the place. These mushrooms point to the often-overlooked thriving network of fungi hidden below our feet. These fungal networks, called mycelium, stay hidden in the soil for years, decades, or even hundreds of years. The oldest and biggest mushroom that we know about is a honey mushroom (*Armillaria ostoyae*) in eastern Oregon that is over 2,000 years old and covers over 890 hectares (8.9 square km)![9] What this means is that if you find a particularly interesting patch of mushrooms, make a note of where you find them and what time of year. Chances are if you come back to the same spot next year, mushrooms may be there again.

GOING ON A MUSHROOM HUNT

Mushrooms grow everywhere, from the bottom of the ocean, tops of mountains, and even in the desert, so it shouldn't be surprising that they also pop up in urban and suburban areas like front lawns, under city trees, in hedgerows along roads, in median strips and boulevards, and in parks, making them perfect for hunting no matter where you live.[10] The humble mushroom often goes unnoticed but once you and your child start paying attention, mushrooms appear everywhere.

Going on a mushroom hunt tends to be the most successful in the autumn, from about mid-September to mid-October, when mushrooms are most abundant. Put your cap on and think like a mushroom: Where would you like to grow? Search for mushrooms in decaying leaves, sticks and logs, near creeks, and in lawns.

There is no need to know everything about mushrooms when you set out but bringing along an identification book or app might help you feel more confident with getting more hands-on with mushrooms. To boost your confidence, connect with local mushroom experts and pay attention to any alerts for poisonous mushrooms in your area.

Cities often send out public warnings for toxic mushrooms like death caps (*Amanita phalloides*) and destroying angel (*Amanita ocreata*), two of the most poisonous mushrooms known that can grow in suburban and urban areas. Eating just one of these mushrooms can lead to death.[11] Remember, *touching* a toxic mushroom won't cause harm, even a death cap. However, if you come across a deadly toxic mushroom in a public area where children play, make note of the location, take a picture, and report it to your city. If you feel comfortable, remove the mushroom, discard it in a garbage (not a home compost bin), and wash your hands.

Identifying Mushrooms

Mushrooms are typically identified based on how they look, feel, smell, sound (when the stem snaps), and where and how they grow. Some mushrooms have gills (radiating blades) under their cap, others do not. Some mushrooms have veils and others do not. Some mushrooms have white spores, or black, brown, yellow, and more. Some mushrooms grow on certain trees, others grow from the ground.

Once you find a mushroom, take a moment to look closely at its cap, stem, as well as where and how it grows. Take a picture or make a sketch. Refer to a mushroom identification book written for your local area. If you don't find a perfect match, don't be discouraged. It can take seeing the same mushroom multiple times before identifying it. Also, not every mushroom makes the pages of an identification book because there are still many waiting to be discovered. Of course, if you plan on harvesting or eating wild mushrooms, you need to know with 100 percent certainty what kind of mushroom it is.

MUSHROOM SPORE PRINTS

Mushrooms release fungal spores into nature for reproduction. These spores are so small we can't see them easily, unless many are collected on paper—spore prints! Not only are mushroom spore prints beautiful to look at, a mushroom's very own "finger" print, but they can be used to identify mushrooms, especially look-alikes where one mushroom is edible, and another isn't.

MATERIALS:

- A sheet of white paper
- A sheet of black paper
- Knife and cutting board
- Large bowl or container (to put over the mushroom cap)
- A mushroom cap (nontoxic)
- Hair spray or fixative (optional, for preserving the spore print)

INSTRUCTIONS:

1. **Harvest a mushroom:** Harvest a fresh nontoxic mushroom with a cap from nearby nature or buy a cultivated mushroom from a farmers' market or grocery store like shitake or portabella mushrooms. Make sure the mushroom isn't too young (no gills exposed) or too old (already released its spores). Place the mushroom into a paper bag to bring home.

2. **Prepare the paper:** At home, in an undisturbed area, place a piece of white paper and black paper side-by-side with one side touching. Using black and white paper will make it possible to see light colored and dark colored spores.

3. **Remove the mushroom cap:** Gently remove the cap of the mushroom by snapping or cutting off the stem with a knife without damaging the underside of the cap.

4. **Place the cap on the paper:** Place the mushroom cap on the papers with the gills (spore side) down so that half of the cap goes on the white paper and half on the black paper. Cover the mushroom cap with a large bowl or container.

5. **Let the spores drop:** Allow the mushroom cap to sit undisturbed for 24 hours so that the spores can drop down. If after 24 hours nothing has happened, the mushroom cap may be too young or too old.

6. **Reveal the spore print:** After 24 hours, gently lift the mushroom cap and notice the spores that dropped on the paper below. The unique shape and color are the mushroom's "finger" print.

7. **Preserve the spore print (optional):** To preserve the mushroom print, gently spray the paper with hair spray or a fixative to make the spores stick.

Shaggymane Painting Ink

Shaggymane mushrooms are common in urban, suburban, and rural environments. They often march together through lawns, meadows, parks, along roads and trails in many parts of the world where soil has been disturbed. Don't let these delicate mushrooms fool you! They can break through concrete before self-digesting into inky black liquid, a unique and safe medium for art.

SAFETY FIRST: SHAGGYMANE IDENTIFICATION AND TOXIC LOOK-ALIKES

Shaggymane mushrooms are nontoxic and safe to eat when harvested early enough. However, these mushrooms have toxic look-alikes, making it important to collect shaggymane mushrooms that have *all* of the following features:

- Cap: Tall bullet-shaped (cylindrical or sausage) white caps (2 to 15 inches high) with soft "shaggy" white to off-white scales
- Gills: Free from stem that turn from white, then pink, and then black then liquify from the edge upward
- Stem: Long, smooth, and hollow stems that sometimes have a moveable ring near the bottom from a veil

TOXIC LOOK-ALIKES TO AVOID:[12]

- Inky Cap/Common Ink Cap (*Coprinopsis atramentaria*) has a smooth cap that is tan or grayish brown and no "shaggy" scales, also self-digests into black ink.
- Magpie inkcap (*Coprinopsis picacea*) has a black cap with white patches.
- Wooly inkcap (*Coprinopsis lagopus*) has a grey cap with hairs.
- Snowy inkcap (*Coprinopsis nivea*) has a white cap with small chalky-looking scales and grows on cow dung.

A FEW OTHER CAUTIONS:

- **Art only:** This ink recipe is for painting only. Keep mushroom "ink" and tools away from food areas.
- **Handwashing:** Wash hands after using any ink.
- **Supervise children:** The ink is nontoxic but best to keep it out of mouths and eyes.

HOW TO MAKE SHAGGYMANE INK

MATERIALS:

- 1–2 shaggymane mushrooms
- A bowl
- ¼ tsp salt
- Paintbrush
- Paper

INSTRUCTIONS:

1. **Harvest a shaggymane mushroom:** Find and properly identify a shaggymane mushroom that is still intact (not self-digested). Carefully harvest the mushroom and place it in a paper bag to keep it safe until returning home.
2. **Place the shaggymane in a bowl:** Shaggymanes are very delicate and will begin to dissolve soon after being harvested, so don't delay! When you get home remove the stem of the shaggymane and place the cap into a bowl large enough to hold it.
3. **Let the shaggymane self-digest:** Leave the cap undisturbed at room temperature for 24 to 48 hours. During this time the cap will break down into a dark black ink.
4. **Strain and preserve shaggymane ink:** Strain out any undigested bits of cap for a smooth paint, then stir in ¼ teaspoon of salt to help preserve the ink. Store the ink in the fridge to keep it fresh.
5. **Painting time:** Dip a paintbrush into the ink and create away!

CREAMY MUSHROOM SOUP (WITHOUT CREAM)

This creamy mushroom soup boasts all the creamy texture without the added cream. Don't get me wrong, I love cream, but without it the mushroom flavors of this soup take center stage and sing! Although, I will admit a drizzle of cream over my soup at the end makes the perfect garnish.

Serves 6–8

INGREDIENTS:

- 2 lbs mushrooms, chopped (a mix of button, cremini, portobello, oyster)
- 6 cups vegetable or chicken stock
- 2 cups milk (whole or 2 percent)
- 4 Tbsp butter (substitutes: bacon fat or olive oil)
- 1 large onion, diced
- 4 garlic cloves, minced
- ¼ to ⅓ cup all-purpose flour
- 1–2 Tbsp soy sauce
- 1 tsp thyme, dried (1 Tbsp thyme, fresh)
- Salt and pepper to taste
- Cream (optional garnish)
- Parsley, fresh, minced (optional garnish)

DIRECTIONS:

1. **Sauté the onions and garlic:** In a large pot over medium-high heat, melt 2 Tbsp butter. Add the diced onion and sauté for 5–8 minutes until soft and golden. Stir in the garlic and cook for 30 seconds, or until fragrant.

2. **Add the mushrooms:** Into the same pot, add the mushrooms along with a generous sprinkle of salt and pepper. Sauté for 8–12 minutes, stirring occasionally, until the mushrooms are soft and golden.

3. **Make the roux:** Add the remaining 2 Tbsp of butter and sprinkle the flour over the mushrooms. For a thicker soup, use ⅓ cup flour, and for a thinner soup ¼ cup flour. Stir together to form a paste at the bottom of the pot. Continue stirring until the paste gets a light golden color. Gradually pour in the stock, whisking constantly to prevent lumps and make a smooth base. Continue to whisk until all the stock is added.

4. **Add the milk and seasonings:** Stir in the milk and thyme. Bring the soup to a gentle boil, then reduce the heat to low and simmer the soup for 15–20 minutes, stirring occasionally.

5. **Puree half the soup:** Working in batches, ladle about ¾ of the soup into a blender and blend until smooth or remove 2 cups of soup from the pot and use an immersion blender.

6. **Add the secret ingredient:** Add 1 to 2 Tbsp of soy sauce and adjust the seasoning with additional salt or pepper if needed.

7. **Serve and enjoy!** Ladle the soup into warm bowls and garnish with a sprinkle of parsley and a drizzle of cream. Serve with crusty bread, hard cheese, and pickles.

Part Five

WINTER

CHAPTER 20

Going Within During Wintertime

WINTER SETTLED IN the Okanagan Valley in layers of thick clouds that brought neither rain nor snow. The frozen earth waited patiently for her crystalline blanket while frosty fingers lazily outlined the edges of purplish bronze Oregon grape leaves. My children met nature's slow pace with impatience.

"When will it snow?" they scowled, noses pressed to cold windows, condensation growing with each frustrated sigh as they willed flurries to fall.

"It will snow soon," I said. I understood their impatience.

The magic of winter's first snowfall is uncontested. The way snowflakes blanket the world, hushing sounds and slowing movement, is a tender embrace for our silent cries of modern-day overwhelm. It forces us to stop in wonder. It begs us outside to play. And yet, winter has been changing, I see it happening right before my eyes. This treasured season is becoming shorter and warmer.

Growing up in northern British Columbia, I remember snow arriving as early as late October and lasting into May. I can count on one hand the number of "green" Christmases I've had in my life, most in the last decade. As I looked at my children's disappointed faces, my mind wandered into worry, about winters with no snow, about what that might mean for this *Land*. It's difficult for me to imagine winter without snow, so intertwined are they that they seemed settled into my very DNA. I crave cold and snow when winter arrives. Nineteen days after the winter solstice, snow covered the valley floor to the great delight of my children. Winter had arrived.

WHEN DOES WINTER BEGIN?

Winter officially begins on the *winter solstice*, a specific moment when the sun is at its lowest (southernmost) point in the sky.

In the Northern Hemisphere, the winter solstice happens on December 21 or 22 when the sun reaches the line of latitude 23.5 degrees north of the Equator (Tropic of Capricorn) and the Northern Hemisphere leans the farthest away from the sun. In the Southern Hemisphere, the winter solstice happens on June 20, 21, or 22 when the sun reaches the line of latitude 23.5 degrees south of the Equator (Tropic of Cancer) and the Southern Hemisphere leans the farthest away from the sun.

On this first day of winter, the amount of daylight is at its shortest and darkness its longest. From this day onward the daylight will begin to lengthen, and the days will feel cooler.

WINTER CELEBRATIONS AND TRADITIONS FOR FAMILIES

There exists in each one of us a deep desire to mark moments in our lives through feasts, celebrations, and festivals. I find that this need is most evident in the winter season when the work of growing and gathering has yielded toward wintering. During this dark and cold season, our ancestors drew close to hearths and sustained themselves on stores of food, stories, and songs. Winter is a season of reflection and rest—one that invites us to slow down and feast.

Our need to feast in the winter, and in all seasons, has been present from our very beginnings. So bound are we to this need that when it is stripped away or lost we become disconnected from our identity, community, and even meaning in life.[1] We've seen this devastation happen to the Indigenous peoples in North America. We've experienced it to a small degree during the restrictions of the COVID-19 pandemic. We continue to experience this loss because of modern society's pressures and our disconnection from nature.

I encourage you to reclaim family winter celebrations. Not in the modern ways of consumerism and constant rushing, but through simple and meaningful moments. Once again, I encourage you to root winter feasts, rituals, and traditions to *your* family values, cultural heritage, beliefs, and *Land* you live on. If you're unsure how to go about celebrating winter, here are a few prompts:

- What winter celebrations and traditions were part of my childhood? Do I want to pass down these traditions to my child?
- What is my cultural background and religious beliefs? Are there specific winter traditions associated with my culture and beliefs that I would like to adopt?
- How has winter been celebrated by the Indigenous peoples living on the *Land* I call home? Are there opportunities to learn about or take part in these celebrations?
- How does the *Land* I call home respond to winter changes? What kind of plants are being harvested? What are the animals doing? How can I take part in these winter changes?

In our home we root ourselves to the unfolding season of winter through several celebrations.

Early Winter Celebrations

Winter sparkles with festivals that honor darkness and the promise of returning light. Here are a few our family and others enjoy:

Winter Solstice (December 21 or 22)

The winter solstice, the shortest day of the year, invites us to slow down and celebrate the return of *light*.

We began by celebrating the winter solstice by eating supper by candlelight, nothing fancy. Year after year, however, we layered on more traditions—making a French stew called coq au vin, a Bûche de Noël (Yule Log) cake, wool lanterns, and beeswax candles, then sharing a winter solstice blessing:

A Winter Solstice Blessing

by Author Unknown

May you find peace in the promise of the solstice night,
That each day forward is blessed with more light.
That the cycle of nature, unbroken and true,
Brings faith to your soul and well-being to you.
Rejoice in the darkness, in the silence find rest,
And may the days that follow be abundantly blessed.

Other families celebrate by sitting around a bonfire, going for a nighttime stroll, telling tales about the winter solstice, making candles, or watching the sun rise or set.

Christmas (December 24/25 or January 6/7)

Rooted in the Christian celebration of Jesus' birth, which aligned with the Roman feast of Sol Invictus, Christmas shines with light, peace, and generosity.[2]

In our home, on Christmas we honor French Canadian Métis traditions like the Réveillon on Christmas Eve, eating tourtière (meat pie), setting up a nativity scene, decorating a tree, giving gifts, and sharing lively music.

Mid-Winter Celebrations

Between winter solstice and spring equinox, the midpoint of winter, several seasonal celebrations continue to bring light among the darkness.

Saint Brigid's Day (February 1)

Saint Brigid is Ireland's greatest female patron saint. Born in Ireland in 451, to a pagan father and Christian mother, Saint Brigid's was known as a protector of women, founder of monasteries, and friend of Saint Patrick.[3] Saint Brigid also shares her name with the Celtic goddess Brigantia and over time history and legend of the two have melded together. Families often craft Brigid's crosses on this day.

Imbolc (February 1–2)

One of the four ancient Gaelic festivals, Imbolc honors their goddess Brigid and commences preparation for the coming spring.[4] Imbolc means "milking" or "in the belly" and was associated with the start of lambing season. During Imbolc people would leave milk and food for the goddess Brigid to receive her blessing. Many families clean their homes, make straw dolls of the goddess, and light bonfires to celebrate.

Candlemas (February 2)

Originating as the Christian Feast of the Presentation of Jesus in the Temple, Candlemas became a winter celebration of light. In our home we celebrate by feasting on crepes, taking stock of our beeswax candles, and selecting one to be blessed and decorated. Other families make their own candles, place a candle in a window to welcome returning light, start indoor seedlings as a symbol of spring's promise, or gather to read a winter blessing before lighting the flame.

Groundhog Day (February 2)

Groundhog Day finds its roots in Candlemas and was brought over by the first German settlers to North America. In German folklore, if a hedgehog saw his shadow on Candlemas Day, spring would be delayed. When the settlers arrived in the United States there were no hedgehogs and so they picked a groundhog instead. Families that celebrate gather at dawn to see if the groundhog spots his shadow, or not, and delight in the hope of spring.

WINTER NATURE KINDNESS WALK

The dark cold days of winter kindle in our hearts a kindness that wraps us with hope and light. When we ignite this kindness through winter celebrations and connecting with nature, it spreads to all who surround us and fortifies us for life's challenges.[5] A winter nature kindness walk is a simple way to share kindness with our children, nature, and our surrounding community. It requires no preparation other than an open door and an open heart.

Steps for Taking a Winter Nature Kindness Walk

Wander around your yard, neighborhood, or in a nearby park or local trail—there's no need to go far from home—and share kindness by:

- Acknowledging others wandering outside, by waving a hand, smiling, saying hello, or having a brief conversation.
- Encouraging your child to introduce themselves to another child at a play park and introducing yourself to their parent or caregiver.
- Noticing wildlife, big and small, and their needs.
- Singing cheerful songs with your child while walking or playing outside. ("You Are My Sunshine," "If You're Happy and You Know It")
- Picking up and discarding bits of trash (if safe to do so).
- Refilling bird feeders with birdseed or hanging birdseed ornaments (Chapter 17: Birding Brings Happiness to Families) on a tree in your yard.
- Using bits of nature like rocks or snow to leave an encouraging message for others to see.
- Noticing three good things in nature (Chapter 16: Back to School, Back to Nature).
- Talking about ways to help animals and plants in nearby nature, or friends, family, and neighbors.

You can continue to cultivate kindness through the winter season by reading picture books about kindness, taking action to show kindness in little ways, and responding to signs of winter in nature.

Signs of Winter in Nature

- After the winter solstice, days slowly get longer but colder.
- Snow, rain, or hail blanket nature.
- Ice forms on puddles, ponds, lakes, and streams.
- Frost covers lawns and windows.
- Leafy (deciduous) trees and bushes are bare.
- Evergreen trees and bushes are green.
- Resident birds are searching for winter foods like berries and seeds.
- Many animals, birds, reptiles, and insects have disappeared (hibernation, migration, etc.).
- Hardy flowers make their appearance in late winter (snowdrops, crocuses, pansies).

SETTING UP A WINTER NATURE TABLE

Our winter nature table begins with boughs of evergreen, candles, and sometimes a string of lights and slowly fills with handmade holiday ornaments and treasures collected from the forest floor. I've listed ideas to fill your own winter nature table below.

- **Evergreen branches:** A handful of different evergreen branches (harvested or purchased) to make into a garland or bough
- **Pine cones:** Pine cones from nearby nature, which can be crafted into pine creatures like owls, hedgehogs, or forest fairies

- **Pieces of bark or log slices:** One or two different pieces of bark collected from the ground or from fallen trees and/or small slices of logs
- **Poinsettia or berries:** Seasonal plants with color like a spring of holly or a small potted poinsettia
- **Lichen or bracket mushroom:** A stick covered in lichen or home to a bracket (shelf) mushroom
- **Fossils, crystals, and rocks:** Rocks with unique features
- **Lanterns and candles:** Glass, wool, or paper lanterns with electric tea lights or natural wax candles to light up the darkness of winter
- **Winter-themed books:** One or two beautifully illustrated picture books to invite children to explore the beauty of winter
- **Play silks:** Winter-colored play silks or fabrics (white, sky blue, deep blue)

DECORATING A TREE FOR WILDLIFE

My children and I often decorate a tree for wildlife close to the Winter Solstice or Christmas Day but occasionally wait until January or February when food for wildlife becomes scarce and winter weather harsh.

Preparing to decorate a tree for wildlife is a multi-day process in our home. We start by making homemade birdseed ornaments, then weave popcorn-cranberry garlands, and finally tie together fresh fruit and veggie bundles. Then we make the trek out to our tree, a small blue spruce on my parents' property, and cover the tree with treats.

Healthy Treats for Wildlife

When deciding what to hang on your outdoor tree, it's important to choose healthy treats for wildlife that live in your area. We typically decorate our tree with birds in mind. In the past, when we lived in a rural area, we added a few things for the local deer too. Deer enjoy things like carrots and apples, but these treats are like candy for them so only hang a few. However, I would not recommend feeding urban deer. While they appear to be peaceful animals, urban deer are overly habituated to humans, which puts them and us at risk.

Healthy treats for birds and other wildlife:

- Dehydrated fruit slices hung on a string (apples, oranges, pears)
- Fresh fruit and veggies hung on a string (apples, pears, berries, watermelon, grapes, oranges, bananas, and carrots)
- Homemade birdseed ornaments or suet cakes
- Pine cone or orange bird feeders
- Popcorn and cranberry garland

What NOT to feed birds and other wildlife:

- Raw meat
- Bread and cookies
- Potato chips
- Avocado
- Chocolate
- Table scraps
- Moldy or rancid birdseed

Tips for decorating an outdoor tree:

Once you and your child have prepared your treats, it's time to decorate a tree.

- Choose a tree on your property or somewhere in nature where feeding animals is permitted. (Public parks and nature areas often do not allow this.)
- Hang treats using materials that are compostable (cotton, wool, twine) in case one gets taken away by an animal.
- Revisit the tree regularly and pick up any uneaten treats and string left behind.
- Read *Night Tree* by Eve Bunting and discover how a young boy and his family go into the quiet woods to decorate their favorite evergreen tree with popcorn chains, apples, tangerines, and pressed millet, honey, and sunflower-seed balls.

TRADITIONAL WINTER FRUIT CAKE

For the longest time, I did everything possible to avoid eating cake riddled with fluorescent bits of "fruit." Then, in my late twenties, I discovered the *traditional* winter fruit cake in *Taproot Magazine*, Issue 12, "Bread," (2014)—now out of print.[6] A cake packed with roasted nuts and real (unsweetened) dried fruit that I had to hide so that it would last more than a few days.

INGREDIENTS:

- 8–9 cups dried fruit (unsweetened, a combination of dried apples, apricot, blueberries, cherries, currants, dates, figs, peaches, pear, prunes, raisins*)
- 2 cups nuts, roasted and chopped (almonds, walnuts, pecans, or hazelnuts. NOT peanuts.)
- ½ cup spiced rum or rum
- 1 cup butter, softened
- 1 cup sugar
- 6 eggs, yolk and whites separated
- ½ tsp salt (omit if using salted butter)

- 2 cups flour, unbleached
- 1 tsp ground cinnamon
- ½ tsp ground cloves
- ½ tsp ground allspice
- ½ tsp ground nutmeg
- ½–1 cup rum or spiced rum (for brushing on cooked loaves)

***Note about dried fruit:** There is no right or wrong combination of dried fruit to use but sweetness and price are a couple factors to consider. Some dried fruit can be very sweet, like dates, so use less of those. Typically, I use a combination of dried cherries (homemade), apricots, dates, figs, and raisins. Raisins are more affordable and are great for the bulk of your dried fruit, especially a combination of different types of raisins. Some years I will also use dried apples, peaches, and pears if I've preserved them over the summer and fall.

INSTRUCTIONS:

1. **Soak the dried fruit (the day before):** The day before baking, chop the dried fruit into smaller pieces (about the size of raisins). Add the chopped dried fruit and ½ cup spiced rum into a large bowl. Stir the mixture, cover the bowl, and let the mixture sit overnight on the counter.

2. **Roast the nuts:** Preheat the oven to 350°F. Spread your nuts on a cookie tray and roast them in the oven for 8–10 minutes or until fragrant and golden. Take the nuts out to cool. Chop the nuts coarsely and set them aside.

3. **Make the fruit cake:** Preheat the oven to 250°F and prepare two 9 by 5 inch or six 5 by 3 inch loaf pans by buttering and lining them with parchment paper.

    a. **Separate the eggs:** Separate the eggs, ensuring there is no egg yolk in the egg white. If there is any egg yolk in the egg whites they will not whip up properly.

b. **Cream butter and sugar:** In a large mixing bowl or stand mixer, cream together the butter and sugar until light and fluffy. Add the egg yolks and beat until well combined.

c. **Mix dry ingredients and combine:** Mix the flour, spices, and salt (if using) in a medium-sized bowl and then add the flour mixture to the butter mixture. Mix until combined.

d. **Add the fruit and nuts:** Before adding the dried fruit and roasted nuts, remove the bowl from the mixer. Most mixers won't be able to mix such a large volume of dried fruit and nuts, and you might break your mixer by trying. Add the rum-soaked dried fruits and roasted chopped nuts to the dough and mix with a sturdy wooden spoon.

e. **Beat the egg whites:** In a medium clean bowl, beat the egg whites until stiff peaks form. Gently fold the beaten egg whites into the thick dough mixture with a wooden spoon.

f. **Bake the cake:** Divide the dough evenly between the prepared bread pans and place them into the preheated oven. Bake large sized loaves (9 by 5 inch) for 3 or 3.5 hours and the small loaves (5 by 3 inch) for 2.5 to 3 hours. Use a wooden skewer or toothpick to check the middle of the cake for doneness. It should come out clean when ready.

g. **Cool the cake:** Cool the fruit cakes on a wire rack for 15 minutes and then remove them from the pans. Let them fully cool to room temperature.

4. **Age the fruit cake:** Winter fruit cake can be eaten right away but it tastes much better after one or two weeks of aging. To store the fruit cake, brush the loaf generously with spiced rum and then wrap each loaf separately in rum-soaked cheese cloth. To soak the cheese cloth, place it in a bowl and pour spiced rum over it until damp but not dripping wet. Then wrap each loaf in plastic and store them in a cool dark place.

CHAPTER 21

Navigating "Bad" Weather as a Family

THE WIND BUFFETED the north side of our house, trying to reach inside. Although the doors remained shut, thin claws of air found purchase around old wooden windows as high-pitched squeals, warnings that danger lurked outside. Within hours, the mild winter weather of the Okanagan Valley gave way to the jaws of a cold snap, trapping families indoors for one of the longest cold snaps since the mid-1980s.[1]

After a few days of staying indoors, my children became restless and irritable. They fought over playdough and had tantrums over spilled soup. I knew they needed fresh air, so I channeled my inner northern girl, bundled them up in layers upon layers, and left the cozy comfort of our home.

"My nose stings!" screeched Theo immediately.

"Keep it covered. That's why you have a scarf," I said, pulling the scarf over his mouth and nose.

"I can't see," he screeched again. His breath, captured by the scarf, coated his glasses in fog.

"Let's take them off," I said, pocketing his glasses.

"My ears are getting cold," Claire complained. I pulled her hood over and cinched it tight.

"You have to move your body," I encouraged.

The goal was to walk to the lake, a venture that normally took five minutes, and we had only made it to the end of our driveway. I pressed on, herding my three children down the street, through an alleyway, and down to Skaha Lake. The moment they set their eyes on the lake they were spellbound.

Cold had transformed the entire shoreline into a series of ice volcanoes that spurted water with each incoming wave. My children crawled over the thick ice shelf to get a better look, peering into the holes. For the next hour, they were lone adventurers in a wild untamed crystalline *Land*, all but forgetting the icy air.

There is a Scandinavian saying, "There's no such thing as bad weather, only inappropriate clothing." In countries like Sweden and Finland, there is a deep appreciation for nature in all its forms—rain, snow, or shine—and families are encouraged to dress appropriately and spend time outside regularly, no matter the weather. In 2017, this saying became popularized in North America when Swedish American writer and author Linda Åkeson McGurk shared her memoir *There's No Such Thing as Bad Weather: A Scandinavian Mom's Secrets for Raising Healthy, Resilient, and Confident Kids.*

When I first read this saying in her book, I nodded with knowing. Growing up in a boreal subarctic climate of British Columbia, Canada, I knew what it meant to play outside no matter the weather. Teachers and parents sent children outside to play snow or shine—there were plenty of both. Recesses were *never* cancelled on the account of "bad" weather, and school buses kept running until they couldn't, typically below -31°F (-35°C) or after a supremely thick snowfall. We celebrated these "snow days" or "cold days" by staying home, and you guessed it, playing outside!

THE REAL CHALLENGES OF BAD WEATHER FOR FAMILIES

In the last few decades, there has been a shift away from embracing nature's varied expressions. Many children aren't playing outside when it's raining, snowing, cold, or hot because their parents are worried that they will be unsafe or uncomfortable, and frankly most children simply don't want to. In schools, this trend is mirrored. Recess gets cancelled when it is raining or snowing out of concern for children's safety, especially when children don't have proper outdoor clothes for the weather.

It's no surprise then that the Scandinavian saying, "There's no such thing as bad weather, only inappropriate clothing," has received backlash, especially in North America. I've heard parents say things like "Not everyone can handle 'bad' weather," "There *is* such bad weather! What about a tornado or snowstorm, no outdoor clothes will protect you from that!," and "I can't afford fancy outdoor clothes for my kids, so we don't play in the rain." In a study of Australian educators and parents, one parent said, "If it's cold and miserable and raining, I am not one to be outside. And if it's 40 degrees (104°F), I don't want to be outside either. [. . .] If the weather is good, I'm good."[2] I think many parents can relate with this statement, and honestly so can I.

Weather can be a major barrier for parents in getting outside with their children, especially when faced with disability, lack of appropriate outdoor gear, and concerns about weather safety. It also doesn't help that extreme weather is becoming more common.[3] While the Scandinavian saying is meant to encourage families to go outside in all weather, I understand why some parents have trouble embracing it. However, instead of feeling discouraged or frustrated by this notion, I still believe that it can be a helpful invitation to reconnect with nature in all her various moods and to learn how to respond to them openly and respectfully.

RETHINKING EVERYDAY WEATHER

All types of weather are necessary for nature to thrive. Wind pollinates flowers and spreads seeds. Rain quenches the thirst of plants and animals. Snow gives nature rest. Everyday weather is part of nature's cycles of the seasons. Truly, there is no such thing as "bad" weather, or "good" weather. Weather simply *is*—part of nature's ebb and flow. When we plaster a label on weather, it impacts our mindset and behavior around these natural rhythms.

I've noticed this reality play out with my own children. If I complain about weather, my kids do the same. If I wait around for "good" weather before going outside, my children do the same. In the end, my mindset around weather either encourages or hampers my children from experiencing nature's unique opportunities for play that only happen when water pools into puddles, snow blows into drifts, and wind dances through trees. It also holds them back from opportunities to build resilience, learn preparedness, and glean important lessons about living life to the fullest.

TALKING ABOUT THE WEATHER

Shifting our mindset around weather starts by noticing *words*, words we say to ourselves and those we say aloud. Words hold incredible power. They shape our thoughts, emotions, habits, and values. Talking about weather in a neutral or positive way shifts us away from seeing weather as a dichotomy of "bad" or "good" and opens our heart to embrace many kinds of weather and find the right words to describe them.

I once heard it said that the Inuit, Indigenous people of the Arctic, have a multitude of words to describe snow and ice. While there has been disagreement around the exact number of Inuktitut words for snow and ice, the general agreement is that their weather lexicon contains many unique words to describe winter weather. In Inuktitut the word *qanik* means "snow falling," *pukak* refers to "crystalline snow on the ground," and *sikuaq* to the "first thin layer of ice" that forms on the ocean or puddles in the fall."[4] What wonderful words! And what's more, most languages, including English, have a great variety of words to describe weather, we just need to rediscover these *lost* words. Words like *graupel* "soft hail," *hoarfrost* "ice crystals on objects," *rime* "a thin layer of ice or frost," *whiffle* "an unsteady gust," or *mizzle* "a misty drizzle" ignite curiosity and wonder about the weather in a fun way.

Learning new words to describe weather can shift the way we experience them. If you are struggling with finding words to describe weather, here are a few prompts:

COLD WEATHER:

- The thermometer says it's below 0°C (32°F) outside. I wonder what Jack Frost has been up to outside. Let's see if we can find some frost (hoarfrost) or thin layers of ice on puddles (rimes).
- Come and peek out the front door. Can you see your breath? Let's get dressed in warm clothing and play outside for a bit.

RAINY WEATHER:

- Look at all that rain! I bet the plants and animals really appreciate it.
- Oh wow! Rain is perfect for making mud pies. Let's go outside and play.

WINDY WEATHER:

- Can you see the trees swaying in the wind? Today would be a great day to fly a kite.
- The wind is swirling leaves through the air. Let's go see if we can catch them.
- Did you know that there are different types of wind? Let's go outside and see what kind of wind is blowing today.

SNOWY WEATHER:

- Look at all those beautiful snowflakes. Let's go outside and see if we can catch some on our tongues.
- The ground is covered in snow. It's a perfect day for making snow sculptures or sledding.
- This sticky snow is just what we need to build a snowman.

CLOUDY WEATHER:

- The sun is hiding behind the clouds. Today would be a great day to look for shapes in the clouds.
- Wow! Those clouds are moving fast. Let's go watch them.
- There's fog outside! We can go walking through clouds.

HOT WEATHER:

- The sun is warm today. It's a good day to wear a hat, bathing suit, and play in some water.
- The thermometer says it's over 30°C (86°F). Today is the perfect day to enjoy a frozen treat outside!
- The sun is getting strong. Let's find a shady spot to play.

DRESSING FOR THE WEATHER

Some of my children's most memorable nature experiences have been when the weather wasn't "perfect." When my eldest was six years old he finally graduated from training wheels to a two-wheeled bike. To celebrate this momentous occasion, I brought him to the nearby rail-trail, a decommissioned railway turned into a pathway, to do his first big bike ride. The ride was 5 miles (8 km), out and back.

On our return I noticed dark foreboding clouds in the sky. Hoping to get back to our van before the rain started, since we hadn't packed rain gear, we pedaled hard, but we weren't fast enough. The sky opened and sheets of summer rain fell hard and fast. Within minutes we were completely soaked. It was such a tremendous downpour that we had to huddle under a tree for the rainfall to slow before continuing.

As the rain slowed to a drizzle, we finished the last section of the trail with smiles on our faces. My son thought the storm was the "best bike ride ever!" It really was quite a fun thing to experience. Even now my teenage son remembers that bike ride as one of his all-time favorites.

NAVIGATING EXTREME WEATHER CHALLENGES

All the advice I've shared up to this point applies to *everyday* weather. Now, let's address an increasing reality on our planet—*extreme* weather. As I mentioned earlier, extreme weather such as severe storms, flooding, droughts, freezes, and wildfires has been increasing in frequency and duration.[5] When I asked parents what barriers kept them indoors, wildfire smoke, pollen, and extreme weather were common responses, more common than I expected.

Living in the southern interior of British Columbia we experience extreme hot, cold, and wildfire smoke on a regular basis, so I'm no stranger to these challenges. Over the years of living with these realities I've developed some strategies that keep my children safe and healthy while keeping their connection with nature thriving.

Extreme Heat and Cold

When it gets very hot or very cold outside, I keep a close eye on the local weather report. During times of extreme heat, we spend time outdoors in the morning and in the evening, taking an indoor break during the heat of the day.

During times of extreme cold we spend time outdoors during the warmest part of the day, which tends to be the afternoon. Movement is key for staying warm in extremely cold weather, so it's important to check in on little ones, babies, and toddlers often. One trick is to feel the back of the neck or quickly remove a glove or boot to feel finger and toe warmth. If either is cold, it may be time to warm up indoors.

Wildfire Smoke, Pollen, and Pollution

Wildfire smoke, pollen, and pollution are trickier barriers to going outdoors, especially for children. My eldest son has asthma and too much time outside breathing in wildfire smoke can trigger an asthmatic reaction. The best tool for understanding air quality and safety is using an air quality index (AQI) report. Plume Labs, IQAir,

BreezoMeter, and AirNow (USA only) all provide accurate data about the quality and safety of outdoor air and guidelines for the type of activities that are safe to do outdoors.

For healthy children, short, non-strenuous outdoor play sessions are alright when the air quality index (AQI) is mild to moderate. Sometimes an area with less smoke is only a short drive away so check the AQI map to find a less smoky area. However, if the AQI is severe, staying indoors might be the safest option.

Bringing Nature Indoors

There are times when extreme weather makes outdoor play unsafe, and when that happens it's great to have a way to stay connected to nature while waiting for the weather to settle. There are many ways to enjoy nature indoors but here are a few of my children's favorites:

- Fill a basket with loose parts from nature such as rocks, shells, sticks, and pine cones. Let your child explore and play with these items.
- Set up a seasonal nature table with nature bits from outside, a seasonal book, and anything else you have on hand.
- Purchase some cut flowers and let your child make a flower display, dissect, or play with flowers.
- Plant some seeds in a pot or make a miniature fairy garden.
- Visit the library and read nature-inspired books together.
- Watch nature from a window—set up a bird feeder!

As parents, we have a powerful choice in how we, and our children, see the world outside our front door. When we trade "bad" weather for curiosity and learn new words to describe snow, wind, or rain, we model resilience and joy. Every drizzle, breeze, or snowflake becomes an invitation rather than a barrier, and our kids learn that can happen in any season. So, the next time "bad" weather rolls in, let's step beyond our comfort zones and discover what nature has to teach us.

CHAPTER 22

Reading the Night Sky

MY MOTHER WRAPPED a scratchy woolen scarf around my nose, making sure I could still see. The clear moonless night sky would be perfect for stargazing, but it was frigid outside.

"Not too long you two," she cautioned, while giving Papa a knowing look, fully aware of my father's propensity for extremes. If it was up to him, we would be climbing up a mountain to see the stars instead of the roof of our house.

"Stay close behind me," Papa urged, while pulling the front door open and vanishing into the darkness.

I sucked in a breath of warm air and stepped outside. Immediately, my nose stung and eyes watered—shocked by the cold, dry air. I tucked my chin into the scarf and blinked rapidly, trying to clear my vision.

"Are you coming?" said Papa, waiting for me by the wooden gate that led to the back of our suburban home. I stumbled onward, following his footsteps through snow so deep it came to my waist and so dry it squeaked with every step.

"Here's the ladder," my dad pointed out. "You go up first so I can help you."

Climbing up a slippery aluminum ladder in a snowsuit is tricky business for an adult, never mind a child of eight, but I did it as quickly as possible. My father followed close behind, prepared to catch me if I slipped. Even if I did fall, the ground was covered with at least six feet of soft snow. The landing would be soft.

On the rooftop I snuggled into the snow and wrapped my arms around my knees. My father joined me.

"Look up!" said Papa.

I peered up into the inky sky. Splatted across the darkness of the moonless sky a sea of pinprick lights shimmered.

"See how they sparkle?" said my father. "It's because of the cold air."

My gloved hand reached out to capture the magic of dancing stars.

"Do you see those three bright stars in a line?" my father asked, while directing my hand to a line of stars. "That's Orion's belt. Orion was a great hunter."

I'm sure that my father told me more about Orion, possibly how he was the son of Poseidon the sea god and Euryale, a Cretan princess, and how his interest in women got him into trouble. I don't recall the details of his story but after locking my eyes on the asterism of stars known as Alnitak, Alnilam, and Mintaka, I have never been able to "unsee" them. We often think of nature as something we experience in daylight, but "dark nature"—the world after sunset—can be just as powerful for our families and for the planet.[1] Gazing up at the night sky not only awakens a sense of wonder, anchoring us in something bigger than ourselves, but it also boosts our sense of happiness.[2] Best of all, the night sky is accessible everywhere, from a balcony in the heart of the city to a quiet field in the country—urban families can join in the magic of stargazing too! And as we learn to spot constellations dimmed by streetlights, we become more aware of how artificial light affects wildlife habitats and our own well-being.[3]

LEGENDS IN THE NIGHT SKY

To this day when I stare at the night sky, I am filled with an overwhelming sense of awe. I know that this feeling isn't unique to me. From the very beginning our ancestors have dipped their quills in the ink of the night sky to pen stories reminding us that we are part of something cosmic. The sun, moon, and stars have played prominent roles in human life, often being honored and revered. These celestial celebrities were the *stars* of our ancestors' most sacred stories.

Many years ago, I sat in a university classroom listening to a professor talk about these stories dismissively. It irked me at the time, but I couldn't explain why. Eventually I came to realize that these stories give us meaning and connect us to *Land*. If we listen carefully to these tales, we can see the veins of place and purpose embedded within. Legends about the moon and stars, about creation, help us and our children connect with nature in a deep and lasting way by giving *meaning* to our lives and our place here on Earth.

DISCOVERING STARS AND CONSTELLATIONS

In each season of the year, as our planet orbits the sun, we can see different constellations in the night sky. There are eighty-eight officially recognized constellations in the night sky; however, some of these constellations are circumpolar.

Circumpolar means that the constellations are at the north and south poles of our planet and never set or rise. They are always there no matter the season. Ursa Major and Ursa Minor, the Great Bear and the Little Bear, also called the Big Dipper and Little Dipper, are circumpolar constellations. They can be seen up in the night sky in every season in the Northern Hemisphere. If someone only went stargazing in the Southern Hemisphere, they would never see them. Just like how I have never seen the circumpolar constellations of the south pole like Chamaeleon and Octans.

Civilizations have studied groups of stars, the constellations, for a long time and have given them different names and stories. That's why constellations are known as legends in the sky. Let's look at the constellation Orion the Hunter. According to astronomer Nadieh Bremer, to the ancient Egyptians this group of stars was known as Sah, the father of gods. To the Navajo it is known as the First Slim One, a protector, and to the Tupi it is an Old Man. Interestingly, the three stars of Orion's belt are included in most constellations of cultures worldwide, but there are way more stars up there than those three.[4]

It's estimated that there are one septillion stars in the universe, or 1,000,000,000,000,000,000,000,000 stars.[5] That's a lot of stars! Stars are born from clouds of gas and dust and can live for millions to trillions of years. Our sun is a star, but not all stars are "suns." Just like our Earth is a planet, but not all planets are "earths." Stars are organized based on how hot they are and what kind of element they absorb. Young stars like our sun are called dwarf stars, old stars like Betelgeuse are giant stars, and dying or dead stars are called white dwarf, brown dwarf, neutron stars, and pulsars. Understanding all the different stars can be confusing, but it can also be very interesting.

SIMPLE ACTIVITIES FOR CONNECTING WITH THE STARS

- **Make your own family legend about a constellation in the night sky:** Create a legend about a group of stars that you can see in the night sky. Use your natural surroundings, family stories, or cultural heritage as inspiration.
- **Create constellation nature art:** Use rocks and sticks to create constellations on the ground. This activity will help you and your child be better able to identify the shapes on the constellation in the sky.
- **Download a constellation app:** Constellation apps can be helpful for viewing the night sky.

- **Learn a song, poem, or nursery rhyme about stars:** You can't go wrong with learning "Twinkle, Twinkle Little Star."

THE MOON

The moon is our planet's only natural satellite. As the fifth-largest moon in our solar system, it helps to moderate our climate and manage our tides.[6] As the moon journeys around the Earth it also reflects sunlight into the darkness of night in different shapes, known as *phases.*

Like the stars and constellations, the moon has also captured the imagination of storytellers, poets, and musicians. Often in legends, the moon is a sibling to the sun, like the Greek Olympian light god Apollo and his twin sister Artemis, the moon goddess, but this is not always the case. In Hawaiian mythology, Hina tires of making cloth and dealing with her unruly sons and lazy husband, so she travels on a rainbow to find peace and quiet on the moon. Eventually, Hina decides to stay at her peaceful abode and becomes known as the goddess of the moon, which is called Mahina in native Hawaiian language.[7]

Tuning into the moon and her phases helps us and our children feel more grounded in the rhythm of the month and seasons. Noticing the moon phases and celebrating the monthly full moon are simple activities that can be done even in the city; the only barrier might be a cloudy sky.

MOON PHASES

It takes the moon 27.3 days to go around the Earth, but 29.5 days to go from one new moon to another.[8] As the moon makes its monthly journey around the Earth, different parts are illuminated by the sun, which are called moon phases. The phases of the moon include the new moon, waxing crescent, first quarter, waxing gibbous, full moon, waning gibbous, third quarter, and waning crescent.

When the moon is new, we can barely see it in the sky. That is because the side of the moon reflecting the sun's light is facing away from us. Slowly, however, the moon gets bigger. After the new moon, a crescent-shaped moon peeks through the dark night. Night after night it grows into a half moon and then a full moon before slowly vanishing again.

A simple activity for connecting with the moon phases:

- Collect round flattened rocks and paint a different phase of the moon on each one. Keep the rocks somewhere accessible and try to match them to the moon phases throughout the month.

A YEAR OF MOONS: THE STORIES BEHIND THEIR FOLK NAMES

As the moon reaches the point in its orbit when it is directly opposite the sun, it acts as a round mirror reflecting the sun's rays into the night. The moon can be so bright that it can even cast shadows onto the Earth—moon shadows.

Ancient civilizations had a deep bond to the full moon, using it to guide their rhythm of life. Because of the importance of the full moon for people of the past, each full moon was given a unique name. These names reflected the culture of the people and their unique connection to place. The most common full moon names that are used in North America today are a blend of Native American or First Nation and European traditions.[9]

A quick note on Indigenous Peoples and Native American moon names and calendars

Many communities follow thirteen lunar cycles, so the timing doesn't always line up neatly with our Gregorian calendar (January to December). Names for the moons can also be the names of the months, and they can differ from Nation to Nation. The "other names" shared here are examples from specific communities (some may have more than one name for each full moon!) and are not a complete list.

January: Wolf Moon

In the depth of winter, wolves prowl snowy landscapes, filling the air with haunting howls that echo over frozen terrain. Instead of fear, their call invites us to embrace the wild within ourselves. When the Wolf Moon is full and strong, step outside with your children, howl at the moon, and feel the beat of your own courageous wild hearts.

Other names: Someone's Ears Are Freezing Moon (Oneida), Great Spirit Moon (Ojibwe), Great Moon (Opaskwayak Cree)[10]

February: Snow Moon

By the midpoint of winter cold envelops *Land*, making February one of the coldest and snowiest months of the year in the Northern Hemisphere and one of the most challenging for hunting and survival. The Snow Moon invites us to acknowledge the challenges in life along with resilience and strength that lay within every one of us.

Other names: Bony Moon (Cherokee), Eagle Moon (Opaskwayak Cree), Deep Snow Moon (Mohican)[11]

March: Worm Moon

As the earth thaws, earthworms break free of their frozen burrows and wiggle up through the soil, catching the attention of hungry robins returning to their nesting grounds. The Worm Moon acknowledges the first stirrings of spring that invite us to make rooms in our homes, yards, and hearts for new growth—a time for spring cleaning!

Other names: Goose Moon (Opaskwayak Cree), Windy Moon (Cherokee), Crow Moon (Mohican), Sugar Making/Boiling Moon (Ojibwe)[12]

April: Pink Moon

In early spring, swathes of pink moss, creeping phlox (*P. Subulata*), bloom in eastern North America, covering the landscape in soft pink hues. The Pink Moon is an invitation to soften our hearts and work on healing our relationships with one another and with nature.

Other names: Frog Moon (Opaskwayak Cree), Grass and Geese Moon (Mohican), Flower Moon (Cherokee)

May: Flower Moon

The old English proverb "April showers bring May flowers" holds true for this month's full moon, the Flower Moon. As the month of the year with the most flowers, May's Flower Moon reminds us to notice flowers in nature, the dandelions sprouting in the lawn, and pansies popping out of the ground, and take time to smell them too.

Other names: Budding Moon (Opaskwayak Cree), Planting Moon (Mohican), Flower/Budding Moon (Ojibwe)

June: Strawberry Moon

Strawberries are ripe for picking during this month along with other berries like raspberries and blueberries. The Strawberry Moon is also a good time to taste nature by visiting a local farmers' market, u-pick farm, or choosing the seasonally fresh fruit at the store.

Other names: Heart Berry Moon (Opaskwayak Cree), Green Corn Moon (Cherokee)

July: Buck Moon

In early spring, male deer, also called bucks, shed their antlers. By the middle of July, their velvety antlers have regrown to full size and will gradually harden for the fall mating season. The Buck Moon is a reminder that we grow and strengthen over time, preparing ourselves for the challenges of life's journey.

Other names: Honey Bee Moon (Mohican), Ripe Corn Moon (Cherokee), Blueberry Moon (Ojibwe)

August: Sturgeon Moon

Sturgeons are large ancient fish with bony plates that have been around since the Cretaceous period (65 to 145 million years ago).[13] These fish were harvested in abundance during the month of August, but overfishing, pollution, and loss of habitat were causing sturgeons to slowly disappear. Thanks to conservation efforts, however, their numbers are bouncing back.[14] The Sturgeon moon invites us to reach out and provide care and compassion for nature and one another.

Other names: Flying Up Moon (Opaskwayak Cree), Fruit Month (Cherokee), New or Fresh Corn Moon (Oneida)

September: Corn Moon

As the heat of summer slowly gives way to cooler nights, apples, squash, and corn ripen for the harvest. The Corn Moon glows brightly in the night sky, giving farmers light for harvesting into the evening and night. This full moon is a time for enjoying the bounty of nature and giving thanks for all that it provides. If this full moon is the one closest to the autumn equinox, it takes the special title Harvest Moon.

Other names: Indian Summer Moon (Opaskwayak Cree), Nut Moon (Cherokee), Harvest Moon

Harvest Moon (September or October)

The Harvest Moon is the full moon nearest the autumn equinox. Some years it falls in September; in other years it lands in October. It replaces the usual monthly moon (Corn in September or Hunter's in October) for that year.

October: Hunter's Moon

At this time of year, animals are preparing for winter, but it's not just winter they need to look out for most. Hunters walk silently through forests, looking to harvest animals to help sustain their own families. Traditionally the Hunter Moon is a time of giving and sharing from the bounty that was gathered. If this full moon is the one closest to the autumn equinox, it takes the special title Harvest Moon.

Other names: Freezing Up Moon (Opaskwayak Cree), Falling Leaves Moon (Ojibwe), Someone Stores Food Moon (Oneida), Harvest Moon

November: Beaver Moon

In November beavers are working at a frenetic pace securing their dams and storing food for the winter. It was also the time of year when hunters would lay traps for beavers and harvest their pelts to make warm winter clothing.[15] The Beaver Moon sends families indoors into their cozy homes to share stories and songs.

Other names: Winter Keeper Moon (Opaskwayak Cree), Freezing/Freeze-up (Ojibwe), First Snow Moon (Mohican)

December: Cold Moon

Approaching the winter solstice the temperature outside plummets and darkness descends. The Cold Moon is the last full moon of the calendar year and is a time to reflect on the past year and kindle in us a light to guide us going forward. The Cold Moon is a perfect time to light a candle, make a lantern, or build a fire outside.

Other names: Little Spirit Moon (Ojibwe), It's a Long Night Moon (Oneida), Snow Moon (Cherokee), Long Night Moon (Mohican)

CHAPTER 23

Embracing the Magic of Snow and Ice

WHEN THE FIRST snow of winter finally arrived that January, the excitement in our home couldn't be contained. My children pulled their snow clothes from bins before breakfast was eaten—a race to paint the first brushstrokes onto nature's blank canvas.

No matter how many snowflakes have been caught on tongues, snowballs thrown into the air, or snowmen built in the front yard, these glittering crystals of ice ignite a sense of joy and excitement in my home that can't be explained—we become snow-struck.

The happy feeling of being snow-struck carried me through my childhood years of living in a landscape covered in snow from October to May. As a young mother, however, I experienced a time when snow felt more burdensome than magical. After completing my degree in nursing at the University of British Columbia, in the picturesque ocean-side city of Vancouver, I returned to my hometown with my husband. Not long after our return to the snowy northern interior, we welcomed our firstborn. As I navigated motherhood, snow, once a friend to me, felt like a foe. My home was laid siege by ever growing piles of snow, and my baby and I were captives.

Although I had a snow-filled childhood, I didn't know how to do the same for my own baby as a new parent. It took me several years to accept winter's invitation to embrace the wonders of snow for my family, but when I finally made the leap there was no turning back.

THE JOYS AND BENEFITS OF WINTER NATURE CONNECTION FOR FAMILIES

The winter season, with its cold, snow, and ice, offers unique opportunities for connecting with nature, exploration, and play that aren't available during any other season. This is especially true for families that live in more northern or mountainous regions where snow and ice are synonymous with winter. To see how these opportunities translate into real benefits, let's turn to research on children's winter play.

In a study set in a semi-urban area on the west coast of Norway, researchers observed kindergarten-aged children engaging in winter play and noticed three key themes.[1]

The first theme was that winterscapes, winter landscapes, are always changing. Like other parts of nature, snow and ice take on different shapes, forms, and textures depending on the temperature, humidity, and type of precipitation, offering unique opportunities for exploration and play. Warm, wet snow can be shaped into snowballs or snow sculptures while a fresh snowfall wipes the winter playscape clean, a fresh start. Even the way light falls onto snow can impact the way children experience winterscapes. Playing after sunset or during the day impacts the various themes of play and exploration.

The second observation was that snow and ice offer children unique movement challenges in play. In the study researchers observed children playing on a sledding hill and noticed how they navigate snow and ice, using balance and coordination to navigate the steepness of the hill and slippery properties of ice. Winter play gives children unique opportunities for developing movement skills that can be difficult to replicate in indoor settings, and mastering these skills can boost children's self-confidence.

The third theme from this study looked at the social, cultural, and connection aspect of winter play. When children play in snow and ice, they grow closer to nature and discover their own place in it, and they also gain a better understanding of others and their community. In some ways, this might be the most important theme.

Unfortunately, for many families winter becomes a neglected season.[2] On one hand I understand why this happens; winter can be a difficult season to get outside. I've gone through the struggles of feeling trapped by winter weather. On the other hand, I know that this often-overlooked season can bring immense joy to my entire family when I take the time to embrace it. Also, like other seasons, spending time outside in the winter season can have a positive effect on our health and well-being. While studies on the topic *winter* nature connection and health are fewer than other seasons, simply taking the time to notice *winter* nature can boost our sense of well-being.[3]

THE SCIENCE OF SNOWFLAKES

The beauty of snow only increases as we draw closer to nature's tiny masterpieces. Like soft notes from nature's great symphony, each delicate crystal sings of the magic and mystery of snow, of winter, and of *Land*. Snow isn't just frozen bits of water. Each snowflake is a unique story from the sky; stories that have captivated our ancestors for thousands of years. By the late 1880s, that fascination found its champion in a Vermont farmer whose passion for photographing ice crystals earned him the nickname "Snowflake Man." Today, we remember him as Snowflake Bentley.

Snowflake Bentley was born Wilson Alwyn Bentley in Jericho, Vermont, on February 9, 1865. His mother, herself a former schoolteacher, fostered his curiosity, gifting him a microscope at fifteen. Mesmerized by ice crystals, Bentley moved from sketching snowflakes to photographing them with a bellows camera and microscope lens, ultimately sharing hundreds of snowflake images thanks to a supportive university mentor. In the 1930s, Japanese physicist Ukichiro Nakaya built on Bentley's work, showing how temperature and humidity shape snowflakes.

How Are Snowflakes Made?

A snowflake forms when extremely cold water vapor clings to a bit of pollen or dust (a nucleus) in the sky and forms a hexagonal (six-sided) prism of ice called a snow crystal.[4] This snow crystal then expands as it tumbles through clouds.

The shape of the snow crystal depends on the temperature and humidity of the clouds and the path it takes through the clouds.[5] Scientists have different ways of categorizing the different shapes of snow crystals:[6]

- **Stellar dendrites:** The classic "snowflake" shape that has a star appearance with delicate branches and side-branches. Dendrites means "like a tree." These snow crystals are lovely when they form at temperatures around 5° F (-15°C).
- **Needles and columns:** Tiny cylindrical snow crystals that look like bits of white hair. Some are needle shaped, and some are hollow. They are quite common and form at temperatures around 21° F (-6° C).
- **Capped columns:** Cylindrical snow crystals with hexagonal plates on each end. These snow crystals look like a spool of thread. These are not common because they must experience two different temperatures to form, temperatures around 21° F (-6° C) for the column and then 5° F (-15°C) for the caps.
- **Rimed crystals and graupel:** Snow crystals that have frozen water droplets (rime) attached. Blobs of rime are called graupel.
- **Irregular crystals:** Randomly shaped snow crystals that happen when they collide or melt and stick together.

The magical thing about snow crystals is that each one is unique. Since no snow crystal will take the same journey through a cloud, each one will have a specific print, just like our thumbprints.

SIMPLE ACTIVITIES FOR CONNECTING WITH SNOW AND ICE

I am a firm believer that every child and adult should go through a "Snowflake Bentley" phase and gaze at the intricate symmetrical patterns of snowflakes, whether in real life or through the pictures that were taken by Bentley many years ago. I highly recommend reading the *Snowflake Bentley* by Jacqueline Briggs Martin picture book as well. However, there are many other ways to connect with snow and ice, even if you live somewhere where they don't occur naturally.

FROZEN NATURE WREATHS

Nature ice wreathes have taken social media by storm in recent years, and it's easy to see why—they're simple to make, eco-friendly, and they are absolutely magical. This project is a perfect way to embrace freezing weather and can even be adapted for warmer climates using a freezer.

MATERIALS:

- Bundt or tube cake pan (for one large wreath) or silicone donut molds (for mini wreaths)
- Thick cotton, wool, or twine (strong and durable)
- Water
- Colorful nature materials:
  - Orange and yellow: Citrus slices (orange, lemon)
  - Red: Cranberries, rose hips, berries
  - Green: Evergreen branches, leaves, lime slices
  - Brown: Pine cones, star anise

Alternative molds: Use a cake pan, large ice cream pail, or other circular container. Place and weigh down a cup in the center to create a hole. Alternatively, add a string to create an ice "pane" or "window."

Skip the birdseeds: While tempting, freezing seeds in ice makes them hard to access and prone to mold as the ice melts.

Using plastics: Stick to biodegradable materials that won't warm nature when the wreath melts.

INSTRUCTIONS:

1. Arrange the nature materials in the mold:
    - For mini ice wreaths: Lay the nature bits in a single layer and fill them with water.
    - For a large ice wreath: Add evergreen branches to the bottom, then layer citrus slices, cranberries, and pine cones or star anise. Fill with water until they are just covered.
2. Place the mold outside in freezing weather or in a freezer if it's too warm outside. Allow 12 to 24 hours to freeze completely.
3. Once frozen, run the mold under warm water to release the wreath.
4. Hang your wreath outside with cotton, wool, or twine and allow the sunlight to shine through.

Tracking Animals

Over woven snowflakes critters silently tell stories of their survival—a trail of two-toed hoofprints along a hedge of cedars, a four-print foot pattern jumping into a burrow, the stamp of extended wings on snow. Every mark reveals the busy world of winter wildlife that often goes unnoticed during other seasons.

In the words of Ernest Thompson Seton (1860–1946), a Canadian naturalist who spent a great amount of time with the *nehiyawak* (Cree) in Manitoba, wildlife tracks are the "oldest writing on earth" that can tell us a great deal about the animal that left them.[7] Like learning to read from books, first we have to notice and decipher letters (tracks) and then link them together to form words, sentences, and stories. These stories connect us to the lives of the creatures that meandered through forest and field, along shore or sidewalk.

Noticing signs of wildlife gives us parents and our children a unique and exciting way to connect with *Land*. While a skillful tracker can glean a lot from animal tracks—the species, the size and age, the sex, and even the mood—noticing animal tracks can be done by anyone with keen eyes. Children are especially good at noticing animal tracks.

Where to Find Animal Tracks

Without doubt, the best place to discover animal tracks is outdoors after a fresh snowfall. Snow-covered landscapes offer a clean canvas for capturing the stories silent animals share. The first day or two after a snowfall are the best days to see the tracks. If snow isn't an option, search for places with soft sand, mud, and soil such as along a pond, creek, lake, or ocean, along a forest trail after rain, or in a recently ploughed field. And there's no need to go far in search of animal tracks; after a snowfall in the city there are plenty of interesting wildlife tracks to spot: dogs, cats, birds, urban deer, raccoons, squirrels, rabbits, and more!

HOW TO IDENTIFY ANIMAL TRACKS

The first step to identifying animal tracks is to answer the question: What kinds of animals live in nature near you? The second step is to get familiar with what those tracks might look like. Typically, animal tracks are put into three **track shape** categories and learning to identify these three different shapes is a great place to start.

- Hoofed tracks: Made by animals with hooves that are often heart-shaped or cloven (split into two), which include deer, moose, elk, bighorn sheep, and wild boar.
- Paw tracks: Made by animals that have padded feet, toe pads, and metacarpal (front paw) or metatarsal (hind paw) pads, which can have retractable claws (cats) or fixed claws (dogs, bears) and include domestic cats and dogs, cougars, coyotes, foxes, wolves, raccoons, and bears.

- **Bird prints:** Made by birds that have three forward-pointing toes and sometimes a backward-pointing toe.

SIMPLE MAPLE TAFFY ON SNOW

The sweet sap of the sugar maple was prized by the Indigenous people of the Eastern Woodlands who collected it in birch baskets in the early spring for cooking, curing, and making into sweet syrup and taffy—a tradition shared with European settlers that has become much loved.[8]

INGREDIENTS:

- 1 cup maple syrup (100 percent pure)
- Clean snow or finely shaved ice

EQUIPMENT:

- Saucepot, medium
- Stirring spoon
- Thermometer
- Wooden ice pop sticks
- Rimmed baking tray or large container

DIRECTIONS:

1. **Prepare the snow:** Pack fresh clean snow or finely shaved ice into a rimmed baking sheet or large container, making sure to create a nice even surface. Place the tray in the freezer or outside (if it's freezing) until the syrup is ready.
2. **Boil the syrup:** In a medium saucepot add the maple syrup and bring to a boil over high heat. Continue to cook over medium-high heat until the syrup reaches 115°C (238°F) for the perfect taffy.
3. **Test the maple taffy:** Drizzle a bit of syrup onto the packed snow. If the taffy hardens like hard candy, add a bit of water to the syrup and test

again. If the taffy is runny and doesn't form a soft ball around a wooden stick, boil it a bit longer. The taffy should be firm enough to make a ball on a stick but soft enough to chew.

4. **Pour and shape onto wooden sticks:** When ready, pour the maple taffy into lines onto the packed snow or ice and roll onto the wooden stick—delicious! Store extra taffies in the freezer in a cup or baggie of snow or shaved ice.

CHAPTER 24

Gathering for Storytime

WINTER'S HOLD BEGAN to slip. Over in the neighboring orchard of my parents' acreage there remained only a few patches of dirty snow lying between the rows of skeletal apple trees. The *conk-a-reee!* of a red-winged blackbird pierced the silence of winter, and my honeybees were taking their cleansing flights. Soon winter could give way to a boisterous symphony of spring, but not quite yet.

In these in-between moments as winter transitions to spring, death can visit unexpectedly. A buzzing hive of honeybees falls silent. A late frost damages the swelling buds of a cherry tree. An old doe lays down for the last time.

We didn't see her at first, her dusty brown fur blending into the dead grass. It was the birds that alerted us to her presence. Crows circled overhead, their shrill cries calling others to the feast. My children peered through the wire fencing at the still body of the dead deer.

"Was it the coyotes?" Theo asked.

"Perhaps," I said. I had heard their raucous yips filling the night just before dawn. "But she may have been growing old, become injured, or even was underfed. It's been a long, cold winter."

Over the next two days, we watched with grim wonder as the animals danced around the dead deer, taking turns to the feast. My children watched with a morbid curiosity; brows furrowed at the carnage. Unsure of how to help them understand that endings are part of beginnings, that death is part of nature and of *Land*, I turned to what felt most natural—storytelling.

LIVING STORIED LIVES

Ochre covered handprints on cavernous walls, tales spinning around campfires, and epics echoing in ancient halls—from our very beginning stories have infused human life. For our ancestors, stories were a way of remembering, sharing knowledge, teaching important lessons, and giving meaning to life.

Over time storytelling has shifted from being oral to written, from being connected to nature to being disconnected, with most modern stories being told on paper or through screens. However, for Indigenous and Native people, oral storytelling continues to hold a sacred place in their lives and culture, impacting their sense of identity, community, and belonging, something I have been rediscovering in my own understanding of being Métis.

Although I have always known that I am a Red River Métis, my father grew up during a time when the Métis people were seen as *lesser-than* people. The Métis were despised and denigrated, to such an extent that it was best *not* to be Métis, even if you were. As a result, my father grew up on the ancestral Métis motherland not knowing he was Métis. And yet, despite not knowing his roots, culture, and stories, his grandfather (not Métis) kept the tradition of storytelling alive and fostered in him a deep connection to the *Land*.

Knowing this bit of personal history taught me something important about stories—we all live storied lives, we are all storytellers, and we all have stories to tell. When we take the time to reconnect to the stories of our grandparents, elders, and ancestors, we reconnect to one another and to the *Land* we live on.

RECONNECTING THROUGH ORAL STORYTELLING

Storytelling, whether telling or reading, has a powerful impact on our families and children. They can help heal broken bonds with one another and nature and build a deep resilience in our children for the future.[1]

While most parents see the benefits of reading stories aloud to their children, most shy away from oral storytelling because it feels unfamiliar or awkward. I know the feeling and I think this comes from a place of believing that stories must be structured in a certain way, having an introduction, rising action, a climax, falling action, and a resolution—sound familiar?

These are the structures of storytelling we learn at school. The linear structure we see read in most books. However, Indigenous storytelling doesn't follow this strict format. Instead, Indigenous stories are living and evolving. They adapt to the listeners, to the season, and to the *Land* and may not have a beginning, middle, or ending. Leaning into the wisdom of Indigenous storytellers can help guide our own family's storytelling so that our stories can connect us more deeply with one another and with nature.

If you are interested in exploring storytelling with your child, here are some suggestions for getting started:[2]

- Think about a story you would like to share with your child. This could be a personal story from your childhood, a story about something that happened recently, a retelling of a story you heard from a grandparent or elder, or something completely made up.
- Lean into nature, the season, and *Land* you live on to inspire you.
- Begin by gathering your child close and waiting until they are ready to listen.
- Start with an opening line (e.g. Let me tell you a story . . . , I'd like to tell you a story . . . , Once upon a time . . .).

- Recount the story authentically, remembering it doesn't have a specific beginning or end.
- Use different hand gestures, props, and tones of voice to add interest to the story.
- Pause during parts of the story to let your child think about or guess what might happen next.
- Notice how your child is reacting to your story and adapt the story as needed.

Remember, the more you practice and repeat stories, the more comfortable and confident you will be as the family storyteller, and the deeper the connection you'll build with your children.

CONNECTING TO NATURE THROUGH STORIES, ART, AND WRITING

Apart from oral storytelling and reading, there are many other ways to connect with nature through writing and art.

The Joy of Nature Journaling

Keeping a nature journal is a relatively old practice. It started when people would carefully observe, record, question, and connect what was being noticed in nature through drawing, painting, and writing. Beatrix Potter (1866–1943), author of the classic children's books *The Tale of Peter Rabbit* and *The Tale of Benjamin Bunny*, among many others, started nature journaling in her childhood. She loved looking closely at nature and drawing pictures of the items she collected from the outdoors. Eventually her keen observations would pave the way to stories we are so familiar with today.

Others that practiced nature journaling include British naturalist and father of evolutionary theory Charles Darwin (1809–1882), American naturalist and educator Anna Botsford Comstock (1854–1930), naturalist and conservationist John Muir (1838–1914), and more recently American naturalist, conservationist, and artist known for the Peterson nature guides, Roger Tory Peterson (1908–1996).

Keeping a nature journal and encouraging our children to do the same provides an engaging pathway toward nature connection. Slowing down to feel the pattern of veins in a maple leaf or the soft black and orange hairs of a woolly bear caterpillar and then recording what was noticed helps us "see" nature's beauty more clearly. Keeping a nature journal also helps us parents and our children learn and practice the language of nature while fostering a deep sense of awe and wonder of the world that surrounds us.

FOR ALL AGES AND ABILITIES

What I love about nature journaling is that it is an activity that embraces every age and ability, and it can be done as a family. When I started nature journaling with my children, they were quite young. Their nature journals were filled with abstract scribbles and crumpled pages. As they got older, they started to trace leaves and rocks, filling them in with a kaleidoscope of color. Then in later childhood their journaling became more intentional. Sometimes I would offer them gentle prompts, but for the most part I let them be.

What's important to remember is that a nature journal is a *journal.* It should be a safe space for discovery, questioning, and reflection. As parents we shouldn't criticize or judge what goes onto the pages of our children's nature journals, or even our own. If anything, gentle encouragement can be helpful if your child is struggling with perfectionism or lack of trying.

RECOMMENDED SUPPLIES

Nature journaling doesn't require any fancy supplies to get started, all you need is something to draw with and something to draw on: a piece of paper and pencil. Beyond that it's all a matter of preference; however, I have found that children are more *drawn* to art when they use good quality supplies.

The pleasure of using a nicely sharpened pencil, deeply colored crayons, or vibrant paints adds to the joy of nature journaling.

Children, like adults, become frustrated with poorly made tools, and nature journaling is no exception. It is better to provide a few good quality art items than a bunch of cheap supplies that won't last or don't work. If you and your child want to make a consistent habit of nature journaling, I recommend the following supplies:

- **Spiral-bound art journal:** Look for a spiral-bound art journal with thicker paper that can handle watercolor paint, markers, ink, pencil, and glue, and is easy to carry around outside.
- **Sketching pencils:** Some parents prefer mechanical pencils because they're always sharp, a bonus while outside. However, I prefer sketching pencils, specifically an HB or F pencil and a 2B pencil. If in doubt, a regular school pencil works perfectly.
- **Pencil sharpener and eraser:** These two important tools are must-haves.
- **Watercolor paints:** A small watercolor pan set or watercolor pencils are easy to carry around and perfect to add color to nature journals.
- **Paintbrushes:** Don't forget a few round-tipped paintbrushes.
- **Black waterproof fine markers:** Often called Micron pens, these are used for outlining or writing. Typically, a Micron size 02 works well, but for younger children something a bit more robust like a permanent marker pen is better.

Those are the basic supplies for nature journaling, but here are a few other things I will throw into my bag: water, rag, eraser, sharpener, colored pencils, magnifying loop or glass, and field guide. Typically, I keep all our supplies together in a bag that I can easily transfer from car to backpack.

HOW TO START NATURE JOURNALING

Nature journaling is best approached without pressure or expectations. Remember, you don't have to be artistic to do this activity with your children. Once you've gathered nature journaling supplies, start by visiting somewhere that's familiar to you and your children and go on a hunt to find three different things that you and your child find interesting (a wildflower, a bug, a feather, a leaf, etc.).

Talk about what you found and why you find them interesting. Choose one of the times to draw and look at it closely. Draw what you see. Remember that the drawing doesn't need to be perfect. It can even be a quick sketch. Add a few words to describe what was drawn, where it was found, and why you and your child found it interesting. You can add the date to your page too.

MAKING STORY STONES

Story stones are smooth rocks decorated with images or words that inspire storytelling. They are easy to make, perfect for little hands, and wonderful tools for budding storytellers that can be used inside or outside to encourage connection and imagination.

MATERIALS:

- Smooth, flat stones (collected from nature or purchased at a craft store)
- Acrylic paint pens or paints (for drawing or painting images)
- Stickers, craft paper, fabric, printed images, or magazine cutouts (for gluing images)
- Decoupage medium for gluing and sealing (e.g. Mod Podge)
- Paintbrush

DIRECTIONS:

1. **Set up a workspace:** Cover a flat workspace with recycled newspaper or an art cloth to simplify cleanup and lay out your supplies.

2. **Pick a theme:** Choose a theme for your story stones inspired by the season, your child's interest, or favorite stories (e.g. winter animals, magical creatures, family outings). Explore nature, books, and online resources for inspiration.
3. **Option 1: Painted images**
    a. Use acrylic paint or pens to paint or draw images onto the flat surface of the stones.
    b. Allow the paint to fully dry before adding a layer of decoupage medium to seal the design.
4. **Option 2: Glued images**
    a. Cut out small images from paper, fabric, magazines, or stickers that fit the size of the stones.
    b. Glue the image to the flat surface and use a paintbrush to paint a layer of decoupage medium over the images and seal the stones.
5. **Dry and enjoy:** Let the stones dry completely before using them. Once dry, place them in a basket on your nature table or child's play area and let the storytelling begin.

Part Six

GOING FORTH

It Takes a Village of Families

It takes a village to raise nature-connected families.

"YOU SEEM DIFFERENT," my friend noted. "Brighter, I'd say."

I sent a beaming smile her way. "I *feel* different. Happier, calmer, more connected to nature," I replied.

It had been a year, almost exactly to the day, since I ran away from home, but it feels like ages ago. When I remember that cardinal moment, I can still feel the icy grip of the lake burning into my skin like a fire to a wick, setting me alight. That light was tremulous at first but with care and support it grew stronger, eventually bursting forth like a lighthouse.

My friend and I sat in silent comfort watching our children play along the shore of Okanagan Lake. I wondered how my story would have been different without her kindness over the last three years. We met right before the global pandemic. She was curious about homeschooling, and I was new to town. We connected immediately. Without her consistent efforts to get me outside, perhaps my tenuous thread of connection to nature might have snapped altogether. She was a lighthouse to me during a time of perpetual darkness. There were others too. My father, my sister, my husband . . . each one a supporting hand guiding me out the front door.

We aren't meant to journey along the pathways to nature connection alone, but to walk hand in hand with our children, extended family members, friends, elders, community members, educators, researchers, and more. In the words of Linda Åkeson McGurk, author of *There's No Such Thing as Bad Weather*, "It takes a village to raise an outdoor child." I wholeheartedly agree, but before we raise nature-connected children, we need to raise, to become, nature-connected parents, and *it takes a village to raise a nature-connected parent.*

Building Villages of Nature-Connected Parents

Parenting in the twenty-first century can be a lonely and isolating experience.[1] Even though we are hyperconnected through social media, texting, and emails, many of us parents feel disconnected and carry a deep longing for meaningful connections with others. I have felt this loneliness many times in my years as a parent. The crushing loneliness of being a new mother. The loneliness of moving to a rural community and then to a bustling city. The loneliness of being so overscheduled that I don't have time to foster friendship. Loneliness is *real*, expanding, and painful.

So, how do you move away from loneliness toward connection? How do we build villages of families connected with one another and nature? The short answer: We must begin at the beginning—going beyond the front door! We need to take that first step and seek out connection and offer it to others. Just how reconnecting with nature doesn't need to be grandiose commitments or epic adventures into the backcountry, building a village can happen through intentional moments of noticing, of kindness and openness close to home.

As you probably know, parents tend to stick close to home so great places to spot other parents in the wild include local playgrounds, nature trails, and community recreation areas. If you spot another parent with wildlings in tow, tuck your phone away and make a move, as in, be the first to make eye contact, smile, and say "Hi!" If you feel shy or awkward about making the first move, remember that most parents feel equally nervous. The world of making new parent friends can be as fraught as the world of dating! But a simple "Hello" and "How do you do?" can break the ice quickly, and so can a meaningful compliment about the other parent's child or something you noticed.

If looking for friendship at parks or along trails feels a little overwhelming, look for already established groups that welcome new members, such as groups that go on walks or hikes with young children, family nature clubs, or community family nature initiatives, events, and festivals. These are wonderful places to meet new people, and if these opportunities aren't in your community, then starting your own could be a great way to build community. For those of you that love the idea of building a village of families connected with nature, starting a Family Nature Club can be a wonderful way to bring families together.

HOW TO START A FAMILY NATURE CLUB

A Family Nature Club is a group of families that get outside on a regular basis to connect with nature together. The idea initially came from Richard Louv, author of *Last Child in the Woods: Saving Our Children from Nature-Deficit Disorder*: "What if parents, grandparents, and kids around the country were to band together to create nature clubs for families? What if this new form of social/nature networking were to spread as quickly as book clubs and Neighborhood Watches did in recent decades? We would be well on our way to true cultural change."[2]

A Family Nature Club is a great way to build a village, make new friends, share knowledge, get motivated, and stay active, and it can be as simple as gathering a few families to meet once or twice a month. Here are three simple steps for starting a Family Nature Club:

Dreaming and Planning

What kind of Family Nature Club do you dream of? There are no right or wrong answers. Your group might be a gathering for unstructured play in a nearby forest, exploring nearby trail systems, or celebrating seasons through nature-connected activities. Your group could be small, with just three or four families, or a large gathering and open to the public. It could meet once a week, twice a month, or once per season. Ultimately, dream of creating something that feels sustainable, inclusive, and exciting for your family and those you hope to connect with.

Here are some ideas for Family Nature Clubs organized by theme. You can mix and match these ideas based on the season, interest, or types of nearby nature that you have access to.

Ideas for Family Nature Club:

1. **Nature play and discovery:**
    - Free play in nearby nature
    - Leisurely strolls along nature trails
    - Storytime in nature (nature-themed stories)
    - Scavenger hunts
    - Nature crafts, art, or nature journaling
    - Seasonal celebrations (solstice and equinox gatherings, leaf walk, or pumpkin patch visit in the autumn)
    - Observing birds, insects, and animals (birding, pond dipping, searching for insects)
    - Stargazing, Full Moon Club, astronomy

2. **Sustainability and stewardship:**
    - Community gardening (vegetable, pollinator, seed exchanges)
    - Organic farming
    - Nature conservation projects (invasive species removal)
    - Wildcrafting or foraging (ethically and responsibly)

3. **Exploration and adventure:**
    - Hiking or backcountry adventures
    - Camping

- Rock climbing or bouldering
- Trail or mountain biking
- Skiing, snowshoeing, and other winter sports
- Swimming, canoeing, snorkeling, and other water sports
- Fishing and hunting
- Survival skills

Find a Location

After dreaming up your Family Nature Club, the next step is to find a location, or multiple, that would work for your gatherings. This could be a nearby nature trail, a park, or even a backyard. Scouting out a location is a great way to find the best location for your club. Here are some things to think about:

- How long does it take to get there?
- Is there enough parking space?
- What kind of features are there? (streams, rocks, viewpoints)
- Is the space large enough for your group?
- Do you need permission or a permit to use the space?
- Are there any facilities? (toilet, outhouse, potable water, shelter)
- What kind of gear and clothes are needed for the area?
- Are there safety considerations? (busy roads, deep or rushing water, cliffs, poison ivy)

Remember, nature is everywhere! There is no need to look far afield. Sometimes the best places to gather will be close to home; even a backyard can be a wonderful place to start. Also, don't be afraid to ask around. Sometimes there are hidden gems nearby.

Invite Families

You've got a plan and a location—well done! Now it's time to invite families to join your club. Start by reaching out to friends, extended family, friends from your child's school, church, or even a Facebook group. Be open to inviting families from diverse backgrounds.

If you want, collect emails from interested families and send them a write-up describing your Family Nature Club and all the necessary meeting details, or keep it casual and share the details by word of mouth.

In your invitation include:

- The purpose of the Family Nature Club (connecting with nature and one another!)
- Meeting frequency and location
- Example of planned activities
- Appropriate gear and clothing

Don't forget to remind parents that this is a family affair (not a drop-off situation!) and that parents are responsible for taking care of their own children. Also, remember that a Family Nature Club should be a welcome space for all on their journey toward great connection with nature and one another.

RADICAL HOPE FOR THE FUTURE

Throughout the process of writing this book, I often encountered the haunting phrase "there is no hope" spoken by academics, writers, and elders when it comes to the future of our planet and our children living on it. Hearing this hopeless statement both unsettled and saddened me. I won't deny that we are on a dangerous and challenging course. Yet, embedded within the pages of this book is a glowing kernel of *radical hope*—one that I wish to pass along to you.

The idea of radical hope, as described by philosopher Jonathan Lear, refers to a kind of hope that endures even in the face of great adversity and loss. Lear wrote about it in the context of the great cultural loss experienced by Indigenous and Native American communities, but I believe that we too can embrace this approach as we experience the great losses and upheavals facing our planet, our families, and our connection with nature.

In his book *Radical Hope: Ethics in the Face of Cultural Devastation*, Jonathan Lear wrote a prophetic line said by Søren Kierkegaard: "If there were a genuine knight of faith in our midst we would be unlikely to recognize him: in terms of outward appearance, he is just another one of our neighbors taking a stroll in the park."[3]

My friend, hold on to these words as you step beyond your front door, down the street, and through the neighborhood park with your child. In these simple acts of connection—with nature, with your family, and with your community—you become a genuine "*knight of faith*" as Lear quotes it. Not only are you nurturing the health and well-being of your loved ones, but you are planting seeds of radical hope for the future on our one precious blue planet.

Live wildly, friend, knowing that each small step outdoors together with your child has the power to transform the future for good.

ACKNOWLEDGMENTS

A book is rarely written alone, and while my names sits on the cover, many have impacted the words on its pages. To my Creator, who has given me this one wild and precious life and the tug on my heart to write this book. To my father, who wove stories into my childhood while showing me that nature is home. To my mother, for her caring heart and constant support. To my husband, for encouraging me and cheering me on. To my five children, for helping me rediscover the beauty of nature, one step at a time. To Shasta Grant from One Lit Place, for keeping me accountable for beginning and continuing this project. To my mentor at The Writing Studio, Claudia Cornwall, and the wonderful writers in my creative nonfiction writing group. To the researchers and academics who took the time to answer my many questions. To everyone at Morehouse Publishing, especially my wonderful editor, Fiona Hallowell, for pulling me out of the weeds many times over. And finally, to my literary agent, Joëlle Delbourgo, for championing my book!

ENDNOTES

Chapter 1: The Night I Slipped Away

1. "Parents Under Pressure: The U.S. Surgeon General's Advisory on the Mental Health & Well-Being of Parents," U.S. Public Health Service, 2024, https://www.hhs.gov/sites/default/files/parents-under-pressure.pdf.

2. "Burn-Out an 'Occupational Phenomenon': International Classification of Diseases," World Health Organization, May 28, 2019, https://www.who.int/news/item/28-05-2019-burn-out-an-occupational-phenomenon-international-classification-of-diseases.

3. Gordon Parker and Gabriela Tavella, "Burnout: A Case for Its Formal Inclusion in Classification Systems," *World Psychiatry* 21, no. 3 (2022): 467–68, https://doi.org/10.1002/wps.21025.

4. Isabelle Roskam et al., "Parental Burnout Around the Globe: A 42-Country Study," *Affective Science* 2, no. 1 (2021): 58–79, https://doi.org/10.1007/s42761-020-00028-4.

Chapter 2: Last Parent in the Woods

1. Robert Michael Pyle, *The Thunder Tree: Lessons from an Urban Wildland* (Houghton Mifflin, 1993).

2. Richard Louv, *The Nature Principle: Human Restoration and the End of Nature-Deficit Disorder* (Algonquin Books, 2011), 3.

3. "Munson Pond Park," City of Kelowna, accessed July 7, 2016, https://www.kelowna.ca/parks-recreation/parks-beaches/parks-beaches-listing/munson-pond-park.

4. Madison Reeve, "Turtles Being Removed from Natural Habitats in Kelowna," *Kelowna News*, April 23, 2021, https://www.castanet.net/news/Kelowna/331819/Turtles-being-removed-from-natural-habitats-in-Kelowna.

5. Linda Åkeson McGurk, *There's No Such Thing as Bad Weather: A Scandinavian Mom's Secrets for Raising Healthy, Resilient, and Confident Kids (from Friluftsliv to Hygge)* (Touchstone, 2018), 34–37.

6. "Urbanization | Population Division," United Nations, accessed June 29, 2023, https://www.un.org/development/desa/pd/content/urbanization-0.

7. Guangdong Li, et al., "Global Impacts of Future Urban Expansion on Terrestrial Vertebrate Diversity," *Nature Communications* 13, no. 1628 (2022), https://doi.org/10.1038/s41467-022-29324-2.

8. Jasmine Gustafsson et al., "Parental Mental Well-Being and Frequency of Adult-Child Nature Visits: The Mediating Roles of Parents' Perceived Barriers," *International Journal of Environmental Research and Public Health* 18, no. 13 (2021): 6814, https://doi.org/10.3390/ijerph18136814.

9. Miles Richardson, *Reconnection: Fixing Our Broken Relationship with Nature* (Pelagic, 2023), 33.

10. "Screen Time vs. Lean Time Infographic," Centers for Disease Control and Prevention, accessed January 23, 2019, https://www.cdc.gov/nccdphp/dnpao/multimedia/infographics/getmoving.html.

11. Masashi Soga et al., "The Vicious Cycle of Biophobia," *Trends in Ecology & Evolution* 38, no. 6 (2023): 512–20, https://doi.org/10.1016/j.tree.2022.12.012.

Chapter 3: Families and Nature Flourishing Together

1. Scott D. Sampson, *How to Raise a Wild Child: The Art and Science of Falling in Love with Nature* (Houghton Mifflin, 2016), 27.

2. Marika Schalla, "Metis Relationality of lii lway di la tayr Through the Teachings of Interconnectedness and Balance," *Pawaatamihk: Journal of Métis Thinkers* 1, no. 2 (2024): 171–74, https://doi.org/10.36939/pawaatamihk/vol1no2/art31 (Original work published June 21, 2024); Sandra Styres et al., "Towards a Pedagogy of Land: The Urban Context," *Canadian Journal of Education* 36, no. 2 (2013): 34–67, https://journals.sfu.ca/cje/index.php/cje-rce/article/view/1293.

3. Darius Kalvaitis and Rebecca Monhardt, "Children Voice Biophilia; the Phenomenology of Being in Love with Nature," *Journal of Sustainability Education* 9 (2015), https://www.susted.com/wordpress/content/children-voice-biophilia-the-phenomenology-of-being-in-love-with-nature_2015_03/.

4. Emma Marris, "Nature Is Everywhere—We Just Need to Learn to See It," TED Talk," TEDSummit, June 2016, 15 min., 42 sec., https://www.ted.com/talks/emma_marris_nature_is_everywhere_we_just_need_to_learn_to_see_it.

5. Chia-Chen Chang et al., "People's Desire to Be in Nature and How They Experience It Are Partially Heritable," *PLOS Biology* 20, no. 2 (2022): e3001500, https://doi.org/10.1371/journal.pbio.3001500.

6. Allana G. LeBlanc et al., "Correlates of Total Sedentary Time and Screen Time in 9–11 Year-Old Children Around the World: The International Study of Childhood Obesity, Lifestyle and the Environment," *PLOS One* 10, no. 6 (2015): e0129622, https://doi.org/10.1371/journal.pone.0129622.

7. Cheryl D. Fryar, Margaret D. Carroll, and Joseph Afful, "Prevalence of Overweight, Obesity, and Severe Obesity Among Children and Adolescents Aged 2–19 Years: United States, 1963–1965 Through 2017–2018," *NCHS Health E-Stats* (December 2020), https://www.cdc.gov/nchs/data/hestat/obesity-child-17-18/overweight-obesity-child-H.pdf.

8. "Obesity Statistics in Canada: Report," Public Health Agency of Canada, Government of Canada, modified June 5, 2025, https://www.canada.ca/en/public-health/services/publications/healthy-living/obesity-statistics-canada.html. Note: Canada reports only *measured* BMI for children/youth and notes it is awaiting nationally representative measured data collected since the COVID-19 pandemic.

9. U.S. Department of Health and Human Services, *Physical Activity Guidelines for Americans*, 2nd ed. (U.S.Department of Health and Human Services, 2018); "Canadian 24-Hour Movement Guidelines for the Children and Youth: An Integration of Physical Activity, Sedentary Behaviour, and Sleep," *Applied Physiology, Nutrition, and Metabolism* 41, no. 6 (June 2026): 311–27, https://csepguidelines.ca/guidelines/children-youth/.

10. Kylie A. Dankiw et al., "The Impacts of Unstructured Nature Play on Health in Early Childhood Development: A Systematic Review," *PLOS One* 15, no. 2 (2020): e0229006, https://doi.org/10.1371/journal.pone.0229006.

11. Casey Gray et al., "What Is the Relationship Between Outdoor Time and Physical Activity, Sedentary Behaviour, and Physical Fitness in Children? A Systematic Review," *International Journal of Environmental Research and Public Health* 12, no. 6 (2015): 6455–74, https://doi.org/10.3390/ijerph120606455.

12. Arja Sääkslahti and Donna Niemistö, "Outdoor Activities and Motor Development in 2–7-Year-Old Boys and Girls," *Journal of Physical Education and Sport* 21, no. 1 (2021): 463–68, https://doi.org/10.7752/jpes.2021.s1047.

13. Centers for Disease Control and Prevention, "Data and Statistics on Children's Mental Health," *Children's Mental Health*, updated June 5, 2025, https://www.cdc.gov/children-mental-health/data-research/index.html.

14. "Mental Health Initiatives," American Academy of Pediatrics, last updated April 14, 2025, https://www.aap.org/en/patient-care/mental-health-initiatives/.

15. "Child and Youth Mental Health," Canadian Paediatric Society, last updated June 5, 2024, https://cps.ca/en/child-and-youth-mental-health.

16. Suzanne Tillmann et al., "Mental Health Benefits of Interactions with Nature in Children and Teenagers: A Systematic Review," *Journal of Epidemiology & Community Health* 72, no. 10 (2018): 958–66, https://doi.org/10.1136/jech-2018-210436.

17. Tillmann et al., "Mental Health Benefits of Interactions with Nature in Children and Teenagers."

18. Mandi Wojciehowski and Julie Ernst, "Creative by Nature: Investigating the Impact of Nature Preschools on Young Children's Creative Thinking," *The International Journal of Early Childhood Environmental Education* 6, no. 1 (2018): 3–20, https://files.eric.ed.gov/fulltext/EJ1193490.pdf.

19. Christine Kiewra and Ellen Veselack, "Playing with Nature: Supporting Preschoolers' Creativity in Natural Outdoor Classrooms," *The International Journal of Early Childhood Environmental Education* 4, no. 1 (2016), 71.

20. Mariana Brussoni et al., "Landscapes for Play: Effects of an Intervention to Promote Nature-Based Risky Play in Early Childhood Centres," *Journal of Environmental Psychology* 54, no. 1 (2017): 139–50, https://doi.org/10.1016/j.jenvp.2017.11.001.

21. Colin A. Capaldi et al., "The Relationship Between Nature Connectedness and Happiness: A Meta-Analysis," *Frontiers in Psychology* 5 (2014): 976, https://doi.org/10.3389/fpsyg.2014.00976; Leanne Martin et al., "Nature Contact, Nature Connectedness and Associations with Health, Wellbeing and Pro-Environmental Behaviours," *Journal of Environmental Psychology* 68 (2020): 101389, https://doi.org/10.1016/j.jenvp.2020.101389; Alison Pritchard et al., "The Relationship Between Nature Connectedness and Eudaimonic Well-Being: A Meta-Analysis," *Journal of Happiness Studies* 21, (2020): 1145–67, https://doi.org/10.1007/s10902-019-00118-6.

22. Jickling Bob et al., *Wild Pedagogies: Touchstones for Re-Negotiating Education and the Environment in the Anthropocene* (Palgrave Macmillan, 2018).

23. Thea Cameron-Faulkner et al., "Responding to Nature: Natural Environments Improve Parent-Child Communication," *Journal of Environmental Psychology* 59 (2018): 9–15, https://doi.org/10.1016/j.jenvp.2018.08.008.

24. Dina Izenstark and Aaron T. Ebata, "Why Families Go Outside: An Exploration of Mothers' and Daughters' Family-Based Nature Activities," *Leisure Sciences* 44, no. 5 (2022): 559–77, https://doi.org/10.1080/01490400.2019.1625293.

25. Jillisa R. Overholt, "Role Shifts and Equalizing Experiences Through Father-Child Outdoor Adventure Programs," *Leisure Sciences* 44, no. 5 (2022): 614–33, https://doi.org/10.1080/01490400.2019.1627966.

26. Jeffrey L. Marion and Scott E. Reid, "Development of the U.S. Leave No Trace Program: An Historical Perspective," Leave No Trace, Inc., January 2001, https://lnt.org/sites/default/files/Leave_No_Trace_History_Paper.pdf.

27. David N. Cole, "Leave No Trace: How It Came to Be," *International Journal of Wilderness* 24, no. 3, (2018), https://ijw.org/leave-no-trace-how-it-came-to-be/.

28. "The 7 Principles," Leave No Trace, accessed January 27, 2025, https://lnt.org/why/7-principles/.

29. Ryan Lumber, in discussion with the author via Zoom, 2024.

30. Chris Loynes, "Leave More Trace," *Journal of Outdoor Recreation, Education, and Leadership* 10, no. 3 (2018), https://doi.org/10.18666/JOREL-2018-V10-I3-8444.

31. Loynes, "Leave More Trace."

32. Ryan Lumber, in discussion with the author via Zoom, 2024.

33. Julie Whitburn et al., "Meta-Analysis of Human Connection to Nature and Proenvironmental Behavior," *Conservation Biology* 34, no. 1 (2020): 180–93, https://doi.org/10.1111/cobi.13381; Caroline M. L. Mackay and Michael T. Schmitt, "Do People Who Feel Connected to Nature Do More to Protect It? A Meta-Analysis," *Journal of Environmental Psychology* 65 (2019): 101323, https://doi.org/10.1016/j.jenvp.2019.101323.

Chapter 4: The Five Pathways to Reconnecting with Nature

1. Miles Richardson and Carly W. Butler, "The Nature Connection Handbook: A Guide for Increasing People's Connection with Nature," 2022, https://findingnatureblog.wordpress.com/wp-content/uploads/2022/04/the-nature-connection-handbook.pdf.

2. Ryan Lumber et al., "Nature Connections 2016 Conference Report: Implications for Research and Practice," University of Derby, March 2016, https://www.natureconnected.org/wp-content/uploads/2016/01/NCx2016-Report.pdf.

3. Alison Pritchard et al., "The Relationship Between Nature Connectedness and Eudaimonic Well-Being: A Meta-Analysis," *Journal of Happiness Studies* 21 (2020): 1145–67, https://doi.org/10.1007/s10902-019-00118-6; Julie Whitburn et al., "Meta-Analysis of Human Connection to Nature and Proenvironmental Behavior," *Conservation Biology* 34, no. 1 (2020): 180–93, https://doi.org/10.1111/cobi.13381; Caroline M. L. Mackay and Michael T. Schmitt, "Do People Who Feel Connected to Nature Do More to Protect It? A Meta-Analysis," *Journal of Environmental Psychology* 65 (2019): 101323, https://doi.org/10.1016/j.jenvp.2019.101323.

4. Ryan Lumber et al., "Beyond Knowing Nature: Contact, Emotion, Compassion, Meaning, and Beauty Are Pathways to Nature Connection," *PLOS One* 12, no. 5 (2017): e0177186, https://doi.org/10.1371/journal.pone.0177186.

5. Lumber et al., "Beyond Knowing Nature."

6. Ryan Lumber, Nottingham Trent University, accessed February 10, 2025, https://www.ntu.ac.uk/staff-profiles/social-sciences/ryan-lumber.

7. Ryan Lumber, in discussion with the author via Zoom, 2024.

8. Lumber et al., "Beyond Knowing Nature."

9. Matthew T. Ballew and Allen M. Omoto, "Absorption: How Nature Experiences Promote Awe and Other Positive Emotions," *Ecopsychology* 10, no. 1 (2018): 26–35, https://doi.org/10.1089/eco.2017.0044.

10. Miles Richardson and David Sheffield, "Three Good Things in Nature: Noticing Nearby Nature Brings Sustained Increases in Connection with Nature," *PsyEcology*, January 12, 2017, https://repository.derby.ac.uk/item/9457v/three-good-things-in-nature-noticing-nearby-nature-brings-sustained-increases-in-connection-with-nature.

11. Holli-Anne Passmore et al., "Parental/Guardians' Connection to Nature Better Predicts Children's Nature Connectedness Than Visits or Area-Level Characteristics," *Ecopsychology* 13, no. 2 (2021): 103–13, https://doi.org/10.1089/eco.2020.0033.

12. Xiaoyan Chen et al., "Parental Nature Orientation and Children's Interpersonal Relationships and Behavioral Problems: The Mediating Role of Children's Nature Connectedness," *Current Psychology* 43 (2024): 13598–607, https://doi.org/10.1007/s12144-023-05316-3.

13. Alexia Barrable and David Booth, "Nature Connection in Early Childhood: A Quantitative Cross-Sectional Study," *Sustainability* 12, no. 1 (2020): 375, https://doi.org/10.3390/su12010375.

Chapter 5: Welcoming Springtime

1. Stephen Tomkins and Sue Dale Tunnicliffe, "Nature Tables: Stimulating Children's Interest in Natural Objects," *Journal of Biological Education* 41, no. 4 (2007): 150–55, https://doi.org/10.1080/00219266.2007.9656090.

2. Tomkins and Tunnicliffe, "Nature Tables."

3. "Shell Eggs from Farm to Table," Food Safety and Inspection Service, U.S. Department of Agriculture, accessed September 13, 2024, http://www.fsis.usda.gov/food-safety/safe-food-handling-and-preparation/eggs/shell-eggs-farm-tale.

Chapter 6: Raising a Nature-Connected Baby

1. Marjo Tourula et al., "Children Sleeping Outdoors in Winter: Parents' Experiences of a Culturally Bound Childcare Practice," *International Journal of Circumpolar Health* 67, no. 2–3 (2008): 269–78, https://doi.org/10.3402/ijch.v67i2-3.18284.

2. "Impacts on Newborns," State of Global Air, accessed September 19, 2024, https://www.stateofglobalair.org/health/newborns.

3. "Vitamin D Supplementation in Infants," World Health Organization, last updated August 9, 2023, https://www.who.int/tools/elena/interventions/vitamind-infants.

4. José Luis Mansur et al., "Vitamin D: Before, During and After Pregnancy: Effect on Neonates and Children," *Nutrients* 14, no. 9 (2022): 1900, https://doi.org/10.3390/nu14091900.

5. Tourula et al., "Children Sleeping Outdoors in Winter"; "Neonatal Mortality," UNICEF Data, last updated March 2025, https://data.unicef.org/topic/child-survival/neonatal-mortality/.

6. Marjo Tourula et al., "Infants Sleeping Outdoors in a Northern Winter Climate: Skin Temperature and Duration of Sleep," *Acta Paediatrica* 99, no. 9 (2010): 1411–17, https://doi.org/10.1111/j.1651-2227.2010.01814.x.

7. Tourula et al., "Children Sleeping Outdoors in Winter."

8. Tourula et al., "Children Sleeping Outdoors in Winter."

9. Ellen Hall et al., "What Can We Learn Through Careful Observation of Infants and Toddlers in Nature?" *Children, Youth and Environments* 24, no. 2 (2014): 192–214, https://doi.org/10.7721/chilyoutenvi.24.2.0192.

10. Nicola Kemp and Jo Josephidou, "Babies and Toddlers Outdoors: A Narrative Review of the Literature on Provision for Under Twos in ECEC Settings," *Early Years* 43, no. 1 (2023): 137–50, https://doi.org/10.1080/09575146.2021.1915962.

11. Ann E. Bigelow and Lela Rankin Williams, "To Have and to Hold: Effects of Physical Contact on Infants and Their Caregivers," *Infant Behavior and Development* 61 (2020): 101494, https://doi.org/10.1016/j.infbeh.2020.101494.

Chapter 7: Discovering Dirt Isn't *Dirty*

1. B. Brett Finlay and Marie-Claire Arrieta, *Let Them Eat Dirt: Saving Our Children from an Oversanitized World* (Greystone Books, 2016), 135.

2. Finlay and Arrieta, *Let Them Eat Dirt*, 130–143.

3. Jan White and Liz Edwards, *Making a Mud Kitchen: Opening up the Wonderful World of Mud Play* (Opening Up the Outdoors, 2012), https://muddyfaces.co.uk/content/files/Making_a_mud_kitchen_LowResAW.pdf.

Chapter 8: Rewilding Playtime

1. Øyvind Kvalnes and Ellen Beate Hansen Sandseter, *Risky Play: An Ethical Challenge* (Springer International, 2023), 13–29.

2. G.A. Res. 44/25, Convention on the Rights of the Child, art. 31 (Nov. 20, 1989), https://www.ohchr.org/en/instruments-mechanisms/instruments/convention-rights-child.

3. Peter Gray, "#5. Play Is How Children Practice All Essential Human Skills," *Play Makes Us Human* (Substack), May 16, 2023, https://petergray.substack.com/p/5-play-is-how-children-practice-all?utm_medium=reader2.

4. Gray, "#5. Play Is How Children Practice All Essential Human Skills"; Kenneth R. Ginsburg et al., "The Importance of Play in Promoting Healthy Child Development and Maintaining Strong Parent-Child Bonds," *Pediatrics* 119, no. 1 (2007): 182–91, https://doi.org/10.1542/peds.2006-2697.

5. Peter Gray, "#2. What Exactly Is Play?" Substack newsletter, *Play Makes Us Human* (Substack), April 25, 2023, https://petergray.substack.com/p/2-what-exactly-is-this-thing-we-call.

6. Asiye İvrendi et al., "Children, Mothers, and Preschool Teachers' Perceptions of Play: Findings from Turkey and Norway," *Erken Çocukluk Çalışmaları Dergisi* 3, no. 1 (2019): 32–54, https://doi.org/10.24130/eccd-jecs.1967201931119.

7. Julie Ernst and Firdevs Burcak, "Young Children's Contributions to Sustainability: The Influence of Nature Play on Curiosity, Executive Function Skills, Creative Thinking, and Resilience," *Sustainability* 11, no. 15 (2019): 4212, https://doi.org/10.3390/su11154212.

8. Kylie A. Dankiw et al., "The Impacts of Unstructured Nature Play on Health in Early Childhood Development: A Systematic Review," *PLOS One* 15, no. 2 (2020): e0229006, https://doi.org/10.1371/journal.pone.0229006.

9. Mariana Brussoni et al., "What Is the Relationship Between Risky Outdoor Play and Health in Children? A Systematic Review," *International Journal of Environmental Research and Public Health* 12, no. 6 (2015): 6423–54, https://doi.org/10.3390/ijerph120606423.

10. Ellen Beate Hansen Sandseter and Leif Edward Ottesen Kennair, "Children's Risky Play from an Evolutionary Perspective: The Anti-Phobic Effects of Thrilling Experiences," *Evolutionary Psychology* 9, no. 2 (2011): 257–84, https://doi.org/10.1177/147470491100900212.

11. Mariana Brussoni et al., "Risky Play and Children's Safety: Balancing Priorities for Optimal Child Development," *International Journal of Environmental Research and Public Health* 9, no. 9 (2012): 3134–48, https://doi.org/10.3390/ijerph9093134.

12. Kumara Ward, "What's in a Dream? Natural Elements, Risk and Loose Parts in Children's Dream Playspace Drawings," *Australasian Journal of Early Childhood* 43, no. 1 (2018): 34–42, https://doi.org/10.23965/AJEC.43.1.04.

13. Natalie E. Houser et al., "Let the Children Play: Scoping Review on the Implementation and Use of Loose Parts for Promoting Physical Activity Participation," *AIMS Public Health* 3, no. 4 (2016): 781–99, https://doi.org/10.3934/publichealth.2016.4.781.

Chapter 9: Picking Pockets Full of Posies

1. Qian, Hong, Jian Zhang, and Jingchao Zhao, "How Many Known Vascular Plant Species Are There in the World? An Integration of Multiple Global Plant Databases," *Biodiversity Science* 30, no. 7 (2022): 22254, https://doi.org/10.17520/biods.2022254; Eimear Nic Lughadha et al., "Counting Counts: Revised Estimates of Numbers of Accepted Species of Flowering Plants, Seed Plants, Vascular Plants and Land Plants with a Review of Other Recent Estimates," *Phytotaxa* 272, no. 1 (2016):

82–88, https://doi.org/10.11646/phytotaxa.272.1.5; Brian J. Enquist et al., "The Commonness of Rarity: Global and Future Distribution of Rarity across Land Plants," *Science Advances* 5, no. 11 (2019): eaaz0414, doi:10.1126/sciadv.aaz0414.

2. Jeannette Haviland-Jones et al., "An Environmental Approach to Positive Emotion: Flowers," *Evolutionary Psychology* 3, no. 1 (2005): 104–32, https://doi.org/10.1177/147470490500300109.

3. Ryan Lumber, in discussion with the author via Zoom, 2024.

4. Chris Loynes, "Leave More Trace," *Journal of Outdoor Recreation, Education, and Leadership* 10, no. 3 (2018), https://doi.org/10.18666/JOREL-2018-V10-I3-8444.

Chapter 10: Celebrating Summertime

1. "June Solstice in 2026: All You Need to Know," June 21, 2026, https://earthsky.org/astronomy-essentials/everything-you-need-to-know-june-solstice/.

2. "Significance of Stonehenge," English Heritage, accessed October 10, 2024, https://www.english-heritage.org.uk/visit/places/stonehenge/history-and-stories/history/significance/.

3. "Significance of Stonehenge," English Heritage, accessed October 10, 2024, https://www.english-heritage.org.uk/visit/places/stonehenge/history-and-stories/history/significance/.

4. Fred Chapman, "Medicine Wheel/Medicine Mountain: Celebrated and Controversial Landmark," WyoHistory.Org, accessed October 15, 2024, https://www.wyohistory.org/encyclopedia/medicine-wheel; "Bighorn Medicine Wheel," Stanford SOLAR Center, accessed October 15, 2024, https://solar-center.stanford.edu/AO/bighorn.html.

5. Britannica, "11 Egyptian Gods and Goddesses," accessed October 11, 2024, https://www.britannica.com/list/11-egyptian-gods-and-goddesses.

6. "Helios," GreekMythology.com, accessed August 25, 2023, https://www.greekmythology.com/Other_Gods/Helios/helios.html.

7. Britannica, "Huitzilopochtli," accessed August 25, 2023, https://www.britannica.com/topic/Huitzilopochtli.

8. Britannica, "Amaterasu," accessed October 11, 2024, https://www.britannica.com/topic/Amaterasu.

9. "Finding Meaning in the Cosmos," eCUIP: The Digital Library—Science: Cultural Astronomy, accessed August 17, 2025, https://ecuip.lib.uchicago.edu/diglib/science/cultural_astronomy/cultures_inuit-4.html.

10. "Our Sun: Facts," NASA, accessed August 23, 2023, https://solarsystem.nasa.gov/solar-system/sun/in-depth.

11. "Our Sun: Facts."

12. Ankur K. Jindal et al., "Sun Exposure in Children: Balancing the Benefits and Harms," *Indian Dermatology Online Journal* 11, no. 1 (2020): 94–98, https://doi.org/10.4103/idoj.IDOJ_206_19.

13. Sophie J. Balk and the Council on Environmental Health and Section on Dermatology, "Ultraviolet Radiation: A Hazard to Children and Adolescents," *Pediatrics* 127, no. 3 (2011): e791–e817, https://doi.org/10.1542/peds.2010-3502.

14. Anna C. Wood et al., "What Parents Should Know About Sun and Sunburns in Children," *JAMA Pediatrics* 177, no. 5 (2023): 547, https://doi.org/10.1001/jamapediatrics.2022.5907.

15. "A Guide to the UV Index," United States Environmental Protection Agency, May 2004, https://www.epa.gov/sites/default/files/documents/uviguide.pdf.

16. Britannica, "Gnomon," accessed October 1, 2024, https://www.britannica.com/technology/gnomon-timekeeping-device.

Chapter 11: Finding a Favorite Tree

1. Bing Yang Tan, "Save a Tree and Save a Life: Estimating the Health Benefits of Urban Forests," *Environmental and Resource Economics* 82, no. 3 (2022): 657–80, https://doi.org/10.1007/s10640-022-00677-y.

2. Michelle C. Kondo et al., "The Association Between Urban Tree Cover and Gun Assault: A Case-Control and Case-Crossover Study," *American Journal of Epidemiology* 186, no. 3 (2017): 289–96, https://doi.org/10.1093/aje/kwx096.

3. Ingrid Jarvis et al., "The Influence of Early-Life Residential Exposure to Different Vegetation Types and Paved Surfaces on Early Childhood Development: A Population-Based Birth Cohort Study," *Environment International* 163 (2022): 107196, https://doi.org/10.1016/j.envint.2022.107196.

4. Sivajanani Sivarajah et al., "Tree Cover and Species Composition Effects on Academic Performance of Primary School Students," *PLOS One* 13, no. 2 (2018): e0193254, https://doi.org/10.1371/journal.pone.0193254.

5. Ming Kuo et al., "Might School Performance Grow on Trees? Examining the Link Between 'Greenness' and Academic Achievement in Urban, High-Poverty Schools," *Frontiers in Psychology* 9 (2018), https://doi.org/10.3389/fpsyg.2018.01669.

6. Eli Paddle and Jason Gilliland, "Orange Is the New Green: Exploring the Restorative Capacity of Seasonal Foliage in Schoolyard Trees," *International Journal of Environmental Research and Public Health* 13, no. 5 (2016): 497, https://doi.org/10.3390/ijerph13050497.

7. Chris Robinson and Duncan Leatherdale, "Sycamore Gap Tree: The Story So Far," BBC, July 16, 2025, https://www.bbc.com/news/uk-england-tyne-66994729.

8. "Sycamore Gap Tree: The Story So Far."

9. Toby Saunders, "The Oldest Trees in World (Top 6, Ranked)," *BBC Science Focus*, July 26, 2023, https://www.sciencefocus.com/nature/oldest-tree-in-world.

10. Taina Laaksoharju and Erja Rappe, "Trees as Affordances for Connectedness to Place—A Framework to Facilitate Children's Relationship with Nature," *Urban Forestry & Urban Greening* 28 (2017): 150–59, https://doi.org/10.1016/j.ufug.2017.10.004.

11. Kaisa Vainio et al., "Do You Have a Tree Friend?—Human–Tree Relationships in Finland," *People and Nature* 6, no. 2 (2024): 646–59, https://doi.org/10.1002/pan3.10593.

12. Vainio et al., "Do You Have a Tree Friend?"

Chapter 12: Delighting in Water Play

1. Carol M. Gross, "Science Concepts Young Children Learn Through Water Play," *Dimensions of Early Childhood* 40, no. 2 (2012), https://www.hookedonscience.org/files/Science_Concepts_Young_Children_Learn_Through_Water_Play_Carol_M_Gross.pdf.

2. World Health Organization, "Global Status Report on Drowning Prevention 2024," 2024, https://iris.who.int/handle/10665/379812.

3. David R. Meddings et al., "Drowning Prevention: Turning the Tide on a Leading Killer," *The Lancet Public Health* 6, no. 9 (2021): e692, https://doi.org/10.1016/S2468-2667(21)00165-1.

Chapter 13: Turning Bug Fear into Curiosity

1. Helena Staňková et al., "The Ultimate List of the Most Frightening and Disgusting Animals: Negative Emotions Elicited by Animals in Central European Respondents," *Animals* 11, no. 3 (2021): 747, https://doi.org/10.3390/ani11030747.

2. Yuya Fukano and Masashi Soga, "Evolutionary Psychology of Entomophobia and Its Implications for Insect Conservation," *Current Opinion in Insect Science* 59 (2023): 101100, https://doi.org/10.1016/j.cois.2023.101100; Jeroen P van der Sluijs, "Insect Decline, an Emerging Global Environmental Risk," *Current Opinion in Environmental Sustainability* 46 (2020): 39–42, https://doi.org/10.1016/j.cosust.2020.08.012.

3. Nigel E. Stork, "How Many Species of Insects and Other Terrestrial Arthropods Are There on Earth?," *Annual Review of Entomology* 63 (2018): 31–45, https://doi.org/10.1146/annurev-ento-020117-043348.

4. Richard Jones, "Bugs vs Insects: What's the Difference?" Discover Wildlife, July 4, 2023, https://www.discoverwildlife.com/animal-facts/insects-invertebrates/bugs-vs-insects-whats-the-difference.

5. "Vector-Borne Diseases," World Health Organization, September 26, 2024, https://www.who.int/news-room/fact-sheets/detail/vector-borne-diseases.

6. Michael J. Samways et al., "Solutions for Humanity on How to Conserve Insects," *Biological Conservation* 242 (2020): 108427, https://doi.org/10.1016/j.biocon.2020.108427.

7. Pedro Cardoso et al., "Scientists' Warning to Humanity on Insect Extinctions," *Biological Conservation* 242 (2020): 108426, https://doi.org/10.1016/j.biocon.2020.108426.

8. "Vector-Borne Diseases."

9. A. Ludwig et al., "Increased Risk of Endemic Mosquito-Borne Diseases in Canada Due to Climate Change," *Canada Communicable Disease Report* 45, no. 4 (2019): 90–97, https://doi.org/10.14745/ccdr.v45i04a03.

10. "Creation of Nesting Possibilities -1-: Nesting Aids for Colonizers Existing Cavities -A-," accessed October 29, 2024, https://www.wildbienen.info/artenschutz/nisthilfen_02a.php.

11. Jo-Lynn Teh, "Insect Hotels: A Refuge or a Fad?," *The Entomologist Lounge* (blog), September 18, 2017, https://entomologistlounge.wordpress.com/2017/09/18/insect-hotels-a-refuge-or-a-fad/.

Chapter 14: Navigating the Teenage Dip in Nature Connection

1. Eluned Price et al., "Factors Associated with Nature Connectedness in School-Aged Children," *Current Research in Ecological and Social Psychology* 3 (2022): 100037 https://doi.org/10.1016/j.cresp.2022.100037.

2. Miles Richardson et al., "A Measure of Nature Connectedness for Children and Adults: Validation, Performance, and Insights," *Sustainability* 11, no. 12 (2019): 3250, https://doi.org/10.3390/su11123250.

3. Carmen Viejo et al., "Adolescents' Psychological Well-Being: A Multidimensional Measure," *International Journal of Environmental Research and Public Health* 15, no. 10 (2018): 2325, https://doi.org/10.3390/ijerph15102325.

4. Author interview with Sean Blenkinsop, March 23, 2024.

5. Price et al., "Nature Connectedness in School-Aged Children."

6. Jo Birch et al., "Nature Doesn't Judge You—How Urban Nature Supports Young People's Mental Health and Wellbeing in a Diverse UK City," *Health & Place* 62 (2020): 102296, https://doi.org/10.1016/j.healthplace.2020.102296.

7. "Mental Health Disorders in Adolescents," ACOG, July 2017, https://www.acog.org/clinical/clinical-guidance/committee-opinion/articles/2017/07/mental-health-disorders-in-adolescents.

8. Caroline Piccininni et al., "Outdoor Play and Nature Connectedness as Potential Correlates of Internalized Mental Health Symptoms Among Canadian Adolescents," *Preventive Medicine* 112 (2018): 168–75, https://doi.org/10.1016/j.ypmed.2018.04.020.

9. Terhi Arola, "The Impacts of Nature Connectedness on Children's Well-Being: Systematic Literature Review," *Journal of Environmental Psychology* 85 (2023): 101913, https://doi.org/10.1016/j.jenvp.2022.101913.

10. Andrew Balmford et al., "Why Conservationists Should Heed Pokémon," *Science* 295, no. 5564 (2002): 2367, https://doi.org/10.1126/science.295.5564.2367b.

11. Ryan Lumber et al., "Beyond Knowing Nature: Contact, Emotion, Compassion, Meaning, and Beauty Are Pathways to Nature Connection," *PLOS One* 12, no. 5 (2017): e0177186, https://doi.org/10.1371/journal.pone.0177186.

12. Lumber et al., "Beyond Knowing Nature."

13. To read more about David Sobel's work, see https://www.davidsobelauthor.com.

14. Anna Botsford Comstock, *Handbook of Nature-Study for Teachers and Parents* (Comstock Publishing, 1911), 1.

15. Sabine Pirchio et al., "The Effects of Contact with Nature During Outdoor Environmental Education on Students' Wellbeing, Connectedness to Nature and Pro-Sociality," *Frontiers in Psychology* 12 (2021), https://doi.org/10.3389/fpsyg.2021.648458.

16. Andy Ruck and Greg Mannion, "Stewardship and Beyond? Young People's Lived Experience of Conservation Activities in School Grounds," *Environmental Education Research* 27, no. 10 (2021): 1502–16, https://doi.org/10.1080/13504622.2021.1964439.

17. Edmond P. Bowers, et al., "Urban Youth Perspectives on the Benefits and Challenges of Outdoor Adventure Camp," *Journal of Youth Development* 14, no. 4 (2019): 122–43, https://doi.org/10.5195/jyd.2019.809.

18. Miles Richardson et al., "Moments, Not Minutes: The Nature-Wellbeing Relationship," *International Journal of Wellbeing* 11, no. 1 (2021): 8–33, https://doi.org/10.5502/ijw.v11i1.1267.

Chapter 15: Honoring Autumnal Days

1. Britannica, "Michaelmas," accessed October 25, 2024, https://www.britannica.com/topic/Michaelmas.

2. Britannica, "Squash," accessed October 17, 2024, https://www.britannica.com/plant/squash.

Chapter 16: Back to School, Back to Nature

1. Jingjing Wang, et al., "Time Outdoors Positively Associates with Academic Performance: A School-Based Study with Objective Monitoring of Outdoor Time," *BMC Public Health* 23, no. 1 (2023): 645, https://doi.org/10.1186/s12889-023-15532-y.

2. Hannah R. Thompson and Rebecca A. London, "Not All Fun and Games: Disparities in School Recess Persist, and Must Be Addressed," *Preventive Medicine Reports* 35 (2023): 102301, https://doi.org/10.1016/j.pmedr.2023.102301.

3. Henna L. Haapala, et al., "Recess Physical Activity and School-Related Social Factors in Finnish Primary and Lower Secondary Schools: Cross-Sectional Associations," *BMC Public Health* 14 (2014): 1114, https://doi.org/10.1186/1471-2458-14-1114.

4. Rong Chang et al., "More Recess Time, Please!" *Phi Delta Kappan* 97, no. 3 (2015): 14–17, https://doi.org/10.1177/0031721715614822.

5. Amie K. Patchen et al., "Barriers to Children's Outdoor Time: Teachers' and Principals' Experiences in Elementary Schools," *Environmental Education Research* 30, no. 1 (2024): 16–36, https://doi.org/10.1080/13504622.2022.2099530.

6. Patchen et al., "Barriers to Children's Outdoor Time."

7. Council on School Health et al., "The Crucial Role of Recess in School," *Pediatrics* 131, no. 1 (2013): 183–88, https://doi.org/10.1542/peds.2012-2993.

8. Sandra L. Hofferth, "Changes in American Children's Time—1997 to 2003," *Electronic International Journal of Time Use Research* 6, no. 1 (2009): 26–47, https://www.ncbi.nlm.nih.gov/pmc/articles/PMC2939468; John F. Sandberg and Sandra L. Hofferth, "Changes in Children's Time with Parents: United States, 1981–1997," *Demography* 38, no. 3 (2001): 423–36, https://doi.org/10.1353/dem.2001.0031.

9. Hofferth, "Changes in American Children's Time—1997 to 2003."

10. Lincoln R. Larson et al., "Children's Time Outdoors: Results and Implications of the National Kids Survey," *Journal of Park and Recreation* Administration 29, no. 2 (2011): 1–20, https://www.researchgate.net/publication/258272055_Children's_time_outdoors_Results_and_implications_of_the_National_Kids_Survey.

11. Kelly L. Dahl et al., "Time Playing Outdoors Among Children Aged 3–5 Years: National Survey of Children's Health, 2021," *American Journal of Preventive Medicine* 66, no. 6 (2024): 1024–34, https://doi.org/10.1016/j.amepre.2023.12.011.

12. Ginny Yurich, "Children Should Be Outside for 4–6 Hours Every Day," 1000 Hours Outside, accessed November 27, 2024, https://www.1000hoursoutside.com/blog/children-should-be-outside-for-4-6-hours-everyday.

13. Angela J. Hanscom, *Balanced and Barefoot: How Unrestricted Outdoor Play Makes for Strong, Confident, and Capable Children* (New Harbinger Publications, 2016).

14. Charlotte Mason, *Home Education: Volume I of Charlotte Mason's Original Homeschooling Series* (Wilder Publications, 2008).

15. Shuyu Xiong et al., "Time Spent in Outdoor Activities in Relation to Myopia Prevention and Control: A Meta-Analysis and Systematic Review," *Acta Ophthalmologica* 95, no. 6 (2017): 551–66, https://doi.org/10.1111/aos.13403.

16. Casey Gray et al., "What Is the Relationship between Outdoor Time and Physical Activity, Sedentary Behaviour, and Physical Fitness in Children? A Systematic Review," *International Journal of Environmental Research and Public Health* 12, no. 6 (2015): 6455–74, https://doi.org/10.3390/ijerph120606455.

17. Amber L. Fyfe-Johnson et al., "Nature and Children's Health: A Systematic Review," *Pediatrics* 148, no. 4 (2021): e2020049155, https://doi.org/10.1542/peds.2020-049155.

18. "Home Oral Care," ADA, accessed November 26, 2024, https://www.ada.org/resources/ada-library/oral-health-topics/home-care.

19. "About Handwashing," U.S. Centers for Disease Control and Prevention, February 16, 2024, https://www.cdc.gov/clean-hands/about/index.html.

20. Miles Richardson et al., "Moments, Not Minutes: The Nature-Wellbeing Relationship," *International Journal of Wellbeing* 11, no. 1 (2021): 8–33, https://doi.org/10.5502/ijw.v11i1.1267.

21. Miles Richardson and David Sheffield, "Three Good Things in Nature: Noticing Nearby Nature Brings Sustained Increases in Connection with Nature," *PsyEcology*, January 12, 2017, https://repository.derby.ac.uk/item/9457v/three-good-things-in-nature-noticing-nearby-nature-brings-sustained-increases-in-connection-with-nature.

22. Rosaline Keenan et al., "Three Good Things in Nature: A Nature-Based Positive Psychological Intervention to Improve Mood and Well-Being for Depression and Anxiety," *Journal of Public Mental Health* 20, no. 4 (2021): 243–50, https://doi.org/10.1108/jpmh-02-2021-0029.

23. Holli-Anne Passmore, "Noticing Nature: Individual and Social Benefits of a Two-Week Intervention," *The Journal of Positive Psychology* 12, no. 6 (2016): 537–46, https://www.tandfonline.com/doi/full/10.1080/17439760.2016.1221126; Holli-Anne Passmore et al., "Wellbeing in Winter: Testing the Noticing Nature Intervention During Winter Months," *Frontiers in Psychology* 13 (2022), https://doi.org/10.3389/fpsyg.2022.840273.

24. Nancy J. Cohen et al., "Watch, Wait, and Wonder: An Infant-Led Approach to Infant-Parent Psychotherapy," *Signal* 14, no. 35 (2006), https://www.researchgate.net/publication/237306205_WATCH_WAIT_AND_WONDER_An_Infant-led_Approach_to_Infant-parent_Psychotherapy.

25. Cohen et al., "Watch, Wait, and Wonder."

26. Boris Cheval et al., "Avoiding Sedentary Behaviors Requires More Cortical Resources than Avoiding Physical Activity: An EEG Study," *Neuropsychologia* 119 (2018): 68–80, https://doi.org/10.1016/j.neuropsychologia.2018.07.029.

27. Sean Simpson, "Nine in Ten (87%) Canadians Say They're Happier When They Spend Time in Nature," Ipsos, September 27, 2018, https://www.ipsos.com/en-ca/news-polls/Canadians-happier-in-nature.

28. Benjamin Gardner et al., "Making Health Habitual: The Psychology of 'Habit-Formation' and General Practice," *British Journal of General Practice* 62, no. 605 (2012): 664–66, https://doi.org/10.3399/bjgp12X659466.

Chapter 17: Birding Brings Happiness to Families

1. George F. Barrowclough et al., "How Many Kinds of Birds Are There and Why Does It Matter?" *PLOS One* 11, no. 11 (2016): e0166307, https://doi.org/10.1371/journal.pone.0166307.

2. H. Ken Cordell and Nancy G. Herbert, "The Popularity of Birding Is Still Growing," *Birding* (2002): 54–61, https://www.srs.fs.usda.gov/pubs/ja/ja_cordell002.pdf.

3. "U.S. Fish & Wildlife Service, Birding in the United States: A Demographic and Economic Analysis. Addendum to the 2022 National Survey of Fishing, Hunting, and Wildlife-Associated Recreation," report 2022–24, November 19, 2024, https://www.fws.gov/media/2022-birding-united-states-demographic-and-economic-analysis.

4. Maria E. White et al., "The Joy of Birds: The Effect of Rating for Joy or Counting Garden Bird Species on Wellbeing, Anxiety, and Nature Connection," *Urban Ecosystems* 26, no. 3 (2023): 755–65, https://doi.org/10.1007/s11252-023-01334-y.

5. "Seven Ways to Make Your Home More Bird-Friendly," *Audubon*, Spring 2022, https://www.audubon.org/magazine/spring-2022/seven-ways-make-your-home-more-bird-friendly.

6. "Convention for the Protection of Migratory Birds in the United States (U.S.) and Canada," Environment and Climate Change Canada (ECCC), modified September 2, 2022, https://www.canada.ca/en/environment-climate-change/corporate/international-affairs/partnerships-countries-regions/north-america/canada-united-states-protecting-migratory-birds.html.

7. Jesse Greenspan, "The History and Evolution of the Migratory Bird Treaty Act," *Audubon*, May 22, 2015, https://www.audubon.org/news/the-history-and-evolution-migratory-bird-treaty-act.

8. Greenspan, "History and Evolution of the Migratory Bird Treaty Act."

9. "Migratory Birds Convention Act (MBCA) and Regulations," Government of Canada, Environment and Climate Change Canada (ECCC), modified July 5, 2018, https://www.canada.ca/en/environment-climate-change/services/migratory-birds-legal-protection/convention-act-regulations.html; "Migratory Bird Treaty Act of 1918," 16 U.S.C. 703–712, U.S. Fish & Wildlife Service, accessed April 26, 2020, https://www.fws.gov/law/migratory-bird-treaty-act-1918.

Chapter 18: Preserving the Bounty of Fall

1. Darren Préfontaine et al., "Métis Seasonal Cycles," accessed October 30, 2025, https://www.metismuseum.ca/media/db/00724.

2. Todd Paquin et al., "Traditional Métis Socialization and Entertainment," accessed October 30, 2025, https://www.metismuseum.ca/media/db/00724.

3. "International Data," Population Reference Bureau, accessed December 4, 2024, https://www.prb.org/international/.

4. Britannica, "Canning," accessed October 25, 2024, https://www.britannica.com/topic/canning-food-processing.

Chapter 19: Into the Hidden World of Fungi

1. Helen Briggs, "The Secret Life of Fungi: Ten Fascinating Facts," BBC, September 11, 2018, https://www.bbc.com/news/science-environment-45486844.

2. Chayanard Phukhamsakda et al., "The Numbers of Fungi: Contributions from Traditional Taxonomic Studies and Challenges of Metabarcoding," *Fungal Diversity* 114, no. 1 (2022): 327–86, https://doi.org/10.1007/s13225-022-00502-3.

3. Merry Buckley, "The Fungal Kingdom: Diverse and Essential Roles in Earth's Ecosystem," *American Society for Microbiology* (2008), http://www.ncbi.nlm.nih.gov/books/NBK559443/.

4. Gianluca Rizzo et al., "A Review of Mushrooms in Human Nutrition and Health," *Trends in Food Science & Technology* 117 (2021): 60–73, https://doi.org/10.1016/j.tifs.2020.12.025; María Elena Valverde et al., "Edible Mushrooms: Improving Human Health and Promoting Quality Life," *International Journal of Microbiology* (2015): 376387, https://doi.org/10.1155/2015/376387.

5. Lawrence Barkwell, "La Michinn Traditional Metis Medicines and Healing," 2018, https://www.metismuseum.ca/media/document.php/148985.La%20Michinn%20revised%20and%20catalogued.pdf.

6. Ursula Peintner et al., "Mycophilic or Mycophobic? Legislation and Guidelines on Wild Mushroom Commerce Reveal Different Consumption Behaviour in European Countries," *PLOS One* 8, no. 5 (2013): e63926, https://doi.org/10.1371/journal.pone.0063926.

7. David Arora, *All That the Rain Promises and More* (Ten Speed Press, 1991); "Poisonous Fungi," ScienceDirect, accessed December 9, 2024, https://www.sciencedirect.com/topics/agricultural-and-biological-sciences/poisonous-fungi.

8. "Poisonous Fungi."

9. Paul Stamets and Heather Zwickey, "Medicinal Mushrooms: Ancient Remedies Meet Modern Science," *Integrative Medicine: A Clinician's Journal* 13, no. 1 (2014): 46–47, https://www.ncbi.nlm.nih.gov/pmc/articles/PMC4684114.

10. Chance Noffsinger et al., "A 200-Year History of Arctic and Alpine Fungi in North America: Early Sailing Expeditions to the Molecular Era," *Arctic, Antarctic, and Alpine Research* 52, no. 1 (2020): 323–40, https://doi.org/10.1080/15230430.2020.1771869.

11. Arora, *All That the Rain Promises and More.*

12. "Shaggy Mane Mushrooms," Vancouver Island Mushrooms, accessed Decem-

ber 10, 2024, https://www.westcoastforager.com/wild-edible-mushrooms/shaggy-mane-mushrooms.

Chapter 20: Going Within During Wintertime

1. Juan C. Riofrio, "The Right to Feast and Festivals," *Vanderbilt Journal of Entertainment & Technology Law* 23, no. 3 (2021): 567–623, https://scholarship.law.vanderbilt.edu/jetlaw/vol23/iss3/3.

2. Cyril Martindale, "Christmas," Catholic Answers, accessed December 12, 2024, https://www.catholic.com/encyclopedia/christmas.

3. Britannica, "St. Brigid of Ireland," accessed January 31, 2025, https://www.britannica.com/biography/Saint-Brigit-of-Ireland.

4. Britannica, "Imbolc," accessed February 7, 2025, https://www.britannica.com/topic/Imbolc.

5. Bryant P. H. Hui et al., "Rewards of Kindness? A Meta-Analysis of the Link Between Prosociality and Well-Being," *Psychological Bulletin* 146, no. 12 (2020): 1084–1116, https://doi.org/10.1037/bul0000298.

6. Kirsten K. Shockey, "Old-Fashioned Fruitcake," *Taproot Magazine*, no. 12 (Bread) (November 2014).

Chapter 21: Navigating "Bad" Weather as a Family

1. Jaimie Kehler, "Kelowna, B.C., Residents Bundle Up During January Cold Snap," CBS News, January 5, 2017, https://www.cbc.ca/news/canada/british-columbia/cold-snap-weather-forecast-kelowna-snow-1.3921909.

2. Kylie A. Dankiw et al., "Parent and Early Childhood Educator Perspectives of Unstructured Nature Play for Young Children: A Qualitative Descriptive Study," *PLOS One* 18, no. 6 (2023): e0286468, https://doi.org/10.1371/journal.pone.0286468.

3. "Chapter 11: Weather and Climate Extreme Events in a Changing Climate," IPCC Sixth Assessment Report, accessed December 17, 2024, https://www.ipcc.ch/report/ar6/wg1/chapter/chapter-11/?utm_source=chatgpt.com.

4. "Inuktitut Words for Snow and Ice," The Canadian Encyclopedia, accessed January 6, 2025, https://www.thecanadianencyclopedia.ca/en/article/inuktitut-words-for-snow-and-ice.

5. "Extreme Weather and Climate Change," NASA, accessed January 6, 2025, https://science.nasa.gov/climate-change/extreme-weather/.

Chapter 22: Reading the Night Sky

1. Rebecca Bell, et al., "Dark Nature: Exploring Potential Benefits of Nocturnal Nature-Based Interaction for Human and Environmental Health," *European Journal of Ecopsychology* 5 (2014): 1–15.

2. Christopher Barnes and Holli-Anne Passmore, "Development and Testing of the Night Sky Connectedness Index (NSCI)," *Journal of Environmental Psychology* 93 (2024): 102198, https://doi.org/10.1016/j.jenvp.2023.102198.

3. Barnes and Passmore, "Development and Testing of the Night Sky Connectedness Index (NSCI)."

4. Nadieh Bremer, "Figures in the Sky," Visual Cinnamon, accessed August 28, 2023, https://figuresinthesky.visualcinnamon.com.

5. "Star Basics," NASA, accessed August 28, 2023, https://universe.nasa.gov/stars/basics/.

6. "The Moon," NASA, accessed September 2, 2023, https://solarsystem.nasa.gov/moons/earths-moon/overview.

7. Paul Coleman, "Hina Moves to the Moon: A Hawaiian Story About Our Moon," University of Hawaii, accessed June 15, 2025, https://www.lpi.usra.edu/education/moonPosters/Poster1/backg.pdf.

8. "Top Moon Questions," NASA," accessed January 9, 2025, https://science.nasa.gov/moon/top-moon-questions/.

9. "Native American Moon Names." *AIANTA* (blog), accessed April 7, 2019, https://www.aianta.org/native-american-moon-names/; Brian Jones, ed., *Yearbook of Astronomy 2025* (White Owl, 2024).

10. Oneida Language & Cultural Centre, "Oneida Words for Months," accessed November 14, 2025, https://oneidalanguage.ca/learn-our-language/calendar-resources/calendar/; Ojibwe.net, "Moons & Days," accessed November 14, 2025, https://ojibwe.net/projects/months-moons/; Wilfred Buck, "Nisto Osap Tiposkawi Pisimuk—Thirteen Moons," Canadian Space Agency, modified July 4, 2025, https://www.asc-csa.gc.ca/eng/youth-educators/objective-moon/thirteen-moons.asp.

11. David Wolfe, "Cherokee Moons," Telliquah, accessed November 14, 2025, https://telliquah.com/Moons.htm; Montclair State University Digital Commons, "Days and Months," Montclair State University, accessed November 14, 2025, https://digitalcommons.montclair.edu/lenapelanguage_audio-days-months/.

12. Ojibwe.net, "Moons & Days," accessed November 14, 2025, https://ojibwe.net/projects/months-moons/.

13. "Lake Sturgeon," *National Geographic*, accessed February 25, 2020, https://www.nationalgeographic.com/animals/fish/facts/lake-sturgeon.

14. "Lake Sturgeon Biology," U.S. Fish and Wildlife Service, last updated March 3, 2016, https://web.archive.org/web/20181117014457/https:/www.fws.gov/midwest/sturgeon/biology.htm.

15. Catherine Boeckmann, "Beaver Moon: Full Supermoon in November 2025," last updated January 16, 2025, https://www.almanac.com/full-moon-november.

Chapter 23: Embracing the Magic of Snow and Ice

1. Jostein Rønning Sanderud et al., "'Winter Children': An Ethnographically Inspired Study of Children Being-and-Becoming Well-Versed in Snow and Ice," *Sport, Education and Society* 25, no. 8 (2020): 960–71, https://doi.org/10.1080/13573322.2019.1678124.

2. Kristen Jakstis and Michael R. Barnes, "Winter-Human-Nature Interactions: A Scoping Review for a Neglected Season," *Global Environmental Psychology* 2 (2024): 1–13, https://doi.org/10.5964/gep.11251.

3. Holli-Anne Passmore et al., "Wellbeing in Winter: Testing the Noticing Nature Intervention During Winter Months," *Frontiers in Psychology* 13 (2022), https://doi.org/10.3389/fpsyg.2022.840273.

4. "How Do Snowflakes Form? Get the Science Behind Snow," National Oceanic and Atmospheric Administration," updated December 21, 2022, https://www.noaa.gov/stories/how-do-snowflakes-form-science-behind-snow.

5. "Snowflake Science," SnowCrystals.com, accessed January 14, 2025, https://www.snowcrystals.com/science/science.html.

6. "Guide to Snowflakes," SnowCrystals.com, accessed January 14, 2025, https://www.snowcrystals.com/guide/guide.html?utm_source=chatgpt.com.

7. Ernest Thompson Seton, *Animal Tracks and Hunter Signs* (Read Books Ltd, 2020).

8. Charles A. Bishop, "Eastern Woodlands Indigenous Peoples in Canada," *The Canadian Encyclopedia*, last edited December 21, 2017, https://www.thecanadianencyclopedia.ca/en/article/aboriginal-people-eastern-woodlands.

Chapter 24: Gathering for Storytime

1. Chandra Ramamurthy et al., "The Impact of Storytelling on Building Resilience in Children: A Systematic Review," *Journal of Psychiatric and Mental Health Nursing* 31, no. 4 (2024): 525–42, https://doi.org/10.1111/jpm.13008.

2. Andrew Wright, *Storytelling with Children* (Oxford University Press, 1995).

It Takes a Village of Families

1. "New Survey Finds Loneliness Epidemic Runs Deep Among Parents," The Ohio State University Wexner Medical Center, April 24, 2024, https://wexnermedical.osu.edu/mediaroom/pressreleaselisting/new-survey-finds-loneliness-epidemic-runs-deep-among-parents.

2. Children & Nature Network, "Nature Clubs for Families: Do It Yourself! Do It Now!," pilot ed., accessed August 25, 2025 https://kidsandnature.org/wp-content/uploads/2009/02/familynatureclubskit.pdf.

3. Jonathan Lear, *Radical Hope: Ethics in the Face of Cultural Devastation* (Harvard University Press, 2008), 6.